"Hank Hanegraaff answers questions of life after death while adding exhilarating moments of personal insight. Enjoyable and helpful in more fully understanding this vital subject."

Dr. Brandt Gustavson
PRESIDENT, NATIONAL RELIGIOUS BROADCASTERS

"Hank Hanegraaff is not only a defender of the truth, but he expresses this defense in a clear, understandable way, which strengthens lives."

Josh McDowell
AUTHOR OF *THE NEW EVIDENCE THAT DEMANDS A VERDICT*

"After nearly thirty years of Bible teaching as a Senior Pastor, I thought I had read all the great apologetic works Christianity has to offer. Now, however, Hank Hanegraaff has prepared a masterpiece. *Resurrection* is the perfect tool for equipping saints to survive in Post-Christian America."

Tom Stipe
SENIOR PASTOR, CROSSROADS CHURCH OF DENVER, COLORADO

"This volume by Hank Hanegraaff speaks popularly in order to achieve maximum appeal. But this does not mean that he sacrifices important conclusions drawn from recent scholarship. He distills the work of many recent scholars, both pro and con, dispensing numerous conclusions along the way. He does so in a format that is easily digestible. Prepare yourself for an enjoyable journey from Jesus' resurrection to the bliss of heaven, as believers share with each other and with their resurrected Lord."

Dr. Gary Habermas
PROFESSOR AND CHAIR OF PHILOSOPHY AND THEOLOGY, LIBERTY UNIVERSITY

"Hands down, slam-dunk, the resurrection is the bottom-line for the believer. Hank leaves no stone unturned, thoroughly portraying the resurrection as our grand hope, the glorious springboard from which we will dive into eternity."

Joni Eareckson Tada
AUTHOR OF *HOLINESS IN HIDDEN PLACES* AND *HEAVEN...YOUR REAL HOME*

"Who better to address the vital truth of Christ's resurrection than one of the foremost Christian apologists of our time—Hank Hanegraaff? *Resurrection* will inform believers, appeal to non-believers, and honor the risen Christ. I recommend this book wholeheartedly."

Dr. Jack Graham
SENIOR PASTOR, PRESTONWOOD BAPTIST CHURCH, PLANO, TEXAS

"Few things are more important (1 Corinthians 15:17) and more certain (Acts 1:3) than the resurrection, and I know of no book that makes it more relevant. This up to date defense of the great pillar of Christianity simultaneously brings condemnation to the cults and consolation to believers. Hank Hanegraaff's *Resurrection* is must reading for every believer."

Dr. Norman L. Geisler
PRESIDENT OF SOUTHERN EVANGELICAL SEMINARY

"Lost in all the millennial madness has been the fact that the resurrection of Jesus Christ is still the defining moment in all of human history—the birth, death, and resurrection of the Lord Jesus Christ. Hank Hanegraaff has never been more poignant with his prophetic pen than in this volume. Read it and reap!"

Dr. O.S. Hawkins
PRESIDENT OF THE ANNUITY BOARD, SOUTHERN BAPTIST CONVENTION

"Perhaps due to the sheer meaningless of naturalism, there has been a resurgence of interest in life after death in popular culture. And there has also been a growth of scholarly interest in a number of subjects relevant to life after death. In *Resurrection*, Hank Hanegraaff has sifted through the literature and compressed it into a well-informed, interesting, and readable treatment of one of life's most important issues: What happens to us when we die? This book clears up a number of contemporary confusions about life after death and it provides sure footing on which to build one's expectations of life beyond the grave."

Dr. J. P. Moreland
PROFESSOR OF PHILOSOPHY, TALBOT SCHOOL OF THEOLOGY, BIOLA UNIVERSITY

"Hank Hanegraaff has helped many readers and listeners with questions about the Bible—and there is no more important biblical truth than the resurrection,first of Jesus and then of those who belong to him. Hank's clear thinking will help many more believers and inquirers know the truth."

Phillip E. Johnson
PROFESSOR OF LAW, UNIVERSITY OF CALIFORNIA AT BERKLEY

"Dealing with questions and issues that are rarely explored by other writers and scholars, Hank Hanegraaff maintains his integrity with thorough scholarship anchored in the Word of God. I wish I had this book in my library forty years ago!"

Dr. Jim Henry
SENIOR PASTOR, FIRST BAPTIST CHURCH ORLANDO

"Once again, Hank Hanegraaff masterfully and aggressively goes after a controversial subject. Hank's work is thorough and methodical without being cumbersome. He is neither afraid of the critics nor of their findings; in fact, he engages them and then gracefully pins them to the ground with meticulous documentation. The reader of *Resurrection* will walk away being bolstered in faith, filled with hope for the future, and equipped to handle what skeptics bring his way. Hank's style is refreshing and captivating. He sets forth the truth of the resurrection in a manner that is easy to grasp while treating the subject completely. No stone is left unturned. It is often difficult to write about a theological subject without bogging down. Hank Hanegraaff succeeds leaving the reader wanting more."

Skip Heitzig
SENIOR PASTOR, CALVARY OF ALBUQUERQUE, NEW MEXICO

"Hank Hanegraaff's keen insights have done much to sharpen mine. I was thrilled to learn of this work on the resurrection."

Max Lucado
AUTHOR OF *WHEN CHRIST COMES*

"Hank Hanegraaff's *Resurrection* cuts through the haze, discerning the core truths of our faith. He shows us more than just the cold facts—he shows us how to apply them to our everyday lives."

Dr. David Jeremiah
PRESIDENT, CHRISTIAN HERITAGE COLLEGE

"This book by Hank Hanegraaff is sure to become an instant classic. Dealing with practical questions, it will answer readers' long-held questions about life beyond the grave. I heartily recommend it."

Greg Laurie
HARVEST CRUSADES

"All of Christianity hinges on belief in the resurrection of the dead, and that is why the forces of evil have waged war so fiercely against this doctrine. In his unique and provocative style, Hank Hanegraaff explores the resurrection of Christ, its centrality to the gospel message, and its ramifications for what we believe and how we live. *Resurrection* is a rich resource for the defense of our faith."

Dr. John MacArthur
SENIOR PASTOR, GRACE COMMUNITY CHURCH, SUN VALLEY, CALIFORNIA

"In *Resurrection*, Hank Hanegraaff defends, explains, and provides the answers to questions about the resurrection and what that remarkable event means to us. A must-read for believers who are serious about their faith."

David T. Moore
SENIOR PASTOR, SOUTHWEST COMMUNITY CHURCH, PALM DESERT, CALIFORNIA

"This book brings alive the truth and wonder of the resurrection, which is both essential Christian doctrine and indisputable fact of history. While the book reflects historic theology, it is refreshingly free of dense vocabulary and complicated polemics. Hanegraaff's trademark style combining clear prose and packets of memorable concepts will equip Christians to know what the Bible teaches about the resurrection and life after death and to trust God for our eternal life in His Son."

Bob and Gretchen Passantino
DIRECTORS, ANSWERS IN ACTION

"Hank Hanegraaff is a passionate defender of the faith and a writer who brings us the facts to bear on the way we live our lives."

Dr. John C. Maxwell
FOUNDER, THE INJOY GROUP

"Compelling and fascinating, but at the same time practical, readers will profit from this book. Hank deals clearly and biblically with the cornerstone of our faith—the resurrection."

Dr. Adrian Rogers
PASTOR, BELLEVUE BAPTIST CHURCH, MEMPHIS, TENNESSEE

"Because of its unique blend of documentation, discipline, and devotion, I plan to make *Resurrection*, a modern classic, required reading in our Student Leadership University."

Dr. Jay Strack
PRESIDENT & FOUNDER, STUDENT LEADERSHIP UNIVERSITY

"In *Resurrection*, one of North America's most outstanding communicators writes with clarity as to why the resurrection of Jesus Christ still does and always will matter."

Dr. John D. Hull
SENIOR PASTOR, THE PEOPLE'S CHURCH, TORONTO

"A good source of answers to many common questions, *Resurrection* is entertaining as well as enlightening."

Joseph Tkach
PASTOR GENERAL, WORLDWIDE CHURCH OF GOD

"Hank Hanegraaff has always been a reliable spokesman who has always relied on the biblical inerrancy of Scripture to answer life's toughest questions. Now he has given us *Resurrection*, which is a superb and concise work on the central theme of the Christian faith. *Resurrection* should be in the library of every serious student of the Bible."

Dr. Charles Stanley
SENIOR PASTOR, FIRST BAPTIST CHURCH OF ATLANTA

"Resurrection is a brilliant defense of the cornerstone of Christianity. But Hank Hanegraaff also takes us a step further and gives us the practical application of the truth of the resurrection to our own lives. This is a wonderful book that we've needed for years."

Dr. Rick Warren
AUTHOR OF *THE PURPOSE-DRIVEN CHURCH*

"Look in any dictionary under "Bible Knowledge"—and you will find the name Hank Hanegraaff. Through his many books and programs, he has enlightened us, taught us, encouraged us, and instructed us—all in the name of Christianity. And now he tackles the fulcrum of Christianity—the Resurrection. Get ready to have your most often asked questions answered straight from Scripture. Want to know if your favorite animal will be in heaven? Will you age there? Who is resurrected? Is there sex in heaven? Pick up a copy of *Resurrection* — easy to read and comprehend, and a great conversation starter with friends and family."

Dr. Karen J. Hayter
COPE T.V. BROADCAST, SOUTHERN BAPTIST CONVENTION

"This is a journey to the center of the core teaching of the Christian faith—a must-read!"

Greg Albrecht
EDITOR-IN-CHIEF, *THE PLAIN TRUTH*

"I wish I had this book when I was an atheist! Clear, creative, compelling, convincing — Hank Hanegraaff has produced a stirring and powerful defense of the central event of Christianity. This masterful book will give Christians and seekers confidence in the truth that because Jesus conquered the grave, so will His followers someday, too. Thanks, Hank, for a valuable resource that God will use to change many lives and eternities!"

Lee Strobel
AUTHOR OF *THE CASE FOR CHRIST*

"*Resurrection* is not only Hank's most important literary work, but it is one of the best Christian books written by anyone in the past decade. *Resurrection* has made a lasting impact on my life—no one should be denied experiencing the impact of *Resurrection*."

Richard Bott, Sr.
PRESIDENT, BOTT RADIO NETWORK

RESURRECTION

RESURRECTION

✠

Hank Hanegraaff

RESURRECTION

Published by Word Publishing, a unit of Thomas Nelson, Inc., P.O. Box 141000, Nashville, Tennessee 37214. No portion of this book may be reproduced, stored in a retrieval system, or transmitted in any form or by any means—electronic, mechanical, photocopy, recording, or other—except for brief quotations in printed reviews, without the prior permission of the publisher.

ISBN 0-8499-1643-7

Printed in the United States of America
01 02 03 04 05 BVG 11 10 9 8 7

Dedication

To Lena Hanegraaff, my mother, who longs to see my father in the resurrection.

Your dead will live;
their bodies will rise.
You who dwell in the dust,
wake up and shout for joy.
Your dew is like the dew of the morning;
the earth will give birth to her dead.

—Isaiah 26:19

RESURRECTION

CONTENTS

Part Two: Defense of the Resurrection of Creation

Part Three: Definitive Answers to Questions Regarding Resurrection

Contents

FOREWORD

✛

A Personal Message about This Book from Joni Eareckson Tada

Not long ago, my mother-in-law purchased a family grave plot at Forest Lawn; however, she would not sign the papers until my husband, Ken, and I looked at the lot and gave our approval. I could have come up with better ways to spend a Sunday afternoon, but, being the submissive wife, I trekked to Forest Lawn. We looked at my grave site located in a section called Murmuring Pines and listened to the realtor (that's what her Forest Lawn tag said) remind me that with my head "here," and my feet "there," I would have a grand view of the valley and distant mountains. "That's important," I mumbled with a hint of sarcasm. I told her I did not have plans to stay there very long.

The realtor and my family conferred over papers as they wandered toward the next plot. I powered my wheelchair onto the top of my grave site and turned to gaze at the range of mountains. A gust of wind rippled the grass, and the pines above me did, indeed, murmur. A breeze tossed my hair. A profound peace settled over the scene.

Suddenly, it struck me that I was sitting on the exact spot where my actual body will rise, should I die before Christ comes. "Do not be amazed at this," Jesus is quoted in John 5:28, "for a time is coming when all who are in their graves will hear his voice and come out." Astounding! One day actual spirits will return to actual graves and reunite with stone-cold dead forms and—in the twinkling of an eye—we shall be changed. We shall come forth and rise strong and brilliant, with hands and arms, feet and legs, and, like Jesus with his glorious body, we shall be perfectly fitted for both earth and heaven.

Sitting in my wheelchair under the pines, it was enough to spill tears. That grassy hillside ignited the reality of the resurrection, wrapping sight, sound, and touch around all the sermons and essays I'd ever read on the subject.

And now, with Hank Hanegraaff's book, *Resurrection,* I have more to devour on the subject. You do too. Hank leaves no stone unturned, thoroughly portraying the resurrection as our grand hope, our glorious springboard from which we will dive into eternity. He underscores it as the core and crux, the main cog of the Christian faith. If it doesn't work, nothing else does. Hands down, slam dunk, the resurrection is the bottom-line for the believer, and one cannot do better than to study the subject with all diligence.

Why? A study of the resurrection will give deep and profound meaning to your labors. It will energize your work. It will, like nothing else, shore up your soul and enable you to stand firm. How do I know? First Corinthians 15:58, the final verse in the magnificent chapter on the resurrection, tells me so. So does my wheelchair.

As a quadriplegic for more than three decades, and as a happy-hearted believer, I've got a lot invested in eternity; the resurrection will be my first step into the resplendent kingdom our resurrected Lord is, even now, putting the finishing touches on.

Turn the page, friend. Study on. I'll be waiting for you by the courts of heaven.

ACKNOWLEDGMENTS

First, I would like to acknowledge the board and staff of the Christian Research Institute for their encouragement and support. I am especially grateful for the prayers of Everett Jacobson, who has served as a CRI board member for going on forty years; for Paul Young, executive vice president—only from the perspective of eternity will I fully appreciate all the unnoticed things he does to lift up my arms; for Stephen Ross, special assistant to the president—his friendship, ferocious commitment to detail, and fantastic mind are a daily blessing; for Elliott Miller, editor-in-chief of the *Christian Research Journal*—who constantly challenges my thinking; for Bob Hunter, who collated the bibliography and indices; for Sam Wall and the research staff—examples of men and women dedicated to touching hearts as well as heads.

Furthermore, I would like to express appreciation to the staff of Word Publishing for their support—I am particularly grateful for Lee Gessner and his enthusiastic encouragement during each phase of the process; for Dr. Norman Geisler, who carefully reviewed this manuscript before it went to press—to have a scholar of his caliber provide an enthusiastic endorsement is an extraordinary blessing; for Joni Eareckson Tada, who has taught me more by her example than all of the great exegetes combined; for Bob and Gretchen Passantino, who are always available for brainstorming sessions; and for a host of other great Christian thinkers, past and present, whose writings have greatly enriched my thinking.

Finally, I would like to acknowledge Kathy and the kids—Michelle, Katie, David, John Mark, Hank Jr., Christina, Paul Stephen, and Faith—who have blessed me beyond measure! Above all, I am supremely thankful to the Lord Jesus Christ: Because he lives we can face the future without fear.

BEFORE YOU BEGIN

✠

As I begin writing, I am filled with a sense of thankfulness and joy. Just moments ago, I experienced the miracle of birth for the tenth time—I have now had the privilege of seeing eight children and two grandchildren birthed into this world! Only moments before I actually laid eyes on her, my granddaughter Elise was safe and secure in a wondrous water wonderland, her every need attended. There is absolutely no way she could have imagined a completely different environment merely inches away from the comforting beat of her mother's heart. Yet, through a series of violent contractions, she was delivered into a whole new realm of existence. In the twinkling of an eye, she emerged into a world of sights and sounds, of smells and sensations—an unexplored existence, just waiting to be experienced. As I watched Elise transition from the womb to the world, the words of the psalmist flooded my mind: "For you created my inmost being; you knit me together in my mother's womb. I praise you because I am fearfully and wonderfully made; your works are wonderful, I know that full well. My frame was not hidden from you when I was made in the secret place. When I was woven together in the depths of the earth, your eyes saw my unformed body. All the days ordained for me were written in your book before one of them came to be" (Psalm 139:13–16).

Two years ago, I witnessed a birth of a radically different sort—it was my first such experience. I stood beside my father, Johannis, as he breathed his last and was transported from this world to the next. One last heartbeat and Dad entered a realm of reality beyond our wildest imaginings. As I watched him transition, words penned long ago on Patmos echoed back faintly through the corridors of time:

> Then I saw a new heaven and a new earth, for the first heaven and the first earth had passed away, and there was no longer any sea. I saw the Holy City, the new Jerusalem, coming down out of heaven from God, prepared as a bride beautifully dressed for her husband. And I heard a loud voice from the throne saying, "Now the dwelling of God is with men, and he will live with them. They will be his people, and God himself will be with them and be their God. He will wipe every tear from their eyes. There will be no more death or mourning or crying or pain, for the old order of things has passed away."
>
> He who was seated on the throne said, "I am making everything new!" (Revelation 21:1–5)

Several days later, I found myself standing beside a casket, cradling my one-year-old daughter, Faith, in my arms. She looked down quizzically at my father, no doubt wondering why he wouldn't wake up. Paul Stephen, then only three, scrunched up his nose and asked, "Where did Grampa go?" Five-year-old Christina looked down at him knowingly and retorted, "He's up in heaven, silly." Hank Jr., my irrepressible seven-year-old, blurted out, "Can Grandpa see us right now?" John Mark, just one year his senior, stared forlornly at his grandfather through tear-stained eyes. "I'll miss Grampa," he sighed dejectedly. My twelve-year-old,

David, put an arm around his younger brother. "Don't worry," he said softly. "We'll all see Grampa again someday." Katie my teenager, looking incredibly mature in her black funeral dress, asked, "Daddy, will we recognize Grampa in heaven?" Michelle, the oldest of my treasures, chimed in, "Yeah, Dad, what will our resurrected bodies look like?"

In the ensuing moments, my wife, Kathy, and the kids fired a seemingly endless barrage of questions at me. They were the very questions that have reverberated through the parlors of mortuaries for centuries. As I answered each question, I noticed an amazing transformation taking place. The more we talked about resurrection, the less foreboding death seemed to be. It was almost as though we had been transported from the funeral parlor to the front porch. In my mind's eye, I saw a familiar scene: Kathy and the kids were huddled together, smiling and waving as Mom and Dad backed out of the driveway and headed for home. We hated to see them leave, but we knew that they would return again soon.

As I looked back down at my dad's lifeless body, a smile crept over my face. I was certain of one thing: I *would* see my dad alive again one day! Not in a body ravaged by sickness and suffering but in a glorious body transformed like unto Christ's resurrected body. A real, flesh-and-bone body perfectly engineered for a renewed universe.

As Elise had emerged from the security of her water wonderland into an existence just waiting to be experienced and explored, so too my father had exited the familiar and entered into the fantastic. Today he is more alive than he ever was. His death was just the beginning—the best is yet to come. At the resurrection, his body will undergo a metamorphosis and reemerge imperishable, glorious, powerful, supernatural, sinless, and Spirit dominated.

The more I learn about the resurrection, the more excited I become! It is mind-boggling to think that our physical carcasses will be resurrected, that the physical cosmos will be renewed, and that the physical Christ will return. Eden lost will become Eden restored and then some, and Christ himself will live with us. We will evermore explore the grandeur and glory of God's creative handiwork.

But what if I'm wrong? What if Jesus Christ never really rose from the tomb? What if the faith that I'll see my dad again is just a fleeting fancy? What if the hope that this physical cosmos will be renewed is misplaced? Would a good God really create a place called hell?

And what about all those questions my children asked me? Will we really have tangible, physical bodies in the resurrection? What age will we be? And what about rewards? Will there be pets and platypuses in the resurrection? If heaven is perfect, won't it be perfectly boring? Can souls really survive without bodies and brains? Will there be sex after the resurrection? What happens to people who were cremated? Are reincarnation and resurrection mutually exclusive? And when do we get our resurrected bodies—when we die or at Christ's Second Coming?

These are the very questions this book is designed to answer. By the time you put this book back on the shelf, it is my prayer that you will be ready to live the remainder of your life with renewed purpose and passion, that you will see your existence as more than marking time, and that you will see this lifetime as an opportunity to make a difference. It is my hope that, like Peter, Paul, James, and John, you will become a world changer who sees prosperity, platforms, and political correctness in the here and now for what they really are compared with your promise and position in paradise. Above all, it is my hope and prayer that you will live life day by day with eternity in mind.

—Hank Hanegraaff

Rancho Santa Margarita, California

On the eve of the new millennium

CHARTING THE COURSE

✚

Before you start down the road to resurrection—a pilgrimage that for some will be measured in days and for others in decades—we would do well to chart the course. Allow me to start by underscoring the importance of the trek. This is not just any journey; it is a journey of enormous consequence. You see, without resurrection, there is no hope. Indeed, without resurrection, there is no Christianity.

As you travel through these pages, you will encounter attacks on resurrection ranging from Judaism, which swears it never happened; to Jehovah's Witnesses, who suggest that Jesus' physical body was discarded, destroyed, or dissolved into gases; and to Jesus Seminar fellows, who say that resurrection is wishful thinking.

When you reach your destination, however, you will have encountered all the evidence necessary to demonstrate not only that Christ's resurrection is an immutable fact of history, but that your own resurrection is just as certain. Along the way, a host of frequently asked questions will be answered as well. In short, the journey will take place in 3-D—*defense* of the resurrection of Christ, *details* on the resurrection of creation, and *definitive* answers to questions regarding resurrection.

PART ONE:
Defense of the Resurrection of Christ

We begin the journey with chapter 1, titled "Mythologies." In this chapter, we travel through a never-ending stream of imaginative stories designed to demonstrate that the resurrection is a crutch for weak-minded Christians. In the following four chapters, we will see that, far from being a gargantuan fraud, the resurrection of Jesus Christ is the greatest *feat* in the annals of recorded history:

Fatal Torment

Empty Tomb

Appearances of Christ

Transformation

The letter *F* in the acronym FEAT serves to remind us of *fatal torment.* In chapter 2, we see that believing anything other than that Jesus suffered fatal torment takes more faith than the resurrection itself. In today's modern age of scientific enlightenment, both liberal and conservative New Testament scholars confirm that Jesus died on the cross, that he was buried in the tomb of Joseph of Arimathea, and that his death drove his disciples to despair. Additionally, in this chapter, I confirm that, although we no longer have the original New Testament documents that chronicle the life and death of Jesus Christ, we can be absolutely certain that the Scriptures we do have are faithful representations of those original writings.

The *E* represents the *empty tomb.* Chapter 3 begins with a coalition of so-called "scholars" who were determined to take their false views out of private academia and demolish the biblical Jesus in the public arena. They attracted huge headlines by depicting evangelicals as naive fundamentalists who uncritically bought into the biblical account of the empty tomb. However, as we will see, their stereotyping is not based on solid scholarship. Contrary to what the Jesus Seminar fellows purport, we can be absolutely certain that, on Easter morning some two thousand years ago, Jesus' tomb was indeed empty.

A stands for the *appearances of Christ* after his resurrection. In chapter 4, we discover that the apostles did not merely proliferate Christ's teachings; they were absolutely positive that he had appeared to them in the flesh. Despite the fact that we are two thousand years removed from the actual event, we, too, can be absolutely confident in Christ's post-resurrection appearances. Additionally, we will cover some of the more extreme measures that critics have taken to explain away Christ's appearances, including the hallucination, hypnosis, and hypersuggestibility hypotheses.

Finally, *T* represents *transformation*. In chapter 5, we see that what happened as a result of the resurrection is unprecedented in human history. In the span of a few hundred years, a small band of seemingly insignificant believers succeeded in turning an entire empire upside down. These believers faced torture, vilification, and even cruel deaths for what they fervently believed to be true. Their willingness to face persecution is further proof of Christ's resurrection, since it is inconceivable that the disciples would have been willing to die for what they knew to be a lie. As we will see, within weeks of the resurrection, an entire community of Jews willingly changed age-old sociological and theological traditions, such as the Sabbath, the sacrifices, and the sacraments, that had previously given them their national identity.

PART TWO:
Defense of the Resurrection of Creation

Part Two begins with a defense of the physical resurrection of believers. In chapter 6, we discover that only in a biblical world-view do we become greater after death than we were before. Christianity is the only religion that holds the view that our lowly bodies will someday be transformed into glorious, resurrected bodies, like unto Christ's resurrected body. Far from being platonic, Christianity is a physical religion—our bodies will be real, physical, flesh-and-bone bodies perfectly engineered for "a new heaven and a new earth" (Revelation 21:1).

In chapter 7, we broach the horrifying reality that unbelievers will be physically resurrected to eternal torment. In hell, people who choose to reject Christ in this life will suffer eternal, excruciating pain in the resurrection, with no hope that it will ever end. The biblical language used to describe hell is grim and ghastly—it is variously described as "darkness, where there will weeping and gnashing of teeth" (Matthew 8:12); as a "fiery furnace" (Matthew 13:42); and as a "lake of burning sulfur" (Revelation 21:8). Additionally, we will discover that the alternative to hell would be worse than hell itself—and that common sense itself dictates that hell exists.

Chapter 8 presents the grand and glorious truth that this physical cosmos will be "resurrected." As there is continuity between our present bodies and our resurrected bodies, so too there will be continuity between the present universe and the one we will inhabit throughout eternity. Christ will not resurrect an entirely different group of created beings; rather, he will resurrect the same humans who have populated this planet. In like manner, God will not renew another cosmos; rather, he will redeem the very world he once called "very good" (Genesis 1:31).

PART THREE:
Definitive Answers to Questions Regarding Resurrection

In Part Three, answers are provided to ten crucial questions regarding the resurrection. These are not only frequently asked questions on the *Bible Answer Man*, the call-in radio show I host, but they include some of the questions my children asked after my father died:

Chapter 9—*Was Christ's physical body resurrected from the dead or did he raise an immaterial spirit?*

Chapter 10—*Does the soul continue to exist after the death of the body?*

Chapter 11—*Do believers receive resurrected bodies when they die or when Christ returns?*

Chapter 12—*If heaven is perfect, won't it be perfectly boring?*

Chapter 13—*Will God raise pets and platypuses from the dead?*

Chapter 14—*Are reincarnation and resurrection mutually exclusive?*

Chapter 15—*Is cremation commensurate with the Christian concept of resurrection?*

Chapter 16—*Will we be resurrected at the same age that we died?*

Chapter 17—*Will there be sex after the resurrection?*

Chapter 18—*What about rewards in the resurrection?*

The Reality of Resurrection

Resurrection is a reality for everyone reading these words. As has been well said, the death rate is one per person, and everyone alive is going to make it. Some will be physically resurrected to eternity with the Savior, others to eternal separation from the Savior. I urge you to read on—and realize that resurrection is not merely an important issue; understanding of the biblical nature of the resurrection will literally transform the way you live your life today.

PART ONE

✦

Defense of the Resurrection of Christ

CHAPTER 1

MYTHOLOGIES

✛

When they had crucified him, above his head they placed the written charge against him: THIS IS JESUS, THE KING OF THE JEWS. Those who passed by hurled insults at him, shaking their heads and saying, "You who are going to destroy the temple and build it in three days, save yourself! Come down from the cross, if you are the Son of God!"

In the same way the chief priests, the teachers of the law, and the elders mocked him—and the robbers who were crucified with him also heaped insults on him.

About the ninth hour, Jesus cried out in a loud voice, "Eloi, Eloi, lama sabachthani?"—which means, "My God, My God, why have you forsaken me?"

Then Jesus, knowing that the Passover plot was nearing completion, cried out, "I am thirsty."

As if on cue, an unidentified friend of Joseph of Arimathea ran, filled a sponge with a sleeping potion, put it on a stick, and offered it to Jesus to drink.

When he had received it, Jesus cried out, "It is finished." With that, he bowed his head and swooned.

RESURRECTION

Because the Jews did not want the bodies left on the crosses during the Sabbath, they asked Pilate to have the legs broken and the bodies taken down. But when they came to Jesus and found that he was already dead, they did not break his legs. Instead, one of the soldiers pierced Jesus' side with a spear.

As evening approached, Joseph of Arimathea went boldly to Pilate and asked for the body of Jesus. He took the body, wrapped it in a clean linen cloth, and placed it in a tomb cut out of rock.

There Joseph and the unidentified Jew worked feverishly to nurse Jesus back to life.

Tragically, the Roman spear led to the death of Christ and the virtual destruction of the Passover plot. Jesus regained consciousness only long enough to cry out, "Do not let me die in vain. Deceive my disciples into believing I have overcome death and the grave." With that, he bowed his head and died. Immediately Joseph and the unidentified Jew took the body of Jesus and disposed of it.

During the next forty days the unidentified Jew appeared to the disciples and through many convincing fabrications deluded them into believing that he was the resurrected Christ. Beginning with Moses and all the Prophets, he explained to them everything that the Scriptures had taught concerning the Messiah—how he should suffer, die, and be raised again. The hearts of the disciples burned within as they believed the lie. To this very day, the Passover plot engineered by Jesus, Joseph, and the unidentified Jew continues to delude millions into believing that Jesus Christ has risen from the dead.

MYTHOLOGIES 27:35–50*

✢

In 1965, Hugh Schonfield published a 287-page volume titled *The Passover Plot*.[1] In this runaway bestseller, Schonfield contends that Jesus "deliberately plotted" his crucifixion and subsequent resurrection. According to *The Passover Plot*, "Jesus contrived to be arrested the night

---

*Adapted from Matthew (NIV) but radically altered to accommodate Hugh Schonfield's "Passover plot" hypothesis

before the Passover, fully aware that he would be nailed to the cross the following day, but taken down before the onset of the Sabbath in accordance with Jewish law. He would survive the agony of but three hours on the cross."[2] Rather than suffering fatal torment, Jesus merely swooned.

To ensure Jesus' safe removal from the cross, Joseph and an unidentified Jew concocted a plan in which Jesus would be given "not the traditional vinegar but a drug that would render him unconscious and make him appear dead. He would then be cut down from the cross in a deathlike trance, removed by accomplices to the tomb where he would be nursed back to health and then 'resurrected.'"[3] Thus, the tomb was empty due not to resurrection, but to resuscitation.

This new interpretation of the life and death of Jesus captured the imagination of the world. Magazines and ministers immediately lauded it as perhaps the most important book published in a decade. *Time* magazine contended, "Schonfield . . . does not discredit Christ. Instead, he argues that Christ was indeed the Messiah—the Son of Man, as he thought of himself, but not the Son of God—who had been foretold by Jewish prophets of old, and that this is glory enough."[4] Bible scholar William Barclay called *The Passover Plot* "a book of enormous learning and erudition, meticulously documented."[5] This despite the fact that Schonfield himself admitted that it is "an imaginative reconstruction of the personality, aims and activities of Jesus," in which such characters as the unidentified Jew emerge out of thin air.[6]

The Swoon Theory

While the critics of historic Christianity have passionately proclaimed the virtues of Schonfield and his scholarship, *The Passover Plot* is little more than a novel regurgitation of swoon theories that were popular in the first half of the nineteenth century. As noted investigative journalist Lee Strobel points out in *The Case for Christ,* the swoon hypothesis is an urban legend that is continually being resuscitated.[7]

Despite the fact that the swoon theory has been soundly refuted by academia,[8] it is still regurgitated ad nauseum in the public arena. Swoon theorists dismiss the resurrection by contending that Jesus never really died on the cross; instead, he merely fainted and was later revived. A never-ending stream of imaginative stories has flowed from this basic thesis.

In 1929, D. H. Lawrence fantasized that, after surviving crucifixion, Jesus ended up in Egypt. There he fell in love with the priestess Isis.[9] In 1972, Donovan Joyce published *The Jesus Scroll.*[10] Christian philosopher Gary Habermas explains that, in Joyce's rendition of the story, Jesus was apparently revived by a doctor who had been planted in the tomb ahead of time. The doctor was assisted by none other than Jesus' uncle, Joseph of Arimathea. In Joyce's fanciful reconstruction, Jesus is an "eighty-year-old defender of Masada who apparently died while fighting the Romans during the Jewish revolt of A.D. 66–73." In this scrolled autobiography, Jesus is married to Mary Magdalene, is a revolutionary zealot who wars with the Romans, and in the end retires as a monk at Qumran.[11]

In 1992, Barbara Thiering produced an even more outrageous version of the swoon theory.[12] Historian Edwin Yamauchi points out that Thiering, who is a professor at the University of Sydney in Australia, uses the New Testament as a "coded commentary" to reinterpret the Dead Sea Scrolls. In Thiering's mind-boggling tale, Jesus is crucified along with Simon Magus and Judas at Qumran, imbibes snake poison to fake his death, upon recovering marries Mary Magdalene, and later falls in love with Lydia of Philippi. Despite the fact that Thiering's revolting reconstruction is devoid of rhyme or reason, it has received rave reviews in a wide variety of public forums, ranging from radio to television.[13]

The Twin Theory

The swoon theory is not the only novel notion that critics of Christianity have used to explain away the resurrection. Another is the twin theory.[14] In a 1995 debate with Christian apologist William Lane Craig, philosopher Robert Greg Cavin contended that Jesus had an identical twin brother, whom he names Hurome.[15] Hurome is separated from Jesus at birth and does not see him again until the time of the crucifixion. Upon stumbling into Jerusalem, he sees his mirror image on the cross and realizes that the Jesus of Nazareth he had previously heard so much about was in reality his identical twin. He immediately concocts a messianic mission for Christ and carries it out by stealing the body and pretending to be the resurrected Christ.[16] During the debate, Craig summarizes Cavin's version of the story as follows:

> Jesus had an unknown identical twin who impersonated Jesus after the crucifixion, thereby convincing people that he was risen from the dead. Remember the movie *Dave*—you know the one where the presidential double takes over the U.S. presidency when the real president falls into a coma—well [Cavin's] theory is a sort of *Dave* theory of the resurrection. Jesus' unknown twin stole Jesus' body out of the tomb and impersonated Jesus before the disciples. Now, if you are wondering why nobody knew about Jesus' twin brother that's because on [Cavin's] theory unbeknownst to Mary and Joseph their real baby got accidentally switched with one member of a pair of identical twins. So the person that we call Jesus wasn't really Mary's child at all and his twin brother grew up independently of him.

Craig goes on to say that theories like the twin theory may make great comedy, but no one should take them seriously—particularly no one such as Cavin, whose research has forced him to agree that Christ was fatally tormented, that the tomb was empty, that the disciples were convinced Jesus had appeared to them, and that as a result of the resurrection their lives were utterly transformed.

The Muslim Theory

Other hypotheses used to explain away the biblical account of the resurrection emanate from world religions, such as Islam. From a Muslim perspective, Jesus was never crucified and, thus, never resurrected.[17] As Christian philosopher Norman Geisler explains, orthodox Muslims have traditionally held that "Jesus was not crucified on the cross, but that God made someone else look like Jesus and this person was mistakenly crucified as Christ. And the words 'God raised him up unto Himself' have often been taken to mean that Jesus was taken up alive to heaven without dying."[18]

There are a wide variety of opinions in the Muslim world as to whom God substituted for Jesus. Possible candidates range from Judas Iscariot to Pilate to Simon of Cyrene or even to one of Christ's inner circle. Some Muslims contend that one of the disciples volunteered to take on the likeness of Christ while others contend that God involuntarily caused one of Christ's enemies to take on his appearance. Norman Geisler and Abdul Saleeb cite Baidawi, a thirteenth-century scholar whose writings have been regarded as a virtual holy book by Sunni Muslims, as a case in point:

It is related that a group of Jews reviled [Jesus] . . . then the Jews gathered to kill him. Whereupon Allah informed him that he would take him up to heaven. Then [Jesus] said to his disciples, "Which one of you is willing to have my likeness cast upon him, and be killed and crucified and enter Paradise?" One of them accepted, and Allah cast the likeness of [Jesus] upon him, and he was killed and crucified. It is said also that he was one who acted the hypocrite toward [Jesus], and went out to lead the Jews to him. But Allah cast the likeness of [Jesus] upon him, and he was taken and crucified and killed.[19]

Geisler and Saleeb go on to note that "the view that Judas replaced Christ on the cross was again recently popularized in the Muslim world by *The Gospel of Barnabas.*"[20]

Muslims also disagree on what happened to Jesus. A majority, however, "contend that Jesus escaped the cross by being taken up to heaven and that one day he will come back to earth and play a central role in the future events. Based on some of the alleged sayings of Muhammad, Muslims believe that, just before the end of time, Jesus will come back to earth, kill the Antichrist (*al-Dajjal*), kill all pigs, break the cross, destroy the synagogues and churches, establish the religion of Islam, live for forty years, and then he will be buried in the city of Medina beside the prophet Muhammad."[21]

The Watchtower Theory

Other theories concerning the resurrection of Jesus Christ can be found in the kingdom of the cults. Jehovah's Witnesses, for example, are not only famous for denying the deity of Jesus Christ, but for denying his bodily resurrection as well.[22] Their contention is that Jesus was created by God as the archangel Michael,[23] that during his earthly sojourn he became merely human, and that after his crucifixion he was re-created as an immaterial spirit creature. As the Watchtower organization puts it, "the King Christ Jesus was put to death in the flesh and was resurrected an invisible spirit creature. Therefore the world will see him no more. He went to prepare a heavenly place for his associate heirs, 'Christ's body,' for they too will be invisible spirit creatures."[24]

Furthermore, Jehovah's Witnesses assert that a physical resurrection would not have been a tremendous triumph; it would have been a hopeless humiliation. In their view, it would mean that after reigning as the archangel Michael, Jesus was reduced to a human being and did not subsequently regain his former status as an exalted spirit creature. Thus, according to the Watchtower Bible and Tract Society, "Jesus did not take his human body to heaven to be forever a man in heaven. Had he done so, that would have left him even lower than the angels. . . . God did not purpose for Jesus to be humiliated thus forever by being a fleshly man forever. No, but after he had sacrificed his perfect manhood, God raised him to deathless life as a glorious spirit creature."[25]

To explain away the empty tomb, Jehovah's Witnesses argue that the physical body of Jesus was discarded and destroyed. In the words of the Watchtower, "The human body of flesh, which Jesus Christ laid down forever as a ransom sacrifice, was disposed of by God's power."[26] Thus, instead of rising from the dead, "the fleshly body of Jesus Christ was disposed of on earth by Almighty God and not taken to heaven by Jesus."[27] In the view of Watchtower founder Charles Taze Russell, the body that hung on the cross either "dissolved into gasses" or is "preserved somewhere as the grand memorial of God's love."[28]

Finally, it should be noted that Jehovah's Witnesses attempt to explain away the post-resurrection appearances of Christ by suggesting that "the bodies in which Jesus manifested himself to his disciples after his return to life were not the body in which he was nailed to the tree. They were merely materialized for the occasion, resembling on one or two occasions the body in which he died, but on the majority of occasions being unrecognizable by his most intimate disciples."[29] If Jehovah's Witnesses are correct, Jesus fooled his disciples into thinking he had physically risen from the grave by appearing in a variety of disparate bodies. In their words, "he appeared in different bodies. He appeared and disappeared just as the angels had done, because he was resurrected as a spirit creature. Only because Thomas would not believe did Jesus appear in a body like that in which he had died."[30]

The Greatest Feat or a Gargantuan Fraud?

If devotees of the kingdom of the cults, adherents of world religions, or liberal scholars are correct, the biblical account of the resurrection is fiction, fantasy, or a gargantuan fraud. If, on the other hand, Christianity is factually reliable, the resurrection is the greatest feat in human history. As Christian apologist Josh McDowell puts it, "After more than 700 hours of studying this subject and thoroughly investigating its foundation, I have come to the conclusion that the resurrection of Jesus Christ is one of the *most wicked, vicious, heartless hoaxes ever foisted upon the minds of men,* OR *it is the most fantastic fact of history.*"[31]

Wilbur Smith points out that, from the very first, the Christian church has unanimously borne witness to the immutable fact of Christ's resurrection. Says Smith, "It is what we may call one of the great fundamental doctrines and convictions of the church, and so penetrates the literature of the New Testament, that if you lifted out every passage in which a reference is made to the Resurrection, you would have a collection of writings so mutilated that what remained could not be understood."[32]

The Book of Acts is a classic case in point. In Acts 1, Matthias is chosen to replace Judas as a witness of the resurrection. In Acts 2, Peter, in his powerful Pentecost proclamation, thunders, "Brothers, I can tell you confidently that the patriarch David died and was buried, and his tomb is here to this day. But he was a prophet and knew that God had promised him on oath that he would place one of his descendants on his throne. Seeing what was ahead, he spoke of the resurrection of the Christ, that he was not abandoned to the grave, nor did his body see decay. God has raised this Jesus to life, and we are all witnesses of the fact" (vv. 29–32).

In Acts 3, at a place called Solomon's Colonnade, Peter said to the men of Israel, "The God of Abraham, Isaac and Jacob, the God of our fathers, has glorified his servant Jesus. You handed him over to be killed, and you disowned him before Pilate, though he had decided to let him go. You disowned the Holy and Righteous One and asked that a murderer be released to you. You killed the author of life, but God raised him from the dead. We are witnesses of this" (vv. 13–15). In Acts 4, we read that the priests, the captain of the temple guard, and the Sadducees were so disturbed by the preaching of Peter and John that they threw them into prison for "proclaiming in Jesus the resurrection of the dead" (v. 2). Likewise, in Acts 5, the apostles face a flogging for testifying that God "raised Jesus from the dead" (v. 30).

In Acts 10, Peter, at a large gathering of people in the house of Cornelius, testifies to the resurrection, saying, "We are witnesses of everything [Jesus] did in the country of the Jews and in Jerusalem. They killed him by hanging him on a tree, but God raised him from the dead on the third day and caused him to be seen. He was not seen by all the people, but by witnesses whom God had already chosen—by us who ate and drank with him after he rose from the dead" (vv. 39–41).

In Acts 13, the spotlight moves from Peter to Paul. After leaving Perga, Paul went on to Pisidian, Antioch. There in his synagogue sermon this persecutor-turned-proselytizer proclaims that the people of Jerusalem and their rulers asked Pilate to have Jesus condemned to death despite the fact that they found no warrant for his crucifixion. Says Paul:

> When they had carried out all that was written about him, they took him down from the tree and laid him in a tomb. But God raised him from the dead, and for many days he was seen by those who had traveled with him from Galilee to Jerusalem. They are now his witnesses to our people.
>
> We tell you the good news: What God promised our fathers he has fulfilled for us, their children, by raising up Jesus. As it is written in the second Psalm: "You are my Son; today I have become your Father." The fact that God raised him from the dead, never to decay, is stated in these words: "I will give you the holy and sure blessings promised to David." So it is stated elsewhere: "You will not let your Holy One see decay."

For when David had served God's purpose in his own generation, he fell asleep; he was buried with his fathers and his body decayed. But the one whom God raised from the dead did not see decay. (Acts 13:29–37)

In Acts 17, we find Paul in Athens, passionately preaching the good news about Jesus and the resurrection. After a group of Epicurean and Stoic philosophers brought him to a meeting of the Areopagus, Paul stood up and addressed the crowd as follows:

"Men of Athens! I see that in every way you are very religious. For as I walked around and looked carefully at your objects of worship, I even found an altar with this inscription: TO AN UNKNOWN GOD. Now what you worship as something unknown I am going to proclaim to you.

The God who made the world and everything in it is the Lord of heaven and earth and does not live in temples built by hands. And he is not served by human hands, as if he needed anything, because he himself gives all men life and breath and everything else. From one man he made every nation of men, that they should inhabit the whole earth; and he determined the times set for them and the exact places where they should live. God did this so that men would seek him and perhaps reach out for him and find him, though he is not far from each one of us. 'For in him we live and move and have our being.' As some of your own poets have said, 'We are his offspring.'

Therefore since we are God's offspring, we should not think that the divine being is like gold or silver or stone—an image made by man's design and skill. In the past God overlooked such ignorance, but now he commands all people everywhere to repent. For he has set a day when he will judge the world with justice by the man he has appointed. He has given proof of this to all men by raising him from the dead."

When they heard about the resurrection of the dead, some of them sneered, but others said, "We want to hear you again on this subject." (Acts 17:22–32)

Many other such passages from Dr. Luke's Acts of the Apostles could be cited. Suffice it to say, Wilbur Smith was absolutely right. Without the resurrection, not only Acts, but the whole of Scripture would be a disfigured document devoid of definition. The resurrection so radically changed the lives of Christ's followers that it was engraved on their tombs and depicted on the walls of their catacombs. In addition, "it entered deeply into Christian hymnology; it became one of the most vital themes of the great apologetic writings of the first four centuries; it was the theme constantly dwelt upon in the preaching of the ante-Nicene and post-Nicene period. It entered at once into the creedal formulae of the church; it is in our Apostles' Creed; it is in all the great creeds that followed."[33]

Smith goes on to note that "the burden of the good news or gospel was not 'Follow this Teacher and do your best,' but, 'Jesus and the Resurrection.' You cannot take that away from Christianity without radically altering its character and destroying its very identity."[34] Paul, along with the rest of the apostles, made it crystal-clear that no middle ground exists. The resurrection is history or hoax, miracle or myth, fact or fantasy. Says Paul:

If Christ has not been raised, our preaching is useless and so is your faith. More than that, we are then found to be false witnesses about God, for we have testified about God that he raised Christ from the dead. But he did not raise him if in fact the dead are not raised. For if the dead are not raised, then Christ has not been raised either. And if Christ has not been raised, your faith is futile; you are still in your sins. Then those also who have fallen asleep in Christ are lost. If only for this life we have hope in Christ, we are to be pitied more than all men. (1 Corinthians 15:14–19)

Pre-evangelism/Post-evangelism

It is precisely because of the strategic importance of the resurrection that each Christian must be prepared to defend its historicity. Thus, apologetics—the defense of the faith—has a dual purpose. On the one hand, apologetics involves pre-evangelism. In post-Christian America, few people are aware that belief in the resurrection is not a blind leap into the dark, but faith founded on fact. It is historic and evidential. Thus, it is defensible. On the other hand, apologetics involves post-evangelism. During an age in which the resurrection is under siege, knowing how to defend its reliability serves to strengthen our faith.

The resurrection is not merely important to the historic Christian faith; without it, there would be no Christianity. It is the singular doctrine that elevates Christianity above all other world religions. Through the resurrection, Christ demonstrated that he does not stand in a line of peers with Abraham, Buddha, or Confucius. He is utterly unique. He has the power not only to lay down his life, but to take it up again.

Because of its centrality to Christianity, those who take the sacred name of Christ upon their lips must be prepared to defend the reliability of the resurrection. To make the process memorable, I've developed the acronym FEAT. This acronym should serve as an enduring reminder that, far from being a gargantuan fraud, the resurrection is the greatest *feat* in the annals of recorded history. As we will see in the following chapters, each letter in FEAT will serve to remind us of an undeniable fact of the resurrection:

Fatal Torment

Empty Tomb

Appearances of Christ

Transformation

CHAPTER 2

FATAL TORMENT

☩

When they had crucified him, they divided up his clothes by casting lots. And sitting down, they kept watch over him there. Above his head they placed the written charge against him: THIS IS JESUS, THE KING OF THE JEWS. Two robbers were crucified with him, one on his right and one on his left. Those who passed by hurled insults at him, shaking their heads and saying, "You who are going to destroy the temple and build it in three days, save yourself! Come down from the cross, if you are the Son of God!"

In the same way the chief priests, the teachers of the law and the elders mocked him. "He saved others," they said, "but he can't save himself! He's the King of Israel! Let him come down now from the cross, and we will believe in him. He trusts in God. Let God rescue him now if he wants him, for he said, 'I am the Son of God.'" In the same way the robbers who were crucified with him also heaped insults on him.

From the sixth hour until the ninth hour darkness came over all the land. About the ninth hour Jesus cried out in a loud voice, "Eloi, Eloi, *lama sabachthani?"—which means, "My God, my God, why have you forsaken me?"*

When some of those standing there heard this, they said, "He's calling Elijah."

Immediately one of them ran and got a sponge. He filled it with wine vinegar, put it on a stick, and offered it to Jesus to drink. The rest said, "Now leave him alone. Let's see if Elijah comes to save him."

And when Jesus had cried out again in a loud voice, he gave up his spirit.

—MATTHEW 27:35–50

✠

The fatal suffering of Jesus Christ as recounted in the New Testament is one of the most well-established facts of ancient history. Even in today's modern age of scientific enlightenment, there is a virtual consensus among New Testament scholars, both conservative and liberal, that Jesus died on the cross, that he was buried in the tomb of Joseph of Arimathea, and that his death drove his disciples to despair.[1]

The Medical Facts

The best medical minds of ancient and modern times have demonstrated beyond a shadow of a doubt that Christ's physical trauma was fatal.[2] His torment began in the Garden of Gethsemane after the emotional Last Supper. There Jesus experienced a medical condition known as hematidrosis. Tiny capillaries in his sweat glands ruptured, mixing sweat with blood. As a result, Christ's skin became extremely fragile.

The same night, Jesus was betrayed by Judas, disowned by Peter, and arrested by the temple guard. Before Caiaphas the high priest, he was mocked, beaten, and spat upon. The next morning, Jesus, battered, bruised, and bleeding, was led into the Praetorium. There

Jesus was stripped and subjected to the brutality of Roman flogging. A whip replete with razor-sharp bones and lead balls reduced his body to quivering ribbons of bleeding flesh. As Christ slumped into the pool of his own blood, the soldiers threw a scarlet robe across his shoulders, thrust a scepter into his hands, and pressed sharp thorns into his scalp.

After they mocked him, they took the scepter out of his hand and repeatedly struck him on the head. Now Jesus was in critical condition. A heavy wooden beam was thrust upon Christ's bleeding body, and he was led away to a place called Golgotha. There the Lord experienced ultimate physical torture in the form of the cross. The Roman system of crucifixion had been fine-tuned to produce maximum pain. In fact, the word *excruciating* (literally "out of the cross") had to be invented to fully codify its horror.[3]

At "the place of the skull," the Roman soldiers drove thick, seven-inch iron spikes through Christ's hands[4] and feet. Waves of pain pulsated through Christ's body as the nails lacerated his nerves. Breathing became an agonizing endeavor as Christ pushed his tortured body upward to grasp small gulps of air. In the ensuing hours, he experienced cycles of joint-wrenching cramps, intermittent asphyxiation, and excruciating pain as his lacerated back moved up and down against the rough timber of the cross.

As the chill of death crept through his body, Jesus cried out, "'*Eloi, Eloi, lama sabachthani?*'—which means, 'My God, my God, why have you forsaken me?'" (Matthew 27:46). And in that anguished cry was encapsulated the greatest agony of all. For on the cross, Christ bore the sin and suffering of all humanity. And then with his passion complete, Jesus gave up his spirit.

Shortly thereafter, a Roman legionnaire drove his spear through the fifth interspace between the ribs, upward through the pericardium, and into Christ's heart. From the wound rushed forth blood and water, demonstrating conclusively that Jesus had suffered fatal torment.

In light of all the evidence, believing that Jesus merely swooned stretches credulity beyond the breaking point. It means that Christ survived six trials, a lack of sleep, the scourge, being spiked to a cross, and a spear wound in his side.

Adherence to some of the more implausible versions of the swoon theory would take even more faith. It would entail believing that Jesus survived three days without medical attention, single-handedly rolled away an enormously heavy tombstone, subdued an armed guard, strolled around on pierced feet, and seduced his disciples into communicating the myth that he had conquered death while he lived out the remainder of his pathetic life in obscurity.

The Medical Verdict

Dr. Alexander Metherell, a prominent physician who has thoroughly investigated the historical and medical facts regarding the death of Jesus Christ, drove a fatal stake through the heart of the swoon theory. In an interview with investigative journalist Lee Strobel, Dr. Metherell pointed out that a person who had suffered the kind of excruciating torture recounted in the Gospels "would never have inspired his disciples to go out and proclaim that he's the Lord of life who had triumphed over the grave." Metherell went on to say that "after suffering that horrible abuse, with all the catastrophic blood loss and trauma, he would have looked so pitiful that his disciples would never have hailed him as a victorious conqueror of death; they would have felt sorry for him and tried to nurse him back to health." Thus, as he concluded, "it's preposterous to think that if he had appeared to them in that awful state, his followers would have been prompted to start a worldwide movement based on the hope that someday they too would have a resurrection body like his."[5] The inevitable conclusion is that the swoon theory is a leap of faith into a chasm of credulity.

The Major Swoon Flaws

Philosopher and New Testament historian Dr. Gary Habermas dismisses swoon theories for three major reasons. First, as recounted by the apostle John, when the soldiers determined that Jesus was dead, one of them "pierced Jesus' side with a spear, bringing a sudden flow of blood and water" (John 19:34). As a first-century man, John would not likely have known what twentieth-century science has only recently discovered—namely, that blood and water flowed from the side of Jesus due to the fact that the heart is surrounded by a sac of water, called a *pericardium.* The water came from Christ's pierced pericardium; the blood came from his pierced heart. Says Habermas, "Even if Jesus was alive before he was stabbed, the lance would almost certainly have killed him. Therefore, this chest wound also disproves the swoon theory."[6]

Furthermore, as demonstrated by the nineteenth-century liberal scholar David Strauss, even if Jesus had survived his crucifixion, he could never have rolled a massive tombstone uphill out of its gully—especially in his weakened condition and without so much as an edge against which to push from inside the tomb. Had he accomplished this miraculous feat, he would then have had to limp around on pierced feet, find his disciples' hideout, and then convince them that he had conquered death and the grave. Strauss points out that, far from fantasizing that this bleeding shell of a man was their Savior, the disciples would have run and fetched a doctor.[7] Dr. Habermas notes that Albert Schweitzer referred to Strauss's critique as "the 'death-blow' to such rationalistic approaches. After Strauss's views were circulated, the liberal 'lives of Jesus' usually shunned the swoon theory. By the early twentieth century, other critical scholars proclaimed this theory to be nothing more than a historical curiosity of the past. Even critics no longer considered it to be a viable hypothesis."[8]

Finally, as demonstrated by twentieth-century medical research, crucifixion is essentially death by asphyxiation. As the body hangs downward, the intercostal and pectoral muscles surrounding the lungs halt the normal process of breathing. Thus, even if Jesus had been given a drug to put him in a deathlike trance, he would not have been able to survive death by asphyxiation. As Habermas puts it, "one cannot fake the inability to breathe for any length of time."[9]

The late liberal Cambridge scholar John A. T. Robinson suggested that the swoon theory is so fatally flawed that "if the public were not so interested in virtually anyone who writes on Christianity, it 'would be laughed out of court.'"[10] While it is one thing to debunk the swoon theory, it is quite another to defend scriptural truth. Critics are quick to point out that the biblical accounts of the resurrection are patently unreliable. In their view, the Bible is a copy of a copy of a copy, with fresh errors introduced during each stage of the process.[11] That, however, is far from true. Though we no longer have the original New Testament autographs that chronicle the fatal torment and resurrection of Jesus Christ, we can be absolutely certain that the copies we have are faithful representations of those original writings.

The Manuscript Evidence

To begin with, it should be noted that the New Testament has stronger manuscript support than any other work of classical literature—including Homer, Plato, Aristotle, Caesar, and Tacitus. There are presently more than five thousand copies of Greek manuscripts in existence[12] and as many as twenty thousand more translations in such languages as Latin, Coptic, and Syriac. One early manuscript fragment can be dated as far back as A.D. 120. Incredibly, there is now reason to believe that the earliest manuscript fragments may be dated all the way back to the middle of the first century.[13] This is amazing when you consider that only seven of Plato's manuscripts are in existence today—and there is a thirteen-hundred-year gap that separates the earliest of these copies from the original writing! Equally amazing is the fact that the New Testament has been virtually unaltered, as has been well-

accepted by scholars who have compared the earliest written manuscripts with manuscripts written centuries later.

Furthermore, the reliability of Scripture is also confirmed through
the eyewitness credentials of the authors. For example, Luke says that
he gathered eyewitness testimony and "carefully investigated everything" (Luke 1:3). John writes, "That which was from the beginning,
which we have heard, which we have seen with our eyes, which we
have looked at and our hands have touched—this we proclaim concerning the Word of life" (1 John 1:1). Likewise, Peter reminded his
readers that the disciples "did not follow cleverly invented stories" but
"were eyewitnesses of [Jesus'] majesty" (2 Peter 1:16).

Finally, secular historians—including Josephus (before A.D. 100),
Tacitus (c. A.D. 120), Suetonius (A.D. 110), and the Roman governor
Pliny the Younger (A.D. 110)—confirm the many events, people, places,
and customs chronicled in the New Testament. Early church leaders,
such as Irenaeus, Tertullian, Julius Africanus, and Clement of Rome—
all writing before A.D. 250—also shed light on the New Testament's
historical accuracy. Even skeptical historians agree that the New
Testament is a remarkably accurate historical document.

The Massive Archaeological Evidence

As with the manuscript evidence, archaeology is a powerful witness to
the accuracy of the New Testament documents. Over and over again,
comprehensive archaeological fieldwork and careful biblical interpretation affirm the reliability of the Bible. It is telling when secular
scholars must revise their biblical criticism in light of solid archaeological evidence.

One of the most well-known New Testament examples concerns the
Books of Luke and Acts. Biblical skeptic Sir William Ramsay was trained
as an archaeologist and then set out to disprove the historical reliability of
this portion of the New Testament. But through his painstaking

Mediterranean archaeological trips, he became converted as, one after another, the historical allusions of Luke were proved accurate.[14]

Furthermore, archaeologists recently discovered a gold mine of archaeological nuggets that provide a powerful counter to objections raised by scholars against the biblical account of Christ's crucifixion and burial. In the October 25, 1999 issue of *U.S. News and World Report,* Jeffrey Sheler highlights the significance of the recent discovery of the remains of a man crucified during the first century. This discovery calls into question the scholarship of liberals who contend that Jesus was tied rather than nailed to the cross and that his corpse was likely thrown into a shallow grave and eaten by wild dogs rather than entombed. The following is Sheler's account of this archeological find:

> Explorers found the skeletal remains of a crucified man in a burial cave at Giva'at ha-Mitvar, near the Nablus road outside of Jerusalem. It was a momentous discovery: While the Romans were known to have crucified thousands of alleged traitors, rebels, robbers, and deserters in the two centuries straddling the turn of the era, never before had the remains of a crucifixion victim been recovered. An initial analysis of the remains found that their condition dramatically corroborated the Bible's description of the Roman method of execution.
>
> The bones were preserved in a stone burial box called an ossuary and appeared to be those of a man about 5 feet, 5 inches tall and 24 to 28 years old. His open arms had been nailed to the crossbar, in the manner similar to that shown in crucifixion paintings. The knees had been doubled up and turned sideways, and a single large iron nail had been driven through both heels. The nail—still lodged in the heel bone of one foot, though the executioners had removed the body from the cross after death—was found bent, apparently having hit a knot in the wood. The shin bones seem to have been broken, corroborating what the Gospel of John suggests was normal practice in Roman crucifixions.[15]

Finally, recent archaeological finds have also corroborated biblical details surrounding the trial that led to the fatal torment of Jesus Christ—including Pontius Pilate, who ordered Christ's crucifixion, as well as the burial grounds of Caiaphas, the high priest who presided over the religious trials of Christ. As noted by Sheler, in 1990, a burial chamber dating back to the first century was discovered two miles south of Temple Mount. "Inside, archaeologists found 12 limestone ossuaries. One contained the bones of a 60-year-old man and bore the inscription *Yehosef bar Qayafa* —'Joseph, son of Caiaphas.'" Experts believe these remains are probably those of Caiaphas, the high priest of Jerusalem who, according to the Gospels, ordered the arrest of Jesus, interrogated him, and handed him over to Pontius Pilate for execution.[16]

Regarding Pontius Pilate, Sheler notes that excavations at the seaside ruins of Caesarea Maritima—the ancient seat of the Roman government in Judea—uncovered a first-century inscription that confirmed Pilate was the Roman ruler at the time of Christ's crucifixion. Archaeologists working at the Herodian theater found a plaque inscribed with the Latin words, *Tiberieum . . . [Pon]tius Pilatus . . . [praef]ectus Juda[ea]e.* "According to experts, the complete inscription would have read, 'Pontius Pilate, the Prefect of Judea, has dedicated to the people of Caesarea a temple in honor of Tiberias.' The discovery of the so-called Pilate Stone has been widely acclaimed as a significant affirmation of biblical history because, in short, it confirms that the man depicted in the Gospels as Judea's Roman governor had precisely the responsibilities and authority that the Gospel writers ascribe to him."[17] Truly, with every turn of the archaeologist's spade, we continue to see evidence for the trustworthiness of the Scriptures.[18]

The Messianic Prophecies

The Bible records predictions of events that could not be known nor predicted by chance or common sense. Surprisingly, the predictive nature of many Bible passages was once a popular argument among liberals against the reliability of the Bible. Critics argued that various passages were written later than the biblical texts indicated because they recounted events that happened sometimes hundreds of years after they supposedly were written. They concluded that, subsequent to the events, literary editors went back and "doctored" the original, nonpredictive texts.

But this is simply wrong. Careful research *affirms* the predictive accuracy of the Scriptures. Since Christ is the culminating theme of the Old Testament and the Living Word of the New Testament, it should not surprise us that prophecies regarding him outnumber all others. Many of these prophecies would have been impossible for Jesus deliberately to conspire to fulfill—such as his descent from Abraham, Isaac, and Jacob (see Genesis 12:3; 17:19; Matthew 1:1–2; Acts 3:25); his birth in Bethlehem (see Micah 5:2; Matthew 2:1, 6); his crucifixion with criminals (see Isaiah 53:12; Matthew 27:38; cf. Luke 22:37); the piercing of his hands and feet on the cross (see Psalm 22:16; John 20:25); the soldiers' gambling for his clothes (see Psalm 22:18; Matthew 27:35); the piercing of his side (Zechariah 12:10; John 19:34) and the fact that his bones were not broken at his death (see Psalm 34:20; John 19:33–37); and his burial among the rich (see Isaiah 53:9; Matthew 27:57–60).

It is statistically preposterous that any or all of the Bible's specific, detailed prophecies could have been fulfilled through chance, good guessing, or deliberate deceit. When you consider some of the improbable prophecies cited above, it seems incredible that skeptics—knowing the authenticity and historicity of the texts—could reject the statistical verdict: The Bible is the Word of God, and the Gospel accounts of Christ's fatal torment are immutable facts of ancient history.[19]

Having established the scriptural reliability of Christ's fatal torment, we now turn to the *E* in the acronym FEAT, which will serve to remind us of the second unshakable pillar undergirding resurrection: the empty tomb.

CHAPTER 3

EMPTY TOMB

✠

It was Preparation Day (that is, the day before the Sabbath). So as evening approached, Joseph of Arimathea, a prominent member of the Council, who was himself waiting for the kingdom of God, went boldly to Pilate and asked for Jesus' body. Pilate was surprised to hear that he was already dead. Summoning the centurion, he asked him if Jesus had already died. When he learned from the centurion that it was so, he gave the body to Joseph. So Joseph bought some linen cloth, took down the body, wrapped it in the linen, and placed it in a tomb cut out of rock. Then he rolled a stone against the entrance of the tomb. Mary Magdalene and Mary the mother of Joses saw where he was laid.

When the Sabbath was over, Mary Magdalene, Mary the mother of James, and Salome bought spices so that they might go to anoint Jesus' body. Very early on the first day of the week, just after sunrise, they were on their way to the tomb and they asked each other, "Who will roll the stone away from the entrance of the tomb?"

But when they looked up, they saw that the stone, which was very large, *had been rolled away. As they entered the tomb, they saw a young man dressed in a white robe sitting on the right side, and they were alarmed.*

"Don't be alarmed," he said. "You are looking for Jesus the Nazarene, who was crucified. He has risen! He is not here. See the place where they laid him. But go, tell his disciples and Peter, 'He is going ahead of you into Galilee. There you will see him, just as he told you.'"

Trembling and bewildered, the women went out and fled from the tomb. They said nothing to anyone, because they were afraid.

—MARK 15:42–16:8

✠

The year 1985 marked the beginning of one of the most well-publicized wars in history. This was not a war of weapons; rather, it was a war of words. It began with a coalition of "scholars" who dubbed themselves the Jesus Seminar. These scholars were determined to demolish the biblical Jesus in the public arena, rather than merely in private academia. They were determined "to liberate the people of the church from the 'dark ages of theological tyranny.'"[1]

The Fellows of the Jesus Seminar

Jesus Seminar founder Robert Funk is bent on convincing the world that the historical Jesus is not worthy of worship. Said Funk, "Jesus himself should not be, must not be, the object of faith. That would be to repeat the idolatry of the first believers."[2] His stated objective is "to liberate Jesus. The only Jesus most people know is the mythic one. They don't want the real Jesus, they want the one they can worship. The cultic Jesus."[3] Fellow cofounder John Dominic Crossan took dead aim at the resurrection of Jesus Christ. *Time* magazine reports Crossan's pontification: "The tales of entombment and resurrection were latter-day wishful thinking. Instead, Jesus' corpse went the way of all abandoned criminals' bodies: it was probably barely covered with dirt, vulnerable to the wild dogs that roamed the wasteland of the exe-cution grounds."[4]

The founders of the Jesus Seminar make little attempt to hide their disdain for the biblical Jesus. Crossan denigrates him as "a peasant Jewish cynic," and Funk demeans him as "perhaps the first stand-up Jewish comic."[5] At times, the assertions of Jesus Seminar participants are so outrageous that the eminent Jewish scholar Jacob Neusner called the Jesus Seminar "either the greatest scholarly hoax since the Piltdown Man or the utter bankruptcy of New Testament studies—I hope the former."[6]

Multitudes uncritically accept the assertions of the Jesus Seminar, failing to recognize that they fly in the face of well-established facts. Unlike a consensus of credible scholarship, Jesus Seminar scholars are famous for making dogmatic assertions while failing to provide defensible arguments. For example, they dogmatically assert that Jesus did not say more than 80 percent of what is attributed to him by Matthew, Mark, Luke, and John. This indefensible assertion is based on what theologian Dr. Gregory Boyd described as their own unique brand of fundamentalism.[7] The so-called historical Jesus that has emerged is: (1) nonapocalyptic, (2) socially subversive, (3) a stand-up comic, (4) a mere human, (5) focused on the here-and-now, (6) one who did not intend to organize a following, (7) and one whose death was merely an insignificant accident of history. Thus, according to the Jesus Seminar, belief in the resurrection was merely a later Christian myth.[8]

In short, the fellows of the Jesus Seminar begin with an antisuper-natural bias and thus reject the resurrection a priori. In place of reason and evidential substance, they offer rhetoric and emotional stereotypes. Those who disagree with their presuppositions are stereotypically regarded as intellectually retarded and reduced to residing in the Dark Ages. If the Jesus Seminar fellows are anything, they are media savvy. They have attracted huge headlines by painting evangelicals as naive fun-damentalists who uncritically buy into the biblical account of the empty tomb. Using colored beads in a ballot vote, they reject the authenticity of statements attributed to Christ by the Gospel writers. In their view, red beads, black beads, and pink beads mean "yes," "no," and "maybe so," respectively. As an intermediate category, they use gray beads to designate words that "did not originate with Jesus though they may reflect his ideas."[9] In their view, fewer than 20 percent of Christ's sayings are credible.

The False Gospel of Thomas

Jesus Seminar participants clearly loathe the Gospel of John and love the Gospel of Thomas—this despite the fact that Thomas includes such patently ignorant and politically incorrect passages as the following conversation between Peter and Jesus: "Simon Peter said to them, 'Make Mary leave us, for females don't deserve life.' Jesus said, 'Look, I will guide her to make her male, so that she too may become a living spirit resembling you males. For every female who makes herself male will enter the domain of Heaven.'"[10]

The *Christian Research Journal* notes that when the Jesus Seminar released their color-coded "scholars version" of *The Five Gospels* in 1993, the second-century Gospel of Thomas was thrust into prime time: "For all intents and purposes, the Jesus Seminar has 'canonized' this 'Gospel,' known primarily from a Coptic translation found in Egypt at Nag Hammadi in late 1945. . . . In fact, it is quite clear that the scholars of the Seminar consider the Gospel of Thomas far more reliable and important than the Gospel of John, and probably more than Matthew and Luke's Gospels as well, as far as being useful in 'reconstructing' the words of the 'historical Jesus.'"[11]

Even a cursory reading of the Gospel of Thomas should suffice to see how deeply it was influenced by second-century gnostic concepts that came in vogue long after the New Testament period.[12] Yet the Jesus Seminar speculates that the Gospel of Thomas is earlier and more authentic than the biblical accounts.[13] Christian philosopher and theologian William Lane Craig lamented, "It is sobering to think that it is this sort of idiosyncratic speculation that thousands of lay readers of magazines like *Time* have come to believe represents the best of contemporary New Testament scholarship."[14]

The Facts Only the Facts!

As the reliability of the resurrection is undermined in the media, it is crucial that Christians are prepared to demonstrate that Jesus was buried and that, on Easter morning some two thousand years ago, the tomb was indeed empty. Contrary to Crossan, the late liberal scholar John A. T. Robinson of Cambridge conceded that the burial of Christ "is one of the earliest and best-attested facts about Jesus."[15] This statement is not merely a dogmatic assertion, but rather stands firmly upon sound argumentation.

The Fictional Pharisee Fallacy

Liberal and conservative New Testament scholars alike agree that the body of Jesus was buried in the private tomb of Joseph of Arimathea. Craig underscores this fact by noting that, as a member of the Jewish court that condemned Jesus, Joseph of Arimathea is unlikely to be Christian fiction. The noted New Testament scholar Raymond Brown explains that "Joseph's being responsible for burying Jesus is 'very probable,' since a Christian fictional creation of a Jewish Sanhedrist doing what is right for Jesus is 'almost inexplicable,' given the hostility toward the Jewish leaders responsible for Jesus' death in early Christian writings. In particular, Mark would not have invented Joseph in view of his statements that the whole Sanhedrin voted for Jesus' condemnation (Mark 14:55, 64; 15:1)."[16]

Furthermore, no competing burial story exists. Craig points out that "if the burial of Jesus in the tomb by Joseph of Arimathea is legendary, then it is strange that conflicting traditions nowhere appear, even in Jewish polemic. That no remnant of the true story or even a conflicting false one should remain is hard to explain unless the Gospel account is substantially the true account."[17] Additionally, it should be noted that "during Jesus' time there was an extraordinary interest in the graves of Jewish martyrs and holy men, and these were scrupulously cared for and honored. . . .This was so because the bones of the prophet lay in the tomb and imparted to the site its religious value. If the remains were not there, then the grave would lose its significance as a shrine." And in the case of Christ, there is no evidence that the tomb was venerated.[18]

Finally, the account of Jesus' burial in the tomb of Joseph of Arimathea is substantiated by Mark's Gospel and is, therefore, far too early to have been the subject of legendary corruption.[19] Likewise, Paul substantiates Christ's burial in a letter to the Corinthian Christians, in which he recites an ancient Christian creed dating to within a few years of the crucifixion itself (see 1 Corinthians 15:3–7).[20]

The Female Factor

As Lee Strobel notes in *The Case for Christ*, "when you understand the role of women in first-century Jewish society, what's really extraordinary is that this empty tomb story should feature females as the discoverers of the empty tomb."[21] In fact, "any later legendary account would have certainly portrayed male disciples as discovering the tomb—Peter or John, for example. The fact that women are the first witnesses to the empty tomb is most plausibly explained by the reality that—like it or not—they *were* the discoverers of the empty tomb! This shows that the gospel writers faithfully recorded what happened, even if it was embarrassing."[22]

To begin with, it should be noted that females were not even allowed to serve as legal witnesses. Says Craig, their testimony "was regarded as so worthless that they could not even testify in a court of law. If a man committed a crime and was observed in the very act by some women, he could not be convicted on the basis of their testimony, since their testimony was regarded as so worthless that it was not even admitted into court."[23]

Furthermore, Craig notes that "women occupied a low rung on the Jewish social ladder. Compared to men, women were second-class citizens. Consider these Jewish texts: 'Sooner let the words of the Law be burnt than delivered to women!' and again: 'Happy is he whose children are male, but unhappy is he whose children are female!'"[24] Prior to the coming of Christ, women were so denigrated by society that "one of the Jewish prayers dated from that era declared, 'I thank thee that I am not a woman.'"[25]

Finally, if Jesus had been a typical Jewish sage, he would not have encouraged women to be his disciples. While women served as maids and mothers in Jewish society, they would never have been allowed to follow a Jewish master as disciples. Even the Greek philosophers of the day were reticent to count women as their disciples. As Craig Keener notes in *The IVP Bible Background Commentary,* for "women to travel with the group would have been viewed as scandalous. Adult coeducation was unheard of, and that these women are learning Jesus' teaching as closely as his male disciples would surely bother some outsiders as well."[26] According to *Nelson's New Illustrated Bible Dictionary*, however, Christ's example and teachings radically challenged the cultural norms:

> He invited women to accompany Him and His disciples on their journeys (Luke 8:1–3). He talked with the Samaritan woman at Jacob's Well and led her to a conversion experience (John 4). Jesus did not think it strange that Mary sat at His feet, assuming the role of a disciple; in fact, He suggested to Martha that she should do likewise (Luke 10:38–42). Although the Jews segregated the women in both Temple and synagogue, the early church did not separate the congregation by sex (Acts 12:1–17; 1 Corinthians 11:2–16). The apostle Paul wrote, "there is neither Jew nor Greek, there is neither slave nor free, there is neither male nor female; for you are all one in Christ Jesus" (Galatians 3:28).[27]

The First Response

Finally, as Craig emphasizes in *Jesus Under Fire,* the earliest Jewish response to the resurrection of Jesus Christ presupposes the empty tomb. Instead of denying that the tomb was empty, the antagonists of Christ accused his disciples of stealing the body. Their response to the proclamation "He has risen—He is risen indeed" was not "His body is still in the tomb," or "He was thrown into a shallow grave and eaten by dogs." Instead, they responded, "His disciples came during the night and stole him away" (Matthew 28:13).[28] In the centuries following the resurrection, the fact of the empty tomb was forwarded by Jesus' friends and foes alike.

The medieval Jewish polemic *Toledot Yeshu* not only states that Jesus suffered fatal torment but sings the common chorus, "His disciples came during the night and stole him away." In this fifth-century version of the Passover plot hypothesis, a gardener named Juda discovers the disciples' devious plan to steal the body of Jesus. Beating them to the punch, he robs Jesus from the tomb of Joseph and disposes of his body in a freshly dug grave. He then tells the foes of Christ what he had done and offers them the body of the Savior for thirty pieces of silver. The Jewish leaders bought the cadaver and subsequently dragged it through the streets of the city in evidence that Christ had *not* risen from the dead as he said he would.[29]

While this fanciful story has no historical merit, it underscores the earliest evidence extant—the empty tomb! In short, early Christianity simply could not have survived an identifiable tomb containing the corpse of Christ. The enemies of Christ could have easily put an end to the charade by displaying the body as depicted in *Toledot Yeshu.* Even Jesus Seminar founder John Dominic Crossan would be forced by the facts to concede that no one can affirm the historicity of Christ's burial while simultaneously denying the historicity of the empty tomb.[30]

Having demonstrated that the empty tomb is an unassailable reality, we now turn to the letter *A* in the acronym FEAT, which will serve to remind us of the third unshakable pillar supporting the resurrection—namely, the appearances of Christ.

CHAPTER 4

APPEARANCES OF CHRIST

✛

Now that same day two of them were going to a village called Emmaus, about seven miles from Jerusalem. They were talking with each other about everything that had happened. As they talked and discussed these things with each other, Jesus himself came up and walked along with them; but they were kept from recognizing him.

He asked them, "What are you discussing together as you walk along?"

They stood still, their faces downcast. One of them, named Cleopas, asked him, "Are you only a visitor to Jerusalem and do not know the things that have happened there in these days?"

"What things?" he asked.

"About Jesus of Nazareth," they replied. "He was a prophet, powerful in word and deed before God and all the people. The chief priests and our rulers handed him over to be sentenced to death, and they crucified him; but we had hoped that he was the one who was going to redeem Israel. And what is more, it is the third day since all this took place. In addition, some of our women amazed us. They went to the tomb early this morning but didn't find his body. They came and told us that they had seen a vision of angels, who said he was alive. Then some of our companions went to the tomb and found it just as the women had said, but him they did not see."

He said to them, "How foolish you are, and how slow of heart to believe all that the prophets have spoken! Did not the Christ have to suffer these things and then enter his glory?" And beginning with Moses and all the Prophets, he explained to them what was said in all the Scriptures concerning himself.

As they approached the village to which they were going, Jesus acted as if he were going farther. But they urged him strongly, "Stay with us, for it is nearly evening; the day is almost over." So he went in to stay with them.

When he was at the table with them, he took bread, gave thanks, broke it and began to give it to them. Then their eyes were opened and they recognized him, and he disappeared from their sight. They asked each other, "Were not our hearts burning within us while he talked with us on the road and opened the Scriptures to us?"

They got up and returned at once to Jerusalem. There they found the Eleven and those with them, assembled together and saying, "It is true! The Lord has risen and has appeared to Simon." Then the two told what had happened on the way, and how Jesus was recognized by them when he broke the bread.

While they were still talking about this, Jesus himself stood among them and said to them, "Peace be with you."

They were startled and frightened, thinking they saw a ghost. He said to them, "Why are you troubled, and why do doubts rise in your minds? Look at my hands and my feet. It is I myself! Touch me and see; a ghost does not have flesh and bones, as you see I have."

When he had said this, he showed them his hands and feet. And while they still did not believe it because of joy and amazement, he asked them, "Do you have anything here to eat?" They gave him a piece of boiled fish, and he took it and ate it in their presence.

He said to them, "This is what I told you while I was still with you: Everything must be fulfilled that is written about me in the Law of Moses, the Prophets and the Psalms."

Then he opened their minds so they could understand the Scriptures. He *told them, "This is what is written: The Christ will suffer and rise from the dead on the third day, and repentance and forgiveness of sins will be preached in his name to all nations, beginning at Jerusalem. You are witnesses of these things. I am going to send you what my Father has promised; but stay in the city until you have been clothed with power from on high."*

—*Luke 24:13–49*

✛

In the Acts of the Apostles, Dr. Luke writes that Jesus gave the disciples "many convincing proofs that he was alive. He appeared to them during a period of forty days and spoke about the kingdom of God" (Acts 1:3). Likewise, Peter in his powerful Pentecost proclamation confidently communicated that many credible eyewitnesses could confirm the fact of Christ's physical post-resurrection appearances: "Brothers, I can tell you confidently that the patriarch David died and was buried, and his tomb is here to this day. But he was a prophet and knew that God had promised him on oath that he would place one of his descendants on his throne. Seeing what was ahead, he spoke of the resurrection of the Christ, that he was not abandoned to the grave, nor did his body see decay. God has raised this Jesus to life, and we are all witnesses of the fact" (Acts 2:29–32).

Like the apostle Peter, the apostle Paul exudes confidence in the appearances of Christ. In his first letter to the Corinthian Christians, he provides details and descriptions:

Now, brothers, I want to remind you of the gospel I preached to you, which you received and on which you have taken your stand. By this gospel you are saved, if you hold firmly to the word I preached to you. Otherwise, you have believed in vain.

For what I received I passed on to you as of first importance: that Christ died for our sins according to the Scriptures, that he was buried, that he was raised on the third day according to the Scriptures, and that he appeared to Peter, and then to the Twelve. After that, he appeared to more than five hundred of the brothers at the same time, most of whom are still living, though some have fallen asleep. Then he appeared to James, then to all the apostles, and last of all he appeared to me also, as to one abnormally born.

For I am the least of the apostles and do not even deserve to be called an apostle, because I persecuted the church of God. But by the grace of God I am what I am, and his grace to me was not without effect. No, I worked harder than all of them— yet not I, but the grace of God that was with me. Whether, then, it was I or they, this is what we preach, and this is what you believed. (1 Corinthians 15:1–11)

Earliest Christian Creed

One thing can be stated with iron-clad certainty: The apostles did not merely propagate Christ's teachings; they were absolutely positive that he had appeared to them in the flesh. Although we are now two thousand years removed from the actual event, we, too, can be absolutely confident in Christ's post-resurrection appearances. One of the principal reasons for this confidence is that, within the passage cited above (1 Corinthians 15:3–7), Paul is reiterating a Christian creed that can be traced all the way back to the formative stages of the early Christian church.[1] Incredibly, scholars of all stripes agree that this creed can be dated to within three to eight years of the crucifixion itself.[2] In his seminal work titled *The Historical Jesus: Ancient Evidence for the Life of Christ,* Dr. Gary Habermas lists a variety of reasons by which scholars have come to this conclusion.

First, Paul employs technical Jewish terminology used to transmit oral tradition when he uses such words as *delivered* and *received.* Scholars view this as evidence that Paul is reciting information he received from another source. The eminent scholar Joachim Jeremias, a leading authority on this issue, also points to non-Pauline phrases such as *for our sins* (v. 3), *according to the Scriptures* (vv. 3, 4), *he was raised* (v. 4), *third day* (v. 4), *he appeared* (vv. 5, 6, 7, 8), and *the Twelve* (v. 5). Furthermore, "the creed is organized in a stylized, parallel form" that reflects an oral tradition. And finally, Paul's use of the Aramaic word *Cephas* for Peter points to an extremely early Semitic source. [3]

Oxford scholar and philosopher Dr. Terry Miethe concurs. Says Miethe, "Most New Testament scholars point out that one of the ways we know [1 Corinthians 15:3–7] is a creedal statement is that it appears to have been in a more primitive Aramaic, and it's also in hymnic form. This means it was stylized Greek, non-Pauline words, and so on, which indicates that it predated Paul and was widely used, probably even used and recited in worship experiences as a form of worship or a song or a hymn or a creedal statement, and was therefore universally acknowledged."[4]

The enormous implications of the early dating of this creed can hardly be overstated. Jeremias refers to it as "'the earliest tradition of all,' and Ulrich Wilckens says it 'indubitably goes back to the oldest phase of all in the history of primitive Christianity.'"[5] Greco-Roman classical historian A. N. Sherwin-White argues that it would be unprecedented historically for legend to have grown up that fast.[6] He points out that the sources used for Greek and Roman history are not only biased, but generations or even centuries removed from the actual events they chronicle. Nonetheless, these sources are the basis on which historians confidently reconstruct the historical facts concerning Greek and Roman history.[7]

Dr. William Lane Craig points out that the writings of Herodotus[8] provide us with a perspective on the rate at which legend accumulates—the data demonstrates that even two generations is insufficient for embellishments to supplant a specific set of historical facts. The short time span between Christ's crucifixion and the composition of this early Christian creed precludes the possibility of legendary corruption.[9] Legends draw from folklore, not from people and places that are demonstrably rooted in history. Nineteenth-century scholar Julius Müller underscores this truth in the eloquence of post-Elizabethan English:

Most decidedly must a considerable interval of time be required for such a complete transformation of a whole history by popular tradition, when the series of legends are formed in the same territory where the heroes actually lived and wrought. Here one cannot imagine how such a series of legends could arise in an historical age, obtain universal respect, and supplant the historical recollection of the true character and connexion of their heroes' lives in the minds of the community, if eyewitnesses were still at hand, who could be questioned respecting the truth of the recorded marvels. Hence, legendary fiction, as it likes not the clear present time, but prefers the mysterious gloom of grey antiquity, is wont to seek a remoteness of age, along with that of space, and to remove its boldest and most rare and wonderful creations into a very remote and unknown land.[10]

As noted by Craig, Müller "challenged scholars of the mid-nineteenth century to show anywhere in history where within thirty years a great series of legends had accumulated around a historical individual and had become firmly fixed in general belief. *Müller's challenge has never been met.*"[11] It is mind-boggling to realize that Christianity can confidently point to a creed that some of the greatest scholars, theologians, philosophers, and historians have traced to within just three to eight years of Christ's crucifixion. Dr. Gary Habermas makes it crystal-clear that we should never "undermine the persuasive evidence that the creed is early, that it's free from legendary contamination, that it's unambiguous and specific, and that it's ultimately rooted in eyewitness accounts."[12]

Eyewitnesses

Peter, Paul, and the rest of the apostles claimed that Christ appeared to hundreds of people who were still alive and available for cross-examination.[13] For example, Paul claims that Christ "appeared to more than five hundred of the brothers at the same time, most of whom are still living, though some have fallen asleep" (1 Corinthians 15:6). It would have been one thing to attribute these supernatural experiences to people who had already died. It was quite another to attribute them to multitudes who were still alive.

As the famed New Testament scholar of Cambridge University C. H. Dodd points out, "There can hardly be any purpose in mentioning the fact that most of the five hundred are still alive, unless Paul is saying, in effect, 'The witnesses are there to be questioned.'"[14] Says Craig, "Paul could never have said this if the event had never occurred; he could never have challenged people to ask the witnesses if the event had not taken place and there were no witnesses. But evidently there were witnesses to this event, and Paul knew that some had died in the meantime. Therefore, the event must have taken place."[15]

Suppose I announced publicly that I played a private round of golf with Arnold Palmer at Bay Hill Country Club in Orlando. During the round I hit the longest drive Palmer had ever seen, made a hole-in-one, and set a new course record. As long as Palmer was living, my credibility could easily be called into question. Likewise, Paul's assertions regarding the eyewitnesses who had seen the resurrected Christ could have easily been refuted if in fact they were not true.

Furthermore, nothing can account for the utter transformation of Paul on the road to Damascus other than the appearance of Christ. While he was yet "breathing out murderous threats against the Lord's disciples," Christ appeared to him. "Suddenly a light from heaven flashed around him. He fell to the ground and heard a voice say to him, 'Saul, Saul, why do you persecute me?'" (Acts 9:1, 3–4). In that instant Paul was transformed from a persecutor of Christians to a proselytizer for Christ. He had once approvingly watched as Stephen was brutally murdered; now he was willing to be murdered for the same Christian testimony. Only the appearance of Christ can account for that.

Incredibly, Paul gave up his position as an esteemed Jewish leader, a rabbi, and a Pharisee who had studied under the famed teacher Gamaliel. He gave up the mission to stamp out every vestige of what he considered the insidious heresy of Christianity. In his words, "I persecuted the church of God and tried to destroy it" (Galatians 1:13). But after the resurrected Christ appeared to him, he became as committed to the gospel as he had been to Gamaliel. In his second letter to the Corinthian Christians, he outlines how he traded in his position as a Pharisee for poverty, prison, and persecution. Says Paul:

> I have worked much harder, been in prison more frequently, been flogged more severely, and been exposed to death again and again. Five times I received from the Jews the forty lashes minus one. Three times I was beaten with rods, once I was stoned, three times I was shipwrecked, I spent a night and a day in the open sea, I have been constantly on the move. I have been in danger from rivers, in danger from bandits, in danger from my own countrymen, in danger from Gentiles; in danger in the city, in danger in the country, in danger at sea; and in danger from false brothers. I have labored and toiled and have often gone without sleep; I have known hunger and thirst and have often gone without food; I have been cold and naked. Besides everything else, I feel daily the pressure of my concern for all the churches. (2 Corinthians 11:23–28)

Paul was no doubt the most radically converted man in history. In the end, he paid the ultimate price for his faith—martyrdom. The stone inscription beneath the high altar at St. Paul's Basilica in Rome simply reads, "To Paul, Apostle and Martyr."[16] Only the physical appearance of the resurrected Christ is a sufficient explanation for such a radical transformation.

Finally, it should be noted that Christ's appearances to Paul and the five hundred are not isolated incidences. As noted by Craig, Paul provides a list of Christ's appearances in 1 Corinthians 15.[17] Among them is his appearance to Peter—which is vouched for by Peter himself (see 2 Peter 1:16). Dr. Luke adds confirmation to this appearance, "saying, 'It is true!' The Lord has risen and has appeared to Simon" (Luke 24:34). Perhaps the most well-attested appearance of all is Christ's appearance to the Twelve. Independent attestations of this appearance are provided by both Luke and John, who recount Christ eating with the Twelve and showing them his wounds (see Luke 24:36–42; John 20:19–20). Thus, Jesus not only demonstrated "that he was the *same Jesus* who had been crucified," but provided proof for the "*corporeality* and *continuity* of the resurrection body."[18]

No doubt the most amazing appearance listed by Paul is Christ's appearance to his half-brother, James. Before this appearance, James was embarrassed by Jesus. Afterward, James was willing to die for Jesus. As the Jewish historian Josephus reports, "James was stoned to death illegally by the Sanhedrin sometime after A.D. 60 for his faith in Christ."[19] Inevitably, you have to ask yourself the question, What would it take for a person to die willingly for the belief that one of his family members is God? In the case of James, the only reasonable explanation is that Jesus appeared to him alive from the dead.[20] Says Craig, "even the skeptical NT critic Hans Grass admits that the conversion of James is one of the surest proofs of the resurrection of Jesus Christ."[21]

Extreme Measures

Since reason and rhetoric cannot dispense with the resurrection, extreme measures are often the order of the day. Unable to explain away the many physical appearances of Christ, critics are often reduced to explaining them away as merely psychological appearances of Christ. Thus, it is argued that the devotees of Christ may well have been experiencing hallucinations, hypnosis, or hypersuggestibility.

Hallucination Hypothesis

The hallucination hypothesis must surely rank as one of the most extreme measures used to explain away the post-resurrection appearances of Christ. According to this hypothesis, the disciples merely saw things they wanted to see as the result of extravagances ranging from drug use to expectations. The arguments of resurrection critics are fairly straightforward: If devotees of Christianity throughout history have experienced hallucinations, there is reason to think that the disciples of Christ experienced hallucinations as well.

Here's how philosopher and atheist Dr. Michael Martin tells the story. Says Martin, we "know from the history of witchcraft that people who are thought to be bewitched had hallucinations that caused those around them to have hallucinations also. For example, Cotton Mather told the story of Mercy Short, a seventeen-year-old Boston servant girl who, in 1692, was cursed by Sarah Good, 'a hag.' Thinking herself bewitched, Mercy started to exhibit various symptoms, including hallucinations of groups of specters."[22] Martin goes on to note another occasion during which Mercy had a hallucination. This time she saw spectral fire. "Mather reported that 'we saw not the flames, but once the room smelled of brimstone.'" Thus, according to Martin:

> It seems clear that in the context of seventeenth-century New England, where witches and demons were taken for granted, one person's hallucination somehow triggered visual, auditory, tactile, and olfactory hallucinations in those nearby. Surely, it is not beyond the realm of psychological possibility, as [Gary] Habermas seems to assume it is, that in first-century Palestine, among the unsophisticated people who believed in the divinity of Jesus, one disciple's hallucination of Jesus could have triggered corresponding hallucinations in the others. The context, background, and psychological state of the disciples were no less congenial to this sort of collective

hallucination than those of the people in Salem or in Boston about three hundred years ago.[23]

Those, like Martin, who use the hallucination hypothesis as a possible explanation for the post-resurrection appearances of Christ are just as likely to point to current examples of Christian gullibility—such as a hallucination that took place at a Rick Joyner conference, during which participants sang one song "for over three hours."[24] As a result, Joyner said, "the gulf between heaven and earth had somehow been bridged."[25] He went on to report that when that one song finally ended, some of the musicians were lying on the floor: "I looked at Christine Potter and Susy Wills, who were dancing near the center of the stage and I have never seen such a look of terror on the faces of anyone. An intense burning, like a nuclear fire that burns from the inside out, seemed to be on the stage. Christine started pulling at her clothes as if she were on fire, and Susy dove behind the drums. Then a cloud appeared on the center of the stage, visible to everyone, and a sweet smell like flowers filled the area."[26]

While critics of Christianity, such as Michael Martin, may point to examples like those cited above, their attempts to explain away the post-resurrection appearances of Christ as hallucinations do not stand up in the cold, hard light of facts. First, in sharp distinction to Michael Martin's contention that hallucinations are common and contagious, in reality they are subjective and scarce. Yet Christ appeared to many people during a long period of time. As noted by psychologist Dr. Gary Collins, "Hallucinations are individual occurrences. By their very nature only one person can see a given hallucination at a time. They certainly aren't something which can be seen by a group of people. Neither is it possible that one person could somehow induce a hallucination in somebody else. Since an hallucination exists only in this subjective, personal sense, it is obvious that others cannot witness it."[27]

Dr. Collins goes on to assert that for someone to prove that the disciples were hallucinating when they experienced the resurrected Christ, "they would have to go against much of the current psychiatric and psychological data about the nature of hallucinations."[28] Thus, the incontrovertible fact that Christ appeared to multitudes on multiple occasions poses an enormous enigma for hallucination theorists.

Furthermore, hallucinations are typically relegated to people with certain personality disorders, are stimulated by expectations, and do not stop abruptly. However, Christ appeared to all kinds of personality types with no expectations, and then the appearances stopped abruptly. As Dr. Habermas points out:

> Hallucinations can't explain away his appearances. . . . The disciples were fearful, doubtful, and in despair after the Crucifixion, whereas people who hallucinate need a fertile mind of expectancy or anticipation. Peter was hardheaded, for good- ness' sake; James was a skeptic—certainly not good candidates for hallucinations. Also, hallucinations are comparably rare. They're usually caused by drugs or bodily deprivation. Chances are, you don't know anybody who's ever had a hallucination not caused by one of those two things. Yet we're supposed to believe that over a course of many weeks, people from all sorts of back- grounds, all kinds of temperaments, in various places, all expe- rienced hallucinations? That strains the hypothesis quite a bit, doesn't it? Besides, if we establish the gospel accounts as being reliable, how do you account for the disciples eating with Jesus and touching him? How does he walk along with two of them on the road to Emmaus? And what about the empty tomb? If people only thought they saw Jesus, his body would still be in his grave.[29]

One final point should be made: Hallucinations in and of them- selves would not have led to a belief in resurrection on the part of the disciples. Craig explains that hallucinations, "as projections of the mind, can contain nothing new. Therefore, given the current Jewish beliefs about life after death, the disciples would have projected hallucinations of Jesus in heaven or in Abraham's bosom, where the souls of the righteous dead were believed to abide until the resurrection. And such visions would not have caused belief in Jesus' resurrection."[30] The inevitable conclusion, says Craig, is that hallucinations might have led the disciples to believe that Jesus had been *translated*, but not that he had been *resurrected* from the dead:

> Translation is the bodily assumption of someone out of this world into heaven. Resurrection is the raising up of a dead man in the space-time universe. Thus, given Jewish beliefs concerning translation and resurrection, the disciples would not have preached that Jesus had been raised from the dead. At the very most, the empty tomb and hallucinations of Jesus would have only caused them to believe in the translation of Jesus, for this fit in with their Jewish frame of thought. But they would not have come up with the idea that Jesus had been raised from the dead, for this contradicted the Jewish belief.[31]

Hypnosis Hypothesis

Another extreme measure employed by critics of the resurrection is the hypnosis hypothesis.[32] This is the notion that the disciples were in some sort of an altered state of consciousness as a result of sleep deprivation or suffocating despair over the loss of their Master. Dr. Charles Tart, credited with coining the term *altered states of consciousness*, explained that during deep hypnosis a person transitions to a new state of consciousness, which causes him or her to lose touch with reality.[33] As has been well documented from studies of the world of the occult, the dangerous effects of hypnosis may involve depression, detachment, depersonalization, disillusionment, and many equally serious disorders.[34]

As underscored by hypnosis researcher Robert W. Marks, "people in crowds are more easily influenced than people taken singly. This fact has been capitalized on by stage hypnotists as well as evangelists, political orators, and dictators."[35] Says Marks, "the effect of suggestion on crowds seems virtually without limit. It can make black appear white. It can obscure realities, enshrine absurdities, and impel men pitilessly to cleave the skulls of their brothers."[36] Marks also notes that once epidemic suggestion contaminates a movement, human beings can "behave like beasts or idiots and be proud of it."[37] No one "is immune to the force of mass suggestion. Once an epidemic of hysteria is in full force it strikes intellectuals as well as morons, rich and poor alike. Its well-springs are subconscious and biological, not rational."[38] Under mass hypnosis, devotees of a movement can become extremely susceptible to spontaneous suggestions. Researcher Charles Baudouin writes, "a condition of mental relaxation is imposed upon the participants. Secondly, an emotional state is invariably aroused by approximation to the mysterious. Thirdly, there exists an expectation that remarkable things will happen."[39]

A classic case in point can be found in the story of a young Bronx boy named Joseph Vitolo.[40] In his book *The Story of Hypnosis*, Marks recounts that in 1945, nine-year-old Joseph was kneeling on a rock in an empty lot when he saw a vision of the Virgin Mary. Mary promised Joseph that she would appear on successive nights and that on the night of her last appearance, a miraculous spring would emerge from the ground.

Following the announcement, crowds trekked to the scene of the alleged vision. On one night, twenty-five thousand people surged to the scene with flowers, candles, and statues of saints. It was automatically assumed that Joseph had a special anointing. Thus, dozens of the disabled were brought to Joseph so that he would lay hands on them.

While Joseph was not able to accomplish anything out of the ordinary, the expectations of the crowd were such that they began to create their own "miracles." On one of the nights, a light rain began to fall, and a woman screamed, "It's pouring, yet Joseph doesn't get wet." Despite the fact that news reporters standing near Joseph observed that he was as soaked as anyone else, the expectations of the miraculous created the illusion. Another woman claimed she saw an apparition in white materialize behind Joseph. In reality, the apparition was nothing more than another woman protectively covered with a white raincoat.

Marks points out that the expectations of the crowd were such that "if imagination and hysterical contagion had been left to do their hallucinatory work, the crowd would have created its own miracle. And it is highly probable that Joseph could have produced some real 'cures' and real 'visions' if the hypnotic effects of the situation could have progressed far enough."[41] The expectations of the crowd had been heightened to such an extent that, as Marks says, they were "no more capable of resisting the proper hypnotic suggestion than Pavlov's dog was capable of resisting the stimulus to salivate."[42]

Skeptics of the resurrection suggest that this may very well have been what happened to the followers of Christ. In a highly suggestible hypnotic state, the disciples saw what they wanted to see—the appearance of Jesus in the flesh! This notion, however, is completely ad hoc—in other words, there is not a shred of evidence to substantiate it. While it is true that spiritual leaders, political orators, and dictators have capitalized on crowd dynamics to fool the masses, there is no warrant for suggesting that this is what happened to the disciples. The hypnotic hypothesis has been dogmatically asserted by antisupernaturalists, but no one has ever presented a defensible argument to substantiate it. As demonstrated conclusively, the disciples did not just proliferate Christ's teachings; they were absolutely positive that he had risen from the dead.

Further, there is no warrant for believing that the disciples were in the practice of working themselves into altered states of consciousness. Even a cursory reading of the writings of the apostles demonstrates that they had a high regard for the mind. Far from seeking to dull the critical-thinking process, they exhorted one another to be alert and sober minded (see 1 Thessalonians 5:6; 1 Peter 5:8). If there is any doubt that the disciples were committed to reason, one reading of the Book of Romans will forever erase that doubt.

Hindu gurus like Baghwan Shree Rajneesh believed the "goal is to create a new man, one who is happily mindless."[43] Thus, he engaged his devotees in practices designed to subjugate their critical-thinking faculties and empty their minds of coherent thought. In sharp distinction, the Judeo-Christian tradition has a high view of the mind. In the Old Testament, the Israelites were instructed to practice good judgment through inquiring, probing, and thoroughly investigating a teaching and practice (see Deuteronomy 13). Likewise, in the New Testament, the apostle Paul commands the Thessalonians to "test everything" (1 Thessalonians 5:21) and commends the Bereans for using their minds to analyze his teachings in light of an objective frame of reference—Scripture (see Acts 17:11). The Master himself commanded the disciples to judge rightly (see John 7:24) and to love God with all of their hearts, souls, and *minds* (see Matthew 22:37). Thus, while hypnotism is capitalized on frequently in aberrant Christianity and in the kingdom of the cults, it is completely foreign to the kingdom of Christ.

Finally, as underscored by theologian and historian Carl Braaten, "Even the more skeptical historians agree that for primitive Christianity . . . the resurrection of Jesus from the dead was a real event in history, the very foundation of faith, and not a mythical idea arising out of the creative imagination of believers."[44] It is an established historical fact that Jesus was fatally tormented, that he was buried, that his tomb was indeed empty three days later, and that Christ's post-resurrection appearances were a material reality so certain that the disciples were willing to die for it.

Hypersuggestibility Hypothesis

One final extreme measure should be considered before moving on—namely, the hypersuggestibility hypothesis. This is the basic idea that the disciples were by nature highly suggestible and thus susceptible to creating the post-resurrection appearances of Christ out of thin air and then believing them. It is suggested that under the influence of an eastern guru like Jesus, devotees are apt to set aside their ability to think rationally or to exercise their wills. Thus, they become hypersuggestible, "which means that they are likely to accept any 'spiritual truth' that enters their minds. Even more remarkably, they seem to be primed for mystical experiences and may attach great spiritual significance to virtually any event or thought, no matter how mundane or outlandish."[45]

Such fantasy proneness on the part of the disciples is typically referred to as "Grade Five Syndrome."[46] While Grade Five personalities may well be intuitive and intelligent, they also have vivid, visual imaginations. Thus, they are highly susceptible to the power of suggestion. To begin with, they are very trusting. Second, they desire to please (particularly an authority figure, such as Jesus). Third, they have the capacity to accept contradictory experiences. Fourth, they have a marked propensity for affiliation with new or unusual events. Fifth, they are apt to relate everything to their own self-perception.[47]

This complex of characteristics makes Grade Five personalities particularly susceptible to spiritual fantasies, "psychic and out-of-body experiences, and the occasional difficulty of differentiating fantasized events and persons from nonfantasized ones."[48] If one out of twelve Americans is susceptible to such fantasy proneness,[49] it is reasoned, then perhaps it is not unreasonable to believe that a mere twelve disciples could fall into this category as well.

In responding to the notion that the disciples were merely hypersuggestible and thus uncritically accepted the post-resurrection appearances of Christ, Dr. Luke comes immediately to mind. Says Luke, "Many have undertaken to draw up an account of the things that have been fulfilled among us, just as they were handed down to us by those who from the first were eyewitnesses and servants of the word. Therefore, since I myself have carefully investigated everything from the beginning, it seemed good also to me to write an orderly account for you, most excellent Theophilus, so that you may know the certainty of the things you have been taught" (Luke 1:1–4).

A cursory reading of Luke's Gospel or his Acts of the Apostles is sufficient to demonstrate that he was anything but "Grade Five." Far from hypersuggestible, Dr. Luke was committed to history. Thus, he "carefully investigated" the details surrounding the post-resurrection appearances of Christ. In a debate with atheist and philosopher Dr. Antony Flew, Dr. Habermas exploded the contention that the disciples were little more than hypersuggestible visionaries. Cutting through Flew's rhetoric with rigorous reason, Habermas demonstrated why a preponderance of "critical historians, philosophers, theologians, and scripture scholars" have universally accepted the following core set of facts:

> The key evidence for Jesus' Resurrection is (1) the disciple's eyewitness experiences, which they believed to be literal appearances of the risen Jesus; these experiences have not been explained by naturalistic theories and additional facts corroborate this eyewitness testimony. Other positive evidences include (2) the early proclamation of the Resurrection by these eyewitnesses, (3) their transformation into bold witnesses who were willing to die for their convictions, (4) the empty tomb, and (5) the fact that the Resurrection of Jesus was the center of the apostolic message, all of which require adequate explanations. It is also found that the disciples proclaimed this message in Jerusalem itself, where it is related that in repeated confrontations with the authorities, (6) the Jewish leaders could not disprove their message even though they had both the power and the motivation to do so.
>
> Additionally, (7) the very existence of the church, founded by monotheistic, law-abiding Jews who nonetheless (8) worshiped on Sunday demand historical causes as well.
>
> Two additionally strong facts arguing for the historicity of the Resurrection are that two skeptics, (9) James and (10) Paul, became Christians after having experiences that they also believed were appearances of the risen Jesus.[50]

No one summed up the consensus of both liberal and conservative scholarship better than Professor Norman Perrin, the late New Testament scholar at the University of Chicago: *"The more we study the tradition with regard to the appearances, the firmer the rock begins to appear upon which they are based."*[51]

At this point, there should be no doubt that Christ suffered fatal torment, that the empty tomb is a factual reality, and that Christ's post-resurrection appearances cannot be explained away by legends or extreme measures. Thus, we now move on to the final letter in the acronym FEAT, which represents the word *transformation*. There we will underscore the fact that, far from being fantasy prone, the disciples were fearless proselytizers who transformed the world because they had encountered the living, resurrected Christ.

CHAPTER 5

TRANSFORMATION

✟

When they had finished eating, Jesus said to Simon Peter, "Simon son of John, do you truly love me more than these?"

"Yes, Lord," he said, "you know that I love you."

Jesus said, "Feed my lambs."

Again Jesus said, "Simon son of John, do you truly love me?"

He answered, "Yes, Lord, you know that I love you."

Jesus said, "Take care of my sheep."

The third time he said to him, "Simon son of John, do you love me?"

Peter was hurt because Jesus asked him the third time, "Do you love me?" He said, "Lord, you know all things; you know that I love you."

Jesus said, "Feed my sheep. I tell you the truth, when you were younger you dressed yourself and went where you wanted; but when you are old you will stretch out your hands, and someone else will dress you and lead you where you do not want to go." Jesus said this to indicate the kind of death by which Peter would glorify God. Then he said to him, "Follow me!"

Peter turned and saw that the disciple whom Jesus loved was following them. (*This was the one who had leaned back against Jesus at the supper and had said, "Lord, who is going to betray you?"*) *When Peter saw him, he asked, "Lord, what about him?"*

Jesus answered, "If I want him to remain alive until I return, what is that to you? You must follow me." Because of this, the rumor spread among the brothers that this disciple would not die. But Jesus did not say that he would not die; he only said, "If I want him to remain alive until I return, what is that to you?"

—*John 21:15–23*

"Men of Israel, listen to this: Jesus of Nazareth was a man accredited by God to you by miracles, wonders and signs, which God did among you through him, as you yourselves know. This man was handed over to you by God's set purpose and foreknowledge; and you, with the help of wicked men, put him to death by nailing him to the cross. But God raised him from the dead, freeing him from the agony of death, because it was impossible for death to keep its hold on him. David said about him:

"'I saw the Lord always before me.
Because he is at my right hand,
I will not be shaken.
Therefore my heart is glad and my tongue rejoices;
my body also will live in hope,
because you will not abandon me to the grave,
nor will you let your Holy One see decay.
You have made known to me the paths of life;
you will fill me with joy in your presence.'

"Brothers, I can tell you confidently that the patriarch David died and was buried, and his tomb is here to this day. But he was a prophet and knew that God had promised him on oath that he would place one of his descendants on his throne. Seeing what was ahead, he spoke of the resurrection of the Christ, that he was not abandoned to the grave, nor did his body see decay. God has raised this Jesus to life, and we are all witnesses of the fact.

Exalted to the right hand of God, he has received from the Father the prom-
ised Holy Spirit and has poured out what you now see and hear. For David
did not ascend to heaven, and yet he said,
    "'The Lord said to my Lord:
    "Sit at my right hand until I make your enemies a footstool for your
feet."'
    "Therefore let all Israel be assured of this: God has made this Jesus,
whom you crucified, both Lord and Christ."

                                                —ACTS 2:22–36

✛

What happened as a result of the resurrection is unprecedented in human history. In the span of a few hundred years, a small band of seemingly insignificant believers succeeded in turning an entire empire upside down. As has been well said, "they faced the tyrant's brandished steel, the lion's gory mane, and the fires of a thousand deaths,"[1] because they were utterly convinced that they, like their Master, would one day rise from the grave in glorified, resurrected bodies.

While it is conceivable that the disciples would have faced torture, vilification, and even cruel deaths for what they fervently believed to be true, it is inconceivable that they would have been willing to die for what they knew to be a lie. No one drove that point home more eloquently than did Dr. Simon Greenleaf, the famous Royall Professor of Law at Harvard. Greenleaf was undoubtedly the greatest American authority on common law evidence of the nineteenth century. His tome titled *A Treatise on the Law of Evidence* is still considered to be one of the most significant works on legal evidence in existence. In 1846, he wrote:

> The great truths which the apostles declared were that Christ had risen from the dead, and that only through repentance from sin, and faith in Him, could men hope for salvation. This doctrine they asserted with one voice, everywhere, not only under the greatest discouragements, but in the face of the

most appalling terrors that can be presented to the mind of man.

Their master had recently perished as a malefactor, by the sentence of a public tribunal. His religion sought to overthrow the religions of the whole world. The laws of every country were against the teachings of His disciples. The interests and passions of all the rulers and great men in the world were against them. The fashion of the world was against them.

Propagating this new faith, even in the most inoffensive and peaceful manner, they could expect nothing but contempt, opposition, revilings, bitter persecutions, stripes, imprisonments, torments, and cruel deaths. Yet this faith they zealously did propagate; and all these miseries they endured undismayed, nay, rejoicing.

As one after another was put to a miserable death, the survivors only prosecuted their work with increased vigor and resolution. The annals of military warfare afford scarcely an example of the like heroic constancy, patience, and unblenching courage. They had every possible motive to review carefully the grounds of their faith, and the evidences of the great facts and truths which they asserted and these motives were pressed upon their attention with the most melancholy and terrific frequency. It was therefore impossible that they could have persisted in affirming the truths they have narrated, had not Jesus actually risen from the dead, and had they not known this fact as certainly as they knew any other fact.*

If it were morally possible for them to have been deceived

---

* *The Testimony of the Evangelists* contains this note:

If the witnesses could be supposed to have been biased, this would not destroy their testimony to matters of fact; it would only detract from the weight of their judgment in matters of opinion. The rule of law on this subject has been thus stated by Dr. Lushington: "When you examine the testimony of witnesses nearly connected with the parties, and there is nothing very peculiar tending to destroy their credit, when they depose to mere facts, their testimony is to be believed; when they depose as to matters of opinion, it is to be received with suspicion." *Dillon v. Dillon,* 3 Curteis, *Eccl. Rep.,* pp. 96, 102.

in this matter, every human motive operated to lead them to discover and avow their error. To have persisted in so gross a falsehood, after it was known to them, was not only to encounter, for life, all the evils which man could inflict from without, but to endure also the pangs of inward and conscious guilt; with no hope of future peace, no testimony of a good conscience, no expectation of honor or esteem among men, no hope of happiness in this life, or in the world to come.

Such conduct in the apostles would moreover have been utterly irreconcilable with the fact that they possessed the ordinary constitution of our common nature. Yet their lives do show them to have been men like all others of our race; swayed by the same motives, animated by the same hopes, affected by the same joys, subdued by the same sorrows, agitated by the same fears, and subject to the same passions, temptations, and infirmities as ourselves. And their writings show them to have been men of vigorous understandings. If then their testimony was not true, there was no possible motive for this fabrication.[2]

The Twelve

As Greenleaf so masterfully communicates, the Twelve[3] were thoroughly transformed by the resurrection.

Peter, who was once afraid of being exposed as a follower of Christ by a young woman, after the resurrection was transformed into a lion of the faith and suffered a martyr's death.[4] According to tradition, he was crucified upside down, because he felt unworthy to be crucified in the same manner as his Lord.[5]

James, the half-brother of Jesus, who once hated everything his brother stood for, after the resurrection calls himself "a bond-servant . . . of the Lord Jesus Christ" (James 1:1 NASB). He not only became the leader of the Jerusalem church, but in c. A.D. 62 was martyred for his faith.[6] Eusebius of Caesarea describes how James was thrown from the pinnacle of the temple and subsequently stoned.[7]

The apostle Paul, likewise, was transformed. Once a ceaseless persecutor of the growing church, he became the chief proselytizer of the Gentiles. His radical transformation is underscored by his letter to the Philippians:

> But whatever was to my profit I now consider loss for the sake of Christ. What is more, I consider everything a loss compared to the surpassing greatness of knowing Christ Jesus my Lord, for whose sake I have lost all things. I consider them rubbish, that I may gain Christ and be found in him, not having a righteousness of my own that comes from the law, but that which is through faith in Christ—the righteousness that comes from God and is by faith. I want to know Christ and the power of his resurrection and the fellowship of sharing in his sufferings, becoming like him in his death, and so, somehow, to attain to the resurrection from the dead. (Philippians 3:7–11)

Peter, James, and Paul were not alone. As Christian philosopher J. P. Moreland points out, within weeks of the resurrection, not just one, but an entire community of at least ten thousand Jews were willing to give up the very sociological and theological traditions that had given them their national identity.[8]

Traditions

Among the traditions that were transformed after the resurrection were the Sabbath, the sacrifices, and the sacraments.

In Genesis, the Sabbath was a celebration of God's work in creation (see Genesis 2:2–3; cf. Exodus 20:11). After the Exodus, the

Sabbath expanded to a celebration of God's deliverance from the oppression of Egypt (see Deuteronomy 5:15). As a result of the resurrection, the Sabbath shifted once again. It became a celebration of the "rest" we have through Christ who delivers us from sin and the grave (see Colossians 2:16–17; Hebrews 4:1–11). In remembrance of the resurrection, the early Christian church changed the day of worship from the Sabbath to Sunday. God provided the early church with a new pattern of worship through Christ's resurrection on the first day of the week, his subsequent Sunday appearances, and the Holy Spirit's Sunday descent.[9] For the emerging Christian church, the most dangerous snare was a failure to recognize that Jesus was the substance that fulfilled the symbol of the Sabbath.

For Jewish believers, the sacrificial system was radically transformed by the resurrection of Christ as well. The Jews had been taught from the time of Abraham that they were to sacrifice animals as the symbol of atonement for sin. However, after the resurrection, the followers of Christ suddenly stopped sacrificing. They recognized that the new covenant was better than the old covenant, because the blood of Jesus Christ was better than the blood of animals (see Hebrews 8–10). They finally understood that Jesus was the substance that fulfilled the symbol of animal sacrifices. He was the sacrificial "Lamb of God that takes away the sin of the world" (John 1:29).

Like the Sabbath and the sacrificial system, the Jewish "sacraments" of Passover and baptism were radically transformed. In place of the Passover meal, believers celebrated the Lord's Supper. Moreland points out that Jesus had just been slaughtered in grotesque and humiliating fashion, yet the disciples remembered the broken body and shed blood of Christ with joy. Only the resurrection can account for that! Imagine devotees of John F. Kennedy getting together to celebrate his murder at the hands of Lee Harvey Oswald. They may well celebrate his confrontations with communism, his contributions to civil rights, or his captivating charisma, but never his brutal killing.[10]

In like fashion, baptism was radically transformed. Gentile converts to Judaism were baptized in the name of the God of Israel.[11] After the resurrection, converts to Christianity were baptized in the name of Jesus Christ as well (see Acts 2:36–41).[12] Thus, Christians equated Jesus with Israel's God. Only the resurrection could account for that.[13]

Today

Each day, people of every tongue and tribe and nation are baptized in the name of the risen Christ. Recently, before the garden tomb in Jerusalem, I encountered a tourist who had no concept of the resurrection's significance. I explained to him that Christ cloaked himself in human flesh to restore the relationship with God broken by our sin, that Christ lived the perfect life we could never live, and that he died for our sins, was buried, and on the third day rose again from the dead. I went on to explain that this was no mere fantasy but the most well-attested fact of ancient history. After communicating the FEAT that demonstrates the fact of resurrection, this young man took the final step and personally experienced the resurrected Christ. Recognizing that he was a sinner, he repented of his sins and received Jesus Christ as Lord and Savior of his life.

Today he not only knows Christ evidentially, but he knows him experientially as well. Christ has become more real to him than the very flesh upon his bones.

PART TWO

✠

Defense of the Resurrection of Creation

PHYSICAL RESURRECTION OF BELIEVERS TO ETERNAL LIFE

✠

Someone may ask, "How are the dead raised? With what kind of body will they come?" How foolish! What you sow does not come to life unless it dies. When you sow, you do not plant the body that will be, but just a seed, perhaps of wheat or of something else. But God gives it a body as he has determined, and to each kind of seed he gives its own body. All flesh is not the same: Men have one kind of flesh, animals have another, birds another and fish another. There are also heavenly bodies and there are earthly bodies; but the splendor of the heavenly bodies is one kind, and the splendor of the earthly bodies is another. The sun has one kind of splendor, the moon another and the stars another; and star differs from star in splendor.

So will it be with the resurrection of the dead. The body that is sown is perishable, it is raised imperishable; it is sown in dishonor, it is raised in glory; it is sown in weakness, it is raised in power; it is sown a natural body, it is raised a spiritual body. If there is a natural body, there is also a spiritual body.

—*1 CORINTHIANS 15:35–44*

✠

RESURRECTION

To the modern materialist, death is the cessation of being. According to the mythical view of the ancients, when we die we devolve into a ghostly shadow of our present selves. Reincarnationists believe that our souls continuously return dressed up in other bodies. The followers of Plato contend that the body is a prison; at death, the prisoner escapes as a mere individual human spirit. Hindus believe that the body is merely an illusion and that the only thing that ultimately survives is an impersonal cosmic consciousness. Only in a biblical worldview do we become greater after death than we were before. Only in Christianity are our lowly bodies transformed into glorious, resurrected bodies, like unto Christ's resurrected body.[1]

Ever wonder what your glorified body will be like? The older I get, the more I find myself thinking about the transformation of my present body into one that is immortal, incorruptible, and imperishable. Joni Eareckson Tada provides a foretaste of this mystic ecstasy. She says she has been thinking about her heavenly body for years. Paralyzed from the neck down, she writes, "Naturally, you can understand why: My earthly body doesn't work."[2] Joni then goes on to share an exhilarating dream she had in Stavanger, Norway:

> That night, as the cold Norwegian wind rattled my bedroom window, I snuggled down and slipped into the most amazing dream. I saw myself standing in a bright yellow bathing suit at the edge of a pool. This was astonishing since I rarely dream about being on my feet. Usually I can't see or feel my body from the shoulders down; my torso and legs are always hazy and unfinished, like the half-completed edges of a painting. But not in this dream.
>
> I stretched my arms above my head, arched my back, and gracefully dove into the water. When I came up and slicked my hair with my hands, I was stunned to see them glow, all rose-red wet and honey-ivory, bathed in life, beauty, and well-being. I pressed my palms to my nose. They smelled wild and sweet.

Some might have mistaken me for an angel, but I never felt more human, more a woman. I cocked my head and admired my outstretched arms and then looked around. This is hard to describe, but the water and air were brilliant, ablaze in light, like pure gold, as transparent as glass.

Each breath was piercing to my lungs, but with a sweet sting that made me want to breathe deeper. I looked down to see the pool water shimmering like diamonds. You know how we say "the water sparkles"? In my dream it was doing exactly that. The air was sparkling too. Everything was flashing, clear, and golden.

I saw a friend sitting poolside, relaxing in a chair under a white cabana and watching me. Oddly, he looked awash in light too. He seemed more real, more a man than ever before. He was my old friend but a thousand times more himself, and when our eyes met, youth infused my heart. I wondered if he felt the same. I smiled, waved, and then began swimming, smoothly parting the water with long, powerful strokes. The ripples felt cool and slick. More like satin than water. After a while, my friend dove in. He touched my shoulder and it burned, but in a painless way. There was no need to talk; our smiles said that we were friends for the first time again. We swam together stroke-for-stroke. And the longer we swam, the stronger we grew. Not weaker, but stronger.

It was the most remarkable dream I've ever had. When I woke up, I had no doubt it was a dream about heaven. I was convinced "pure gold like transparent glass" existed. It wasn't a gawky image. I saw it with the eyes of my heart.[3]

One day, says Joni, her dream will come true: "No more bulging middles or balding tops. No varicose veins or crow's-feet. No more cellulite or support hose. Forget the thunder thighs and highway hips. Just a quick leapfrog over the tombstone, and it's the body you've always dreamed of. Fit and trim, smooth and sleek."[4] As the apostle Paul explains, "Our citizenship is in heaven. And we eagerly await a Savior from there, the Lord Jesus Christ, who, by the power that enables him to bring everything under his control, will transform our lowly bodies so that they will be like his glorious body" (Philippians 3:20–21).

Savior

Of all the things that can be said concerning our glorified bodies, the first and foremost is this: Our lowly bodies will be transformed "like his glorious body"! Like the Savior's body, our resurrection bodies will be real, physical, flesh-and-bone bodies perfectly engineered for "a new heaven and a new earth" (Revelation 21:1). As emphasized by Dr. Norman Geisler:

> The orthodox fathers unanimously confessed belief in "the *resurrection of the flesh.*" They believed that flesh was essential to human nature and that Jesus, being fully human, was not only incarnated in, but also resurrected in, the same human flesh He had before His death. A resurrected body can be seen with the naked eye. If a picture were taken of it, the image would appear on the film. As Anselm affirmed, it is just as material as Adam's body was and would have remained if Adam had not sinned. It was so physical that were someone to have seen it arise in the tomb, it would have caused dust to fall off the slab from which it arose![5]

Furthermore, it is important to note that Christ's resurrection was a historical event that took place in our space-time continuum. Likewise, our resurrection will be a historical event that takes place when Christ physically returns and transforms our mortal bodies in a microsecond. In Paul's words, "we will all be changed—in a flash, in the twinkling of an eye, at the last trumpet. For the trumpet will sound, the dead will be raised imperishable, and we will be changed" (1 Corinthians 15:51–52).

Finally, it should be emphasized that there is a one-to-one correspondence between the body of Christ that died and the body that rose. Jesus said, "Destroy this temple, and I will raise *it* again in three days" (John 2:19; emphasis added). The apostle John clarifies that "the temple he had spoken of was his body" (v. 21). Says Geisler, "It has always been part of orthodox belief to acknowledge that Jesus was raised immortal in the *same physical body* in which he died. That is, His *resurrection body was numerically the same as his pre-resurrection body.*"[6] Likewise, our resurrection bodies are numerically identical to the bodies we now possess. In other words, our resurrection bodies are not *second* bodies; rather, they are our present bodies transformed.

Seed

To further inform our thinking with respect to the nature of our resurrected bodies, the apostle Paul provides us with a seed analogy. Says Paul, "But someone may ask, 'How are the dead raised? With what kind of body will they come?' How foolish! What you sow does not come to life unless it dies. When you sow, you do not plant the body that will be, but just a seed, perhaps of wheat or of something else. But God gives it a body as he has determined, and to each kind of seed he gives its own body" (1 Corinthians 15:35–38). As a seed is transformed into the body it will become, so too our mortal bodies will be transformed into the immortal bodies they will be. Joni paints a riveting word picture:

Have you ever seen those nature specials on public television? The ones where they put the camera up against a glass to show a dry, old lima bean in the soil? Through time-lapse photography, you watch it shrivel, turn brown, and die. Then, miraculously, the dead shell of that little bean splits open and a tiny lima leg-like root sprouts out. The old bean is shoved aside against the dirt as the little green plant swells. The lima plant came to life because the old bean died.

Not even a Ph.D. in Botany can explain how life comes out of death, even in something so simple as a seed. But one thing is for sure: it's a lima bean plant. Not a bush of roses or a bunch of bananas. There's no mistaking it for anything other than what it is. It has absolute identity. Positively, plain as day, a lima bean plant. It may come out of the earth different than when it went in, but it's the same. So it is with the resurrection body. We'll have absolute identification with our body that died.[7]

Much can be gleaned from Paul's seed analogy. First, we see that the blueprints for our glorified bodies are in the bodies we now possess.[8] While orthodoxy does not dictate that every cell of our present bodies will be restored in the resurrection, it does require continuity between our earthly bodies and our heavenly bodies.[9] Just as there is continuity between our present bodies and the bodies we had at birth—even though all of our subatomic particles and most of our cells have been replaced—so too there will be continuity from death to resurrection, despite the fact that not every particle in our bodies will be restored. In fact, without continuity, there is no point in even using the word *resurrection*.[10]

Furthermore, while the blueprints for our glorified bodies are in the bodies we now possess, the blueprints pale by comparison to the buildings they will be—"an eternal house in heaven, not built by human hands" (2 Corinthians 5:1). It would be impossible for a common caterpillar to imagine becoming a beautiful butterfly and soaring off into the wild blue yonder. Likewise, it is impossible for human beings to fully comprehend what we will be capable of in the resurrection.

Finally, it is significant to note that each seed reproduces after its own kind. The DNA for a fetus is not the DNA for a frog, and the DNA for a frog is not the DNA for a fish. Rather, the DNA for a fetus, frog, or fish is uniquely programmed for reproduction after its own kind. Paul puts it this way:

All flesh is not the same: Men have one kind of flesh, animals have another, birds another and fish another. There are also heavenly bodies and there are earthly bodies; but the splendor of the heavenly bodies is one kind, and the splendor of the earthly bodies is another. The sun has one kind of splendor, the moon another and the stars another; and star differs from star in splendor.

So will it be with the resurrection of the dead. The body that is sown is perishable, it is raised imperishable; it is sown in dishonor, it is raised in glory; it is sown in weakness, it is raised in power; it is sown a natural body, it is raised a spiritual body. (1 Corinthians 15:39–44)

Spiritual Body

The apostle Paul not only wants us to know that our bodies will be transformed like unto our Savior's glorified body and that the seeds of what we will become are in the bodies that we now possess, but he also wants us to know that our natural bodies will be raised spiritual bodies. Some have mistakenly interpreted this to mean that our post-resurrection bodies will be ethereal and immaterial. As previously documented, however, nothing could be further from the truth. Christ's resurrection was demonstrably physical. Jesus invited the disciples to examine his resurrected body. He told Thomas, "Put your finger here; see my hands. Reach out your hand and put it into my side. Stop doubting and believe" (John 20:27). The disciples gave Jesus "a piece of broiled fish, and he took it and ate it in their presence" (Luke 24:42–43). And Jesus overtly told the disciples that his body was comprised of "flesh and bones." "Touch me and see," he said. "A ghost does not have flesh and bones, as you see I have" (Luke 24:39).

Dr. Geisler points out that when Paul referred to the "spiritual man" (1 Corinthians 2:15), he did not intend to imply "immaterial man." Rather, he is describing a human being whose life is supernaturally directed by the power of God.[11] Thus "natural man" does not mean "physical man"; it describes a man who is dominated by his human nature. Likewise, "spiritual man" does not mean "nonphysical man," but rather describes a man who is dominated by the supernatural power of the Spirit.

Paul describes the resurrected body as a "spiritual body" in the same sense that we describe the Bible as a "spiritual book."[12] If "spiritual body" means "immaterial body," Satan would have won a strategic battle. God would have had to dispense with our physical nature and re-create humanity as a different ontological species, such as the angels.

In the words of philosopher Peter Kreeft, "It is irrational to suppose we change our species. God does not rip up his handiwork as a mistake. We are created to fill one of the possible levels of reality, one of the unique rungs on the cosmic ladder, between animals and angels. This is our essence, our destiny, and our glory. We would lose that by becoming angels just as much as by becoming apes."[13]

Kreeft further amplifies the significance of physicality in the resurrection by noting that through our natural bodies we can engage in activities of which mere spiritual beings can only dream. Says Kreeft, "We are better than angels at many things, and those things would be missing from us and those perfections missing from the universe if our souls were simply disembodied. Angels are much better than we are at intelligence, will, and power, but they cannot smell flowers or weep over a Chopin nocturne."[14] As Anthony Hoekema concludes: "Then it would indeed seem that matter had become intrinsically evil so that it had to be banished. And then, in a sense, the Greek philosophers would have been proved right. But matter is not evil; it is part of God's good creation. Therefore the goal of God's redemption is the resurrection of the physical body, and the creation of a new earth on which his redeemed people can live and serve God forever with glorified bodies."[15]

Thus, when Paul talks about the "spiritual body" (1 Corinthians 15:44), he is not communicating that we will be re-created as spirit beings, but rather that our resurrected bodies will be supernatural, Spirit dominated, and sin free. First, our resurrected bodies will be *supernatural* rather than *simply natural*. In this sense, our heavenly bodies will be imperishable, incorruptible, and immortal. As noted by Geisler:

> The complete context indicates that "spiritual" (*pneumatikos*) could be translated "supernatural" in contrast to "natural." This is made clear by the antithetical parallels of perishable and imperishable, corruptible and incorruptible, etc.
>
> In fact, this same Greek word *pneumatikos* is translated "supernatural" in 1 Corinthians 10:4, speaking of the "supernatural Rock which followed them" (RSV). The *Greek-English Lexicon of the New Testament* says, "That which belongs to the supernatural order of being is described as *pneumatikos:* accordingly, the resurrection body is a *soma pneumatikon* [supernatural body]."[16]

Furthermore, Paul is emphasizing that our resurrected bodies will be dominated by the Holy Spirit, rather than dominated by hedonistic sensations or natural proclivities. In other words, our spiritual bodies will be bodies that are completely ruled by the Spirit, rather than enslaved to our sinful natures. In place of "sexual immorality, impurity and debauchery; idolatry and witchcraft; hatred, discord, jealousy, fits of rage, selfish ambition, dissensions, factions and envy; drunkenness, orgies, and the like" (Galatians 5:19–21), we will faithfully manifest the fruit of the Spirit, which is "love, joy, peace, patience, kindness, goodness, faithfulness, gentleness and self-control" (vv. 22–23).

Finally, having a resurrected spiritual body means being set free from our slavery to sin. Although Christians are declared positionally righteous before God, we continue to struggle against our sinful natures. Even the great apostle Paul, who wrote two-thirds of the New Testament epistles, confesses, "I have the desire to do what is good, but I cannot carry it out. For what I do is not the good I want to do; no, the evil I do not want to do—this I keep on doing" (Romans 7:18–19).

When we receive our spiritual bodies, what we are now only in position we will then be in practice. The prophet of Patmos put it this way: "There will be no more death or mourning or crying or pain, for the old order of things has passed away" (Revelation 21:4). The inspired prophet goes on to say that "nothing impure" will enter the new heaven and the new earth, "nor will anyone who does what is shameful or deceitful, but only those whose names are written in the Lamb's book of life" (v. 27).

In the meantime, we eagerly await the metamorphosis that will transform our natural bodies into bodies that are supernatural, Spirit dominated, and sin free.

CHAPTER 7

PHYSICAL RESURRECTION OF UNBELIEVERS TO ETERNAL TORMENT

✠

"Then he will say to those on his left, 'Depart from me, you who are cursed, into the eternal fire prepared for the devil and his angels. For I was hungry and you gave me nothing to eat, I was thirsty and you gave me nothing to drink, I was a stranger and you did not invite me in, I needed clothes and you did not clothe me, I was sick and in prison and you did not look after me.'

"They also will answer, 'Lord, when did we see you hungry or thirsty or a stranger or needing clothes or sick or in prison, and did not help you?'

"He will reply, 'I tell you the truth, whatever you did not do for one of the least of these, you did not do for me.'

"Then they will go away to eternal punishment, but the righteous to eternal life."

—MATTHEW 25:41–46

✠

Let me ask you a question: Do you believe in the resurrection of believers? I mean, do you *really* believe in the resurrection of believers? Or do you just *say* you believe? Are you absolutely certain that one day those who have died in Christ will be resurrected to eternal life in heaven? If you are, then you can be just as certain that unbelievers will be resurrected to eternal torment in hell.

While myriad jokes have surrounded the subject of hell, hell is not a laughing matter. Nothing is more ghastly and grim than the biblical language used to describe hell (see Appendix C). It is variously described as "darkness, where there will be weeping and gnashing of teeth" (Matthew 8:12), as a "fiery furnace" (Matthew 13:42), and as a "lake of burning sulfur" (Revelation 20:10). Its torment is said to be "everlasting" (2 Thessalonians 1:9), "unquenchable" (Matthew 3:12), and "eternal" (Jude 7).

Nothing, however, codifies the horrors of hell more vividly than does the word *gehenna*. *Gehenna* is a Greek word that conjures up images of bones, burning bodies, and birds tearing flesh off rotting corpses—a place where the "worm does not die, and the fire is not quenched" (Mark 9:48). The Old Testament prophets spoke of "a deep, narrow gorge southeast of Jerusalem called *gê ben hinnōm*, 'the Valley of Ben Hinnom,' in which idolatrous Israelites offered up child sacrifices to the gods Molech and Baal (2 Chronicles 28:3; 33:6; Jeremiah 7:31–32; 19:2–6). . . . As a result, the Valley of Ben Hinnom became known as the dump heap, the place of destruction by fire in Jewish tradition. The Greek word *gehenna*, 'hell,' commonly used in the [New Testament] for the place of final punishment, is derived from the Hebrew name for this valley."[1]

As graphic and ghastly as the language describing *gehenna* is, it is merely a symbol of a more suffocating reality. As noted by Dr. R. C. Sproul, symbols invariably convey a higher reality than they contain; thus, we find no relief in them. Says Sproul:

A breath of relief is usually heard when someone declares, "Hell is a symbol for separation from God." To be separated from God for eternity is no great threat to the impenitent person. The ungodly want nothing more than to be separated from

God. Their problem in hell will not be separation from God, it will be the presence of God that will torment them. In hell, God will be present in the fullness of His divine wrath. He will be there to exercise His just punishment of the damned. They will know Him as an all-consuming fire.[2]

Sproul goes on to say that the most horrifying aspect of hell is its eternality. The most excruciating pain can be endured if we know that it will end. In hell, however, no such hope exists. In the words of Dante, "Abandon hope, all ye who enter here."[3]

The horrors of hell are such that they cause us instinctively to recoil in disbelief and doubt. And yet there are compelling reasons that should cause us to erase such doubt from our minds. The first and foremost of such reasons is that Christ, the Creator of the cosmos, clearly communicated hell's irrevocable reality. "Do not be amazed" he said, "for a time is coming when all who are in their graves will hear his voice and come out—those who have done good will rise to live, and those who have done evil will rise to be condemned" (John 5:28–29).[4]

Christ

Christ spent more time talking about hell than he did about heaven. In the Sermon on the Mount alone, he explicitly warned his followers about the dangers of hell a half-dozen or more times.[5] Using hyperbole, he drove home the urgency of his message: "If your right eye causes you to sin, gouge it out and throw it away. It is better for you to lose one part of your body than for your whole body to be thrown into hell. And if your right hand causes you to sin, cut it off and throw it away. It is better for you to lose one part of your body than for your whole body to go into hell" (Matthew 5:29–30).

Furthermore, in the Olivet Discourse, Christ repeatedly warned his followers of the judgment that is to come: "When the Son of Man comes in his glory, and all the angels with him, he will sit on his throne in heavenly glory. All the nations will be gathered before him, and he will separate the people one from another as a shepherd separates the sheep from the goats. He will put the sheep on his right and the goats on his left. . . . Then he will say to those on his left, 'Depart from me, you who are cursed, into the eternal fire prepared for the devil and his angels.' . . . Then they will go away to eternal punishment, but the righteous to eternal life" (Matthew 25:31–33, 41, 46).

Finally, in his famous story of the rich man and Lazarus, Christ portrayed the finality of eternal torment in hell:

> There was a rich man who was dressed in purple and fine linen and lived in luxury every day. At his gate was laid a beggar named Lazarus, covered with sores and longing to eat what fell from the rich man's table. Even the dogs came and licked his sores.
>
> The time came when the beggar died and the angels carried him to Abraham's side. The rich man also died and was buried. In hell, where he was in torment, he looked up and saw Abraham far away, with Lazarus by his side. So he called to him, "Father Abraham, have pity on me and send Lazarus to dip the tip of his finger in water and cool my tongue, because I am in agony in this fire."
>
> But Abraham replied, "Son, remember that in your lifetime you received your good things, while Lazarus received bad things, but now he is comforted here and you are in agony. And besides all this, between us and you a great chasm has been fixed, so that those who want to go from here to you cannot, nor can anyone cross over from there to us."
>
> He answered, "Then I beg you, father, send Lazarus to my father's house, for I have five brothers. Let him warn them, so that they will not also come to this place of torment."

Abraham replied, "They have Moses and the Prophets; let them listen to them."

"No, father Abraham," he said, "but if someone from the dead goes to them, they will repent."

He said to him, "If they do not listen to Moses and the Prophets, they will not be convinced even if someone rises from the dead." (Luke 16:19–31)

Choice

As with these compelling words from the lips of Christ, the concept of choice demands that we believe in hell. Without hell, there is no choice. And without choice, heaven would not be heaven; heaven would be hell. The righteous would inherit a counterfeit heaven, and the unrighteous would be incarcerated in heaven against their wills, which would be a torture worse than hell. Imagine spending a lifetime voluntarily distanced from God only to find yourself involuntarily dragged into his presence for all eternity. As Geisler explains, the alternative to hell is worse than hell itself. It would "rob human beings of freedom and dignity by forcing them into heaven against their free choice. That would be 'hell' since they do not fit in a place where everyone is loving and praising the Person they want most to avoid."[6]

Furthermore, without choice, love would be rendered meaningless. God is neither a cosmic rapist who forces his love on people, nor is he a cosmic puppeteer who forces people to love him. Instead, God, the personification of love, grants us the freedom of choice. This freedom provides a persuasive polemic for the existence of hell. As Peter Kreeft explains, "Scratch freedom and you find Hell. Everyone wants there to be free will and no one wants there to be Hell, yet if there is either one there must be the other. For life is a game, a drama, not a formula."[7] Adds C. S. Lewis, "if a game is played, it must be possible to lose it."[8] Geisler suggests that the possibility to lose in the game of life is not a sufficient reason to suppose that the game should not be played:

> Before the Super Bowl ever begins both teams know that one of them will lose. Yet they all will to play. Before every driver in America takes to the road each day we know that people will be killed. Yet we will to drive. Parents know that having children could end in great tragedy for their offspring as well as for themselves. Yet the foreknowledge of evil does not negate our will to permit the possibility of good. Why? Because we deem it better to have played with the opportunity to win than not to have played at all. It is better to lose in the Super Bowl than not to be able to play in it. From God's standpoint, it is better to love the whole world (John 3:16) and lose some of its inhabitants than not to love them at all.[9]

Finally, we should note that without eternal separation, the very nature of heaven is polluted. "Evil is contagious (1 Corinthians 5:6) and must be quarantined. Like a deadly plague, if it is not contained it will continue to contaminate and corrupt. If God did not eventually separate the tares from the wheat, the tares would choke out the wheat. The only way to preserve an eternal place of good is to eternally separate all evil from it. The only way to have an eternal heaven is to have an eternal hell."[10]

Common Sense

Like choice, common sense dictates that there must be a hell. Without hell, the wrongs of Hitler's holocaust will never be righted. Justice would be impugned if, after slaughtering six million Jews, Hitler merely died in the arms of his mistress with no eternal consequences. The ancients knew better than to think such a thing. Common sense told Abraham that the Judge of all the earth would do right (see Genesis 18:25). Likewise, David knew that for a time it may seem as though the wicked prosper in spite of their deeds, but in the end justice will be served (see Psalm 73). Geisler underscores the fact that hell is necessary for God's justice to be maintained. "Surely, there would be no real justice were there no place of punishment for the demented souls of Stalin and Hitler, who initiated the merciless slaughter of multimillions. God's justice demands that there is a hell."[11] As Jonathan Edwards, arguably the greatest theological mind ever produced in America, explains, it flies in the face of common sense to suppose that hell does not exist:

> It is a most unreasonable thing to suppose that there should be no future punishment, to suppose that God who had made man a rational creature, able to know his duty, and sensible that he is deserving punishment when he does it not; should let man alone, and let him live as he will, and never punish him for his sins, and never make any difference between the good and the bad; that he should make the world of mankind and then let it alone, and let men live all their days in wickedness, in adultery, murder, robbery, and persecution, and the like, and suffer them to live in prosperity, and never punish them; that he should suffer them to prosper in the world far beyond many good men, and never punish them hereafter. How unreasonable is it to suppose that he who made the world, should leave things in such confusion, and never take any care of the government of his creatures, and that he should never judge his reasonable creatures! Reason teaches that there is a God and reason teaches that if there be he must be a wise and just God, and he must take care to order things wisely and justly among his creatures; and therefore it is unreasonable to suppose that man dies like a beast, and that there is no future punishment.[12]

Unfortunately, common sense in our day has given way to credulity. Thus, says Kreeft, we fall for such refutations of hell as, "Are you living in the twentieth century or the Dark Ages?" Says Kreeft, "What is behind the rhetoric is a dying but still dominant humanism, a faith in man despite Auschwitz, Hiroshima, the Gulag, Cambodia, and Jonestown. We are shocked when we hear about such things. Previous generations were not; they believed in evil." Kreeft goes on to explain that common-sense distinctions between good and evil have not only been blurred by our culture, they have virtually been obliterated— which is precisely why Eastern religions have become politically correct and popular in Western regions. Observes Kreeft:

> They, like we, do not believe in sin or Hell. This entails loss of belief in free will, for free will can choose only between two really distinct objects. If all roads lead to the same place, we can only accept and not reject; all are inevitably blended into one Heaven. That is also why totalitarianism, collectivism, and communism are popular today; as in Eastern religions, the individual and his terrible burden of responsibility and freedom are removed. . . .We think of ourselves as having progressed in our appreciation of the value of love. But this is counterbalanced by our subjectivizing and sentimentalizing of love as mere kindness or tolerance. Thus we think of love as the rival of justice, and forget the necessity of justice. It is true that justice without love is hardness of heart; but love without justice is softness of head.[13]

Furthermore, common sense dictates that a God of love and justice does not arbitrarily rub out the crowning jewels of his creation. Far from rubbing us out, God graciously provides us the freedom to choose between redemption and rebellion. It would be a horrific evil to think that God would create people with freedom of choice and then capriciously annihilate them because of their choices. As noted by J. P. Moreland and Gary Habermas, it "would be wrong to destroy something of such value just because it has chosen a life it was not intended to live. Thus, one way God can respect persons is to sustain them in existence and not annihilate them. Annihilation destroys creatures of intrinsic value. . . . Since God cannot force his love on people and coerce them to choose him, and since he cannot annihilate creatures with such high intrinsic value, then the only option available is quarantine. And that is what hell is."[14]

It should also be noted that common sense inevitably leads to the conclusion that nonexistence is not better than existence. Says Geisler, "Nonexistence cannot be said to be a better condition than any kind of existence, since nonexistence is nothing. And to affirm that nothing can be better than something is a gigantic category mistake."[15] It is crucial to recognize that not all existence in hell is equal. We may safely conclude that the torment of Hitler's hell will greatly exceed the torment experienced by a garden-variety pagan. God is perfectly just, and each person who spurns his grace will suffer exactly what he or she deserves. Hell may be torment, but it is not torture. "People in hell are not howling like dogs in mind-numbing pain. There are degrees of anguish in hell. But the endlessness of existence in hell at least dignifies the people there by continuing to respect their autonomy and their intrinsic value as persons."[16]

Finally, and most importantly, common sense dictates that without a hell there is no need for a Savior. Little needs to be said about the absurdity of suggesting that the Creator should suffer more than the cumulative sufferings of all of mankind, if there were no hell to save us from. Without hell, there is no need for salvation. Without salvation, there is no need for a sacrifice. And without sacrifice, there is no need for a Savior. As much as we may wish to think that all will be saved, common sense precludes that possibility. Says Lewis, "I would pay any price to be able to say truthfully 'All will be saved.' But my reason retorts, 'Without their will, or with it?' If I say 'Without their will' I at once perceive a contradiction; how can the supreme voluntary act of self-surrender be involuntary? If I say 'With their will,' my reason replies 'How if they *will not* give in?'"[17] Ultimately, "There are only two kinds of people in the end: those who say to God, 'Thy will be done,' and those to whom God says, in the end, '*Thy* will be done.' All that are in Hell, choose it. Without that self-choice there could be no Hell. No soul that seriously and constantly desires joy will ever miss it. Those who seek find. To those who knock it is opened."[18]

P H Y S I C A L
"R E S U R R E C T I O N" O F
T H E   C O S M O S

✠

The creation waits in eager expectation for the sons of God to be revealed. For the creation was subjected to frustration, not by its own choice, but by the will of the one who subjected it, in hope that the creation itself will be liberated from its bondage to decay and brought into the glorious freedom of the children of God.

We know that the whole creation has been groaning as in the pains of childbirth right up to the present time. Not only so, but we ourselves, who have the firstfruits of the Spirit, groan inwardly as we wait eagerly for our adoption as sons, the redemption of our bodies. For in this hope we were saved.

—*Romans 8:19–24*

✠

One of the most exhilarating experiences I have ever had is memorizing the twenty-first chapter of the Book of Revelation, particularly this powerful paragraph:

Then I saw a new heaven and a new earth, for the first heaven and the first earth had passed away, and there was no longer any sea. I saw the Holy City, the new Jerusalem, coming down out of heaven from God, prepared as a bride beautifully dressed for her husband. And I heard a loud voice from the throne saying, "Now the dwelling of God is with men, and he will live with them. They will be his people, and God himself will be with them and be their God. He will wipe every tear from their eyes. There will be no more death or mourning or crying or pain, for the old order of things has passed away."

He who was seated on the throne said, "I am making everything new!" Then he said, "Write this down, for these words are trustworthy and true." (Revelation 21:1–5)

What does the prophet of Patmos mean when he says, "the first heaven and the first earth had passed away"? Does he mean that this cradle of humanity will indeed be obliterated? Or will this universe, including Planet Earth, be our home throughout eternity? Tragically, many Christians spend precious little time thinking about their eternal home. Instead, they work themselves into oblivion building temporary homes and hideaways.

At this very moment, the news of U.S. Open champion Payne Stewart's death is being flashed around the world via radio, television, and the Internet. Early this morning, Stewart walked out of his dream home near Disney World. Yet now at this very moment, his earthly home is but a distant memory, and eternity is a dynamic reality. Stewart's physical body has fallen out of the sky, but one day soon that body will be materially resurrected, and he will once again stand on the very ground on which he fell.

That, ultimately, is the hope of the Christian: not only that God will resurrect our physical carcasses, but that he will redeem the physical cosmos. In the words of Dr. John Piper, the hope of the historic Christian faith is "not the mere immortality of the soul, but rather the resurrection of the body and the renewal of all creation."[1] God's redemption is both the resurrection of the physical body and the renewal of this universe, including Planet Earth. The grand and glorious truth that we will once again walk this physical planet is made abundantly clear in Scripture. John's expression "a new heaven and a new earth" is not meant to communicate a place that is totally other than this present earth, but rather this universe renewed. Says Anthony Hoekema: "Both in II Peter 3:13 and in Revelation 21:1 the Greek word used to designate the newness of the new cosmos is not *neos* but *kainos*. The word *neos* means new in time or origin, whereas the word *kainos* means new in nature or in quality. The expression *ouranon kainon kai gen kainen* ('a new heaven and a new earth,' Revelation 21:1) means, therefore, not the emergence of a cosmos totally other than the present one, but the creation of a universe which, though it has been gloriously renewed, stands in continuity with the present one."[2]

As there is continuity between our present bodies and our resurrected bodies, so too there will be continuity between the present physical universe and the one we will inhabit throughout eternity.

Continuity

The principle of continuity begins with the resurrection of people and progresses through the renewal of this planet. Christ will not resurrect an entirely different group of human beings; rather, he will resurrect the very people who have populated this planet. In like manner, God will not renew another cosmos; rather, he will redeem the very world he once called "very good" (Genesis 1:31). John Piper points out that when Peter says that the present heavens and earth will pass away (see 2 Peter 3:10), he is communicating that the cosmos will be thoroughly transformed, as opposed to totally terminated:

It does not have to mean that they go out of existence, but may mean that there will be such a change in them that their present condition passes away. We might say, "The caterpillar passes away, and the butterfly emerges." There is a real passing away, and there is a real continuity, a real connection.

And when Peter says that this heaven and earth will be "destroyed" it does not have to mean entirely "put out of existence." We might say, "The flood destroyed many farms." But we don't mean that they vanished out of existence. We might say that on May 18, 1980, the immediate surroundings of Mt. St. Helens in Washington were destroyed by a blast 500 times more powerful than the Hiroshima atomic bomb. But anyone who goes there now and sees the new growth would know that "destroy" did not mean "put out of existence."

And so what Peter may well mean is that at the end of this age there will be cataclysmic events that bring this world to an end *as we know it*—not putting it out of existence, but wiping out all that is evil and cleansing it by fire and fitting it for an age of glory and righteousness and peace that will never end.[3]

Piper goes on to argue that this is precisely what Scripture has in mind. In Romans 8:22–23, Paul specifically connects the redemption of our physical bodies with the restoration of creation. Says Piper, "What happens to our bodies and what happens to the creation go together. And what happens to our bodies is not annihilation but redemption. . . . Our bodies will be redeemed, restored, made new, not thrown away. And so it is with the heavens and the earth."[4]

Conquest

Furthermore, we can rightly conclude that the cosmos will be renewed, not annihilated, on the basis of Christ's conquest over Satan on the cross. As Christ has liberated his children from death and disease, so too he will liberate his cosmos from destruction and decay. As Paul puts it in Romans 8, "the creation was subjected to frustration, not by its own choice, but by the will of the one who subjected it, in hope that the creation itself will be liberated from its bondage to decay" (vv. 20–21). This liberation, which begins with the conquest of the cross, will be completed at Christ's Second Coming. As Christ's conquest ensures our bodily resurrection, so too his conquest ensures the restoration of this cosmos:

> Indeed, in Scripture the resurrection of the body as a glorified body of flesh is inseparably tied to the renewal and glorification of the cosmos.
>
> In contrast to those who would declare this scriptural truth a myth, E. Thurneysen in 1931 expressed his faith in it when he wrote: "The world into which we shall enter in the Parousia of Jesus Christ is . . . not another world; it is this world, this heaven, this earth; both, however, passed away and renewed. It is these forests, these fields, these cities, these streets, these people, that will be the scene of redemption. At present they are battlefields, full of strife and sorrow of the not yet accomplished consummation; then they will be fields of victory, fields of harvest, where out of seed that was sown with tears the everlasting sheaves will be reaped and brought home."[5]

Anthony Hoekema further amplifies Christ's conquest by pointing out that if God annihilated the present cosmos, Satan would have won a decisive victory. He would have succeeded in so corrupting the cosmos that God would have had to completely do away with it. "But Satan did not win such a victory. On the contrary, Satan has been decisively defeated. God will reveal the full dimensions of that defeat when he shall renew this very earth on which Satan deceived mankind and finally banish from it all the results of Satan's evil machinations."[6]

Childbirth

A final assurance that God is not going to scrap this universe and start over with a brand-new one is communicated through the metaphor of childbirth. As Scripture puts it, "the whole creation has been groaning as in the pains of *childbirth* right up to the present time" (Romans 8:22; emphasis added). Paul uses the metaphor of childbirth to describe the longing of creation for the consummation of Christ's conquest on the cross. Says Piper, "Something is about to be brought forth *from* creation, not *in place of* creation. Creation is not going to be annihilated and recreated with no continuity. The earth is going to bring forth like a mother in labor (through the upheavals of fire and earthquake and volcanoes and pestilence and famine) a new earth."[7] From the perspective of her wheelchair, Joni Eareckson Tada paints a most inspiring portrait of what these pains of childbirth will eventually produce. Here is just a sampling of what she so eloquently communicates in *Heaven . . . Your Real Home*:

> When I drive the coastal mountains just a stone's throw from where I live and marvel at the jutted, jagged rocks and canyons, I'm vividly aware I'm in the middle of earthquake country (the Northridge quake of 1994 felt like one of those "pangs of childbirth"). Mud slides and fires happen all the time around here. These hills are restless. They're also scarred by the improbable palaces of Malibu movie stars who litter the landscape with satellite dishes. My heart breaks for these mountains and trees (and movie stars!) to be liberated from their bondage.
>
> This is the earth that Christ will bring into His glorious freedom. Can you hear the sighing in the wind? Can you feel the heavy silence in the mountains? Can you sense the restless longing in the sea? Can you see it in the woeful eyes of an animal? Something's coming . . . something better. . . . It intrigues me to think that after Christ comes back for us, we may inhabit this

very planet again. The paths that I wheel over in my chair now may well be the same ones my glorified feet will walk on when Christ reigns. . . . Heaven is not some never-neverland of thin, ghostly shapes and clouds. It's not a place where you can poke your finger through people only to discover that they are spacey spirit beings you can't really hug or hold. No way! . . . Maybe years ago I assumed heaven was a misty, nebulous home for angels and—gulp!—humans, but not now. I get tickled thinking about how rock-solid real heaven is, and how much of a home.[8]

To provide a further glimpse of what the reborn universe will be like, Joni treats us to a vision of heaven as seen through the eyes of C. S. Lewis, one of the most intelligent, imaginative, and inspiring writers of this or any other century. In *The Great Divorce*, Lewis takes his readers on a fantasy voyage in which unredeemed get a glimpse of a cosmos delivered from its bondage to corruption:

It was the light, the grass, the trees that were different; made of some different substance, so much solider than things in our country. . . . I saw people coming to meet us. Because they were bright I saw them while they were still very distant. . . . The earth shook under their tread as their strong feet sank into the wet turf. A tiny haze and a sweet smell went up where they had crushed the grass and scattered the dew . . . the robes did not disguise in those who wore them the massive grandeur of muscle and the radiant smoothness of flesh . . . no one in that company struck me as being of any particular age. One gets glimpses, even in our country, of that which is ageless—heavy thought in the face of an infant, and frolic childhood in that of a very old man. Here it was all like that.[9]

I don't know about you, but the more I think about the new heaven and the new earth,[10] the more excited I get! It is incredible to think that one day soon we will not only experience the resurrection of our carcasses, but the renewal of the cosmos and the return of the Creator. We will literally have heaven on earth. Eden lost will become Eden restored and a whole lot more! Not only will we experience God's fellowship as Adam did, but we will see our Savior face to face. God incarnate will live in our midst. And we will never come to the end of exploring the infinite, inexhaustible I AM or the grandeur and glory of his incomparable creation.

Those who die in Christ will experience the new heaven and the new earth as both a physical place in creation and as the personal presence of the Creator: "The dwelling of God is with men, and he will live with them. They will be his people, and God himself will be with them and be their God. He will wipe every tear from their eyes. There will be no more death or mourning or crying or pain, for the old order of things has passed away. He who was seated on the throne said, 'I am making everything new!'" (Revelation 21:3–5).

PART THREE

Definitive Answers to Questions
Regarding Resurrection

CHAPTER 9

PHYSICALITY

✛

Was Christ's Physical Body Resurrected from the Dead or Did He Rise an Immaterial Spirit?

While they were still talking about this, Jesus himself stood among them and said to them, "Peace be with you."

They were startled and frightened, thinking they saw a ghost.

He said to them, "Why are you troubled, and why do doubts rise in your minds? Look at my hands and my feet. It is I myself! Touch me and see; a ghost does not have flesh and bones, as you see I have."

When he had said this, he showed them his hands and feet.

And while they still did not believe it because of joy and amazement, he asked them, "Do you have anything here to eat?"

They gave him a piece of broiled fish, and he took it and ate it in their presence.

—LUKE 24:36–43

✛

How you answer this question makes all the difference in the world. Without the bodily resurrection of Christ, you may as well tear up your

Bible, terminate your preacher, and torch your church because Christianity is false and there is no hope for salvation and immortality. Paul goes so far as to say, "If the dead are not raised, 'Let us eat and drink, for tomorrow we die'" (1 Corinthians 15:32). The physical resurrection of Christ is the very capstone of our faith. Without it, Christianity crumbles.

It is precisely because the physical resurrection of Christ strikes at the very heart of Christianity that it is constantly under attack. The culture frequently denies the bodily resurrection of Jesus Christ due to a bias against miracles. Thomas Jefferson, for example, not only dispensed with the bodily resurrection of Christ, but he discarded every other miracle chronicled in the Gospels. The Jefferson Bible ends with the words, "Now, in the place where he was crucified, there was a garden; and in the garden a new sepulchre, wherein was never man yet laid. There laid they Jesus, and rolled a great stone to the door of the sepulchre, and departed."[1]

It is common for aberrant Christianity and cultism to compromise the physical resurrection of Christ as well. As a case in point, Jehovah's Witnesses claim that Christ was resurrected an invisible, immaterial spirit. In the words of the Watchtower: "The fleshly body is the body in which Jesus humbled himself, like a servant, and is not the body of his glorification, not the body in which he was resurrected. . . . He was raised to life divine in a spirit body."[2] "So the King Christ Jesus was put to death in the flesh and was resurrected an invisible spirit creature."[3] "The bodies in which Jesus appeared after his resurrection were neither the body that was crucified nor his glorious spiritual body, but bodies created expressly for the purpose of appearing unto his disciples. Our Lord's human body, the one crucified, was removed from the tomb by the power of God."[4]

It is precisely because Christ's bodily resurrection is being compromised, confused, and contradicted that we must be equipped to defend this essential of essentials. To do so, let's look back at the biblical and historical record. The canon of Scripture, the confessions of the church, and the characteristics of Christ's resurrected body all confirm that there is a one-to-one correspondence between Christ's pre-resurrection and post-resurrection body.[5]

Canon of Scripture

First, the physical resurrection of Christ is affirmed in the canon of Scripture. When the Jewish leaders asked for a miraculous sign, Jesus answered, "Destroy this temple, and I will raise it again in three days" (John 2:19). Scripture confirms that the temple he was speaking of was the temple of his own body (see v. 21). This gave Peter the epistemological warrant for his Pentecost proclamation, in which he declared that Christ "was not abandoned to the grave, nor did his body see decay. God has raised this Jesus to life, and we are all witnesses of the fact" (Acts 2:31–32). John is equally emphatic: "That which was from the beginning, which we have heard, which we have seen with our eyes, which we have looked at and our hands have touched—this we proclaim concerning [Jesus] the Word of life" (1 John 1:1). The bodily resurrection of Christ is so axiomatic to Christianity and the canon so jam-packed with references that I have provided an appendix (Appendix B) for these biblical proofs.

Confessions of the Church

Furthermore, the confessions of Christianity are replete with references to the physical resurrection of the Redeemer. The confessions of the early church fathers are convicting. Justin Martyr rebuked those who maintained that, after his resurrection, Jesus "appeared only as spiritual, and not in flesh, but presented merely the appearance of flesh."[6] In like fashion, Cyril of Jerusalem thundered, "Let no heretic ever persuade thee to speak evil of the Resurrection. For to this day the Manichees say, that the resurrection of the Saviour was phantom-wise, and not real."[7] According to Cyril, believers could ill afford to compromise Christ's physical resurrection.

Like the church fathers, the medieval church produced compelling confessions concerning the bodily resurrection. Augustine, in the fourth century, wrote, "Already both the learned and the unlearned have believed in the resurrection of the flesh and its ascension to the heavenly places."[8] Thomas Aquinas condemns those who "have not believed in the resurrection of the body, and have strained to twist the words of Holy Scripture to mean a spiritual resurrection."[9]

The Reformation codified confessions regarding the bodily resurrection as well. In the great Belgic Confession, we read that "our Lord Jesus Christ will come from heaven, corporally and visibly, as he ascended with great glory and majesty."[10] Likewise, the Westminster Confession asserts that Christ "was crucified, and died; was buried, and remained under the power of death, yet saw no corruption. On the third day he rose from the dead, with the same body in which he suffered; with which also he ascended into heaven, and there sitteth at the right hand of his Father."[11]

Characteristics of Christ's Body

Finally, the characteristics of Christ's body bear eloquent truth to his physical resurrection. Jesus invited the disciples to examine his resurrected body so that they would know beyond the shadow of a doubt that it was the exact same one that had been fatally tormented. He went so far as to say to Thomas, "Put your finger here; see my hands. Reach out your hand and put it into my side. Stop doubting and believe" (John 20:27). If Jesus had been resurrected in an immaterial body, he would be guilty of misleading his disciples by conning them. Jesus also ate food as proof of the nature of his resurrected body. Dr. Luke says the disciples gave Jesus "a piece of broiled fish, and he took it and ate it in their presence" (Luke 24:42–43). In fact, Jesus "was eating" with his disciples prior to being taken up into heaven (Acts 1:4). Jesus provided the final exclamation mark for his physical resurrection by telling the disciples that his resurrected body was comprised of "flesh and bones." "Touch me and see," he said, "a ghost does not have flesh and bones, as you see I have" (Luke 24:39).

Was Christ physically resurrected from the dead? Absolutely! In truth, apart from this affirmation there is no Christian faith.

CHAPTER 10

SOUL

✣

Does the Soul Continue to Exist after the Death of the Body?

"So do not be afraid of them. There is nothing concealed that will not be disclosed, or hidden that will not be made known. What I tell you in the dark, speak in the daylight; what is whispered in your ear, proclaim from the roofs. Do not be afraid of those who kill the body but cannot kill the soul. Rather, be afraid of the One who can destroy both soul and body in hell."
—MATTHEW 10:26–28

✣

One of the reasons I love the game of golf is that it puts me in touch with people whose world-view is radically different from mine. One such person is Matt.[1] This year, Matt and I had an opportunity to team up as partners in a golf tournament. While driving to the tournament, we transitioned from talking about golf to talking about God. Matt, a lawyer by profession, was utterly convinced that humans were mere material beings. To his way of thinking, if we were to die during our drive, we would simply cease to exist. For Matt, the notion of a soul that exists beyond the grave was patently absurd.

Like so many others in our culture, Matt was firmly committed to Carl Sagan's creed—"The Cosmos is all that is, or ever was, or ever will be." In addition, he had embraced the mantra of Madonna—"We are living in a material world, and I am a material girl." From his perspective, human beings are merely material brains and bodies. As we rolled on down the road, I attempted to convince Matt that there are compelling reasons to believe that humans have an immaterial aspect to their being that transcends the material.

I pointed out that, from the perspective of logic, we can demonstrate that the mind is not identical to the brain by proving that the mind and brain have different properties.[2] In other words, "the subjective texture of our conscious mental experiences—the feeling of pain, the experience of sound, the awareness of color—is different from anything that is simply physical. If the world were only made of matter, these subjective aspects of consciousness would not exist. But they *do* exist! So there must be more to the world than matter."[3] An obvious example is color. A moment's reflection is enough to convince a thinking person that the experience of color involves more than a mere wavelength of light.[4]

I went on to argue that, from a legal perspective, if human beings were merely material, they could not be held accountable this year for a crime committed last year, simply because physical identity changes over time. We are not the *same* people today that we were yesterday. Every day we lose multiplied millions of microscopic particles—in fact, every seven years, virtually every part of our material anatomy changes, apart from aspects of our neurological system. Therefore, from a purely material perspective, "the self who did the crime in the past is not literally the same self who is present at the time of punishment."[5] Appealing to Matt's legal background, I suggested that a criminal who attempted to use this line of reasoning as a defense would not get very far. Such legal maneuvering simply does not fly in an age of scientific enlightenment. Legally and intuitively, we recognize a *sameness of soul* that establishes personal identity over time.[6]

Since we were nearing the golf course, I quickly moved on to an argument from libertarian freedom. If we are merely material beings, I said, then libertarian freedom (freedom of the will) does not exist. Instead, we are fatalistically relegated to a world in which everything is determined by mechanistic material processes.[7] Realizing that at this point Matt might have begun thinking about the golf tournament, I transitioned to a golf illustration to make sure I had his attention.

The distance a golf ball flies is fatalistically predetermined by such factors as launch angle, centeredness of contact, ball velocity, and spin rate.[8] Thus, in concert with Newton's laws of motion, the precise distance the ball will travel is determined by the physical processes involved. Likewise, if I am merely material, my choices are merely a function of such factors as genetic makeup and brain chemistry. Therefore, my decisions are not free; they're fatalistically determined.

I pointed out that the implications of such a notion are profound. In a world-view that embraces fatalistic determinism, I cannot be held morally accountable for my actions, since reward and punishment make sense only if we have freedom of the will. In a solely material world, reason itself is reduced to the status of a conditioned reflex. Moreover, even the very concept of love is rendered meaningless. Rather than being an act of the will, love is relegated to a robotic procedure that is fatalistically determined by physical processes. If Madonna is merely a material girl living in a material world, then she really has no freedom of choice.

In short, I presented Matt with three compelling reasons to believe that human beings have a soul that continues to exist apart from the body. First, logically or intuitively, we recognize nonphysical aspects of humanity, such as ego. Furthermore, even though our physical identity changes from year to year, we recognize a sameness of soul that legally establishes personal identity. Finally, libertarian freedom presupposes that we are more than mere material robots. Together these three reasons give us warrant to conclude that human beings have an immaterial nature that transcends the material body. In the Christian world-view, this immaterial aspect of humanity is called the "soul."[9] It is precisely because the human soul is not dependent on material processes for its existence that it can survive the death of the physical body.[10]

I could see the golf course looming on the horizon, so our discussion had to be put on hold. For the next four hours, Matt and I focused on beating a little white ball from one hole to the next. By the time we got back into the car, our visions of golf glory had dematerialized. While we had not crashed on the way to the tournament, we had definitely crashed during it. Nothing seemed to go right. As we headed toward home, we dejectedly replayed every single shot over and over again in our minds, all the while dreaming of what might have been. Eventually, however, we transitioned from mere earthly vanities to eternal verities. As a lawyer, Matt was significantly impressed by the logical, legal, and libertarian freedom arguments I had presented on the way to the tournament. However, he was not yet convinced of life beyond the grave. Thus, during the course of the next few hours, I presented additional arguments that no one with a truly open mind can reject.

I began by suggesting that, in an age of scientific enlightenment, nothing is more compelling than belief in a supreme designer.[11] In Darwin's day, for example, a human egg was thought to be quite simple —for all practical purposes, little more than a microscopic blob of gelatin. Today, however, we know that a fertilized egg is among the most organized, complex structures in the universe. In an age of scientific enlightenment, it is incredible to think that people are willing to maintain that something so vastly complex arose by merely blind natural processes.

Likewise, nineteenth-century science had no concept of what happened when a photon of light hits the human eye. Today, however, we know that "each of the anatomical steps and structures that Darwin thought were so simple actually involves staggeringly complicated biochemical processes"[12] that cannot be accounted for by time and chance.

Like an egg or an eye, the earth is a masterpiece of precision and design that could not have come into existence by chance. Astronaut Guy Gardner, who has seen the earth from the perspective of the moon, points out that "the more we learn and see about our universe the more we come to realize that the most ideally suited place for life within the entire solar system is the planet we call home."[13]

Furthermore, it doesn't take a rocket scientist to understand that an effect such as Planet Earth must have a cause greater than itself. This is plain old common sense. The principle "that every effect must have a cause is a self-evident truth, not only for those who have been trained in logic, but for thinking people everywhere."[14] Cause and effect, "which is universally accepted and followed in every field of science, relates every phenomenon as an effect to a cause. No effect is ever quantitatively 'greater' nor qualitatively 'superior' to its cause. An effect can be lower than its cause but never higher."[15] In stark contrast, the competing theory of evolution attempts to make effects such as organized complexity, life, and personality greater than their causes—disorder, nonlife, and impersonal forces. As has been well said, "design requires a designer, and that is precisely what is lacking in non-theistic [materialistic] evolution."[16]

In the television series *Cosmos*, Carl Sagan boldly pontificated—but never proved—his premise that "the Cosmos is all that is, or ever was, or ever will be."[17] From a purely logical point of view, it should be self-evident that Sagan is dead wrong. In other words, it is illogical to believe that *something* could come from *nothing*.

Finally, it should be noted that philosophical naturalism—the world-view undergirding evolutionism—can provide only three explanations for the existence of the universe in which we live. The first is that the universe is merely an illusion. This notion carries little weight in an age of scientific enlightenment. As has been well said, "even a full-blown solipsist looks both ways before crossing the street."[18] The second is that the universe sprang from nothing. As previously pointed out, this proposition flies in the face of the law of cause and effect. And the third is that the universe eternally existed. This hypothesis is devastated by the law of entropy, which predicts that a universe that has eternally existed would have died an "eternity ago" from heat loss.[19]

There is, however, one other possibility. It is found in the first chapter of the first book of the Bible: "In the beginning God created the heavens and the earth" (Genesis 1:1). In an age of enlightenment and empirical science, nothing could be more certain, clear, or correct.[20]

As the conversation continued, I explained to Matt that the God who created the cosmos condescended to cloak himself in human flesh. He came to live and move among us and demonstrated that there was life beyond the grave through the immutable fact of his resurrection from the dead. As we drove along, I communicated the FEAT that demonstrates the fact of resurrection—documented in Part One of this book. I shared with Matt that Jesus Christ suffered *fatal torment,* that the *empty tomb* is one of the earliest and best-attested facts of ancient history, that no one has ever come up with a credible explanation to explain away the post-resurrection *appearances of Christ,* and that within weeks of the resurrection, not just one, but an entire community of at least ten thousand Jews experienced such an incredible *transformation* that they willingly gave up sociological and theological traditions that had given them their national identity.[21] Dr. Norman Geisler summed up the evidence for the immutable fact of the resurrection as follows:

> The New Testament reveals that more than 500 witnesses saw Christ after his resurrection (1 Corinthians 15:6) on twelve different occasions, scattered over a forty-day period (Acts 1:3). He was seen and heard on each occasion. He was touched at least twice (Matthew 28:9; John 20:17; see also Luke 24:39; John 20:27). He ate (Luke 24:30, 42–43; John 21:12–13; Acts 1:4; cf. 10:41). His crucifixion wounds were visible (Luke 24:39; John 20:27). The disciples saw his empty tomb and the cloths with which his body had been wrapped. These experiences transformed followers of Christ from scared, scattered skeptics to the world's greatest missionary society, preaching the resur-

rection. Nothing else accounts for all this evidence except the literal bodily resurrection of Christ.[22]

By the time I had finished telling Matt about the resurrection, we were already pulling into his driveway. We continued talking, however. I told him that some twenty years earlier, someone had explained to me what I was now explaining to him. I shared that after examining the evidence, the Creator of the cosmos had become the Lord and Savior of my soul and that today he is more real to me than the very flesh upon my bones.

While I would like to tell you that Matt yielded his life to Christ in the driveway that evening, I can't. What I can say is that, since that day, he and I have had numerous conversations about the afterlife and the existence of the soul. As I think about my experience with Matt, I am reminded of a conversation that the apostle Paul had with the Greek philosophers at the Areopagus in Athens. In that conversation, Paul told the Athenians:

"From one man he made every nation of men, that they should inhabit the whole earth; and he determined the times set for them and the exact places where they should live. God did this so that men would seek him and perhaps reach out for him and find him, though he is not far from each one of us. 'For in him we live and move and have our being.' As some of your own poets have said, 'We are his offspring.'

"Therefore since we are God's offspring, we should not think that the divine being is like gold or silver or stone—an image made by man's design and skill. In the past God overlooked such ignorance, but now he commands all people everywhere to repent. For he has set a day when he will judge the world with justice by the man he has appointed. He has given proof of this to all men by raising him from the dead."

When they heard about the resurrection of the dead, some of

them sneered, but others said, "We want to hear you again on this subject." (Acts 17:26–32)

Like some of the philosophers in Athens, Matt has asked to hear more. While I have proven to him beyond a reasonable doubt that the soul continues to exist beyond the death of the body, he remains a skeptic. Thus, I am reminded that all the evidence in the world will not change someone's heart—only the Holy Spirit can do that. People reject the evidence not because they *can't* accept it, but because they *won't* accept it. As I write, Matt has not yet yielded his life to the Creator of his soul—but then again, the whole story has not yet been told.

CHAPTER 11

TIMING

✛

Do Believers Receive Resurrected Bodies When They Die or When Christ Returns?

According to the Lord's own word, we tell you that we who are still alive, who are left till the coming of the Lord, will certainly not precede those who have fallen asleep. For the Lord himself will come down from heaven, with a loud command, with the voice of the archangel and with the trumpet call of God, and the dead in Christ will rise first. After that, we who are still alive and are left will be caught up together with them in the clouds to meet the Lord in the air. And so we will be with the Lord forever.

Therefore encourage each other with these words.

—1 THESSALONIANS 4:15–18

✛

This is a question I encountered frequently after the death of my father. Family members and friends wanted to know whether my dad had become a disembodied soul or whether he had received his resurrection body the moment he died. Dr. Norman Geisler, President of Southern Evangelical Seminary, points out that those who teach that believers receive their resurrection bodies at the moment of death often do so as a result of misunderstanding or misinterpreting the following words in Paul's second letter to the Corinthians:[1]

Now we know that if the earthly tent we live in is destroyed, we have a building from God, an eternal house in heaven, not built by human hands. Meanwhile we groan, longing to be clothed with our heavenly dwelling, because when we are clothed, we will not be found naked. For while we are in this tent, we groan and are burdened, because we do not wish to be unclothed but to be clothed with our heavenly dwelling, so that what is mortal may be swallowed up by life. Now it is God who has made us for this very purpose and has given us the Spirit as a deposit, guaranteeing what is to come.

Therefore we are always confident and know that as long as we are at home in the body we are away from the Lord. We live by faith, not by sight. We are confident, I say, and would prefer to be away from the body and at home with the Lord. So we make it our goal to please him, whether we are at home in the body or away from it. For we must all appear before the judgment seat of Christ, that each one may receive what is due him for the things done while in the body, whether good or bad. (2 Corinthians 5:1–10)

The argument is typically framed in the following manner. Far from being "found naked" (v. 3) when we die, Paul promises that God will give us "an eternal house in heaven, not built by human hands" (v. 1). Thus it is presumed that we either receive another body in place of the body that is being buried or else we receive an intermediate body until our present bodies are raised at the Second Coming of Christ. To determine Paul's meaning, we need to apply a basic principle in the art and science of biblical interpretation called the principle of scriptural harmony. Simply stated, this principle, also known as the analogy of

Scripture, means that individual passages of Scripture must always be harmonized with Scripture as a whole. An isolated passage should never be interpreted in such a way as to conflict with other passages. What appears to be cloudy should be interpreted in light of what is crystal-clear. The biblical interpreter must keep in mind that all of Scripture, though communicated through various human instruments, has a single author: God. And God does not contradict himself.

Thus, to determine what 2 Corinthians 5:1–10 means, we need to consider this passage in light of the immediate and broader context of Scripture. In doing so, we are led to the inevitable conclusion that believers receive their resurrected bodies at the Second Coming of Christ, not when they die.

First and foremost, as noted by Dr. Geisler, the passage under consideration, as well as the rest of Scripture, clearly refers to the moment of death as one of disembodiment, not of re-embodiment.[2] In the immediate context, Paul refers to death as being "naked" (v. 3) or "away from the body" (v. 8). Why would he dread being naked if he were going to receive another body at the moment of death? Says Geisler, "Speaking of death as disembodiment ('absent from the body') and as an undesirable experience makes little sense if that is the moment of one's ultimate triumph with a resurrection body (see 2 Corinthians 5:1, 4; 1 Corinthians 15:50–58 NKJV)."[3] In fact, in verse 8, Paul makes it crystal-clear that being "at home with the Lord" is tantamount to being "away from the body."[4]

Furthermore, Scripture teaches that believers are not resurrected until the Second Coming of Christ (see Philippians 1:23; Hebrews 12:23; Revelation 6:9). Paul explicitly says that when the Lord comes down from heaven, "the dead in Christ will rise first" (1 Thessalonians 4:16). Jesus himself taught that at his Second Coming "all who are in their graves will hear his voice and come out—those who have done good will rise to live, and those who have done evil will rise to be condemned" (John 5:28–29). If believers receive their resurrected bodies at the moment of death, they obviously could not receive them at

Christ's Second Coming. According to theologian Millard Erickson, saying that believers receive their immortal bodies at the moment of death, while their mortal bodies are still in the grave, is tantamount to saying that the resurrection has already come. Paul denounces such notions as godless chatter and explicitly condemns Hymenaeus and Philetus for saying that the resurrection had already taken place (see 2 Timothy 2:16–18).[5]

Finally, as explained in chapter 6, our eternal bodies correspond directly with the bodies we now possess. As Christ rose in the same physical body in which he died, so we will be raised in the same physical bodies in which we die. As mentioned earlier, our resurrection bodies are not second bodies; rather, they are our present bodies transformed. As Geisler explains:

> Upon death the physical body is still in the grave. But the resurrection of the physical body cannot occur while the physical body is still in the grave. If it did, then there would be no continuity between what died (the physical body) and what rose. But Paul declared that "*the body* that is sown is perishable, *it* is raised imperishable." He repeats, "*It* is sown . . . , *it* is raised . . . " (1 Corinthians 15:42–43). That is to say, the body that dies is the very same one to come back to life. Further, resurrection is described by Jesus as the time when "all who are in their graves will hear his voice and come out. . . ." (John 5:28). So while their bodies are in the grave, they are not being raised, and when they are raised their bodies are no longer in the grave. One cannot have it both ways. Resurrection cannot occur while someone's body is still in the grave.[6]

In short, Scripture describes the moment of death as disembodiment, not re-embodiment. Paul makes it clear that being at home with the Lord is tantamount to being "away from the body." Further, if believers received their resurrected bodies at the moment of death, they obviously could not receive them at the Second Coming of Christ, as Scripture teaches. And finally, there is a one-to-one correspondence between the body when it dies and the body when it rises. Thus, our resurrection bodies are not second bodies but our present bodies transformed.

One day, the very body of my father that I watched being lowered into the ground will rise from its grave. It was sown a perishable body, it will be raised imperishable; it was sown in dishonor, it will be raised in glory; it was sown in weakness, it will be raised in power; it was sown a natural body, it is raised a spiritual body (see 1 Corinthians 15:42–44). On that day, Dad's body will no longer be dominated by natural proclivities; instead, he will have a supernatural, spiritual body dominated by the Holy Spirit and set free from slavery to sin—"an eternal house in heaven, not built by human hands" (2 Corinthians 5:1). Apart from that hope, there is no hope. "If the dead are not raised," says Paul, "'let us eat and drink, for tomorrow we die'" (1 Corinthians 15:32).

CHAPTER 12

BORING

✠

If Heaven Is Perfect, Won't It Be Perfectly Boring?

You have made known to me the path of life; you will fill me with joy in your presence, with eternal pleasures at your right hand.

—PSALM 16:11

✠

An all-too-prevalent perception in Christianity and the culture is that heaven is going to be one big bore. Pardon the golf analogy, but I have heard more than one person say that a never-ending repetition of hole-in-ones would make even Tiger Woods want to give up the game. That, however, is far from what heaven will be. Rather, heaven will be a place of continuous learning, growth, and development. By nature, humans are finite, and that is how it always will be. Thus, while we will have an incredible capacity to learn, we will never come to the end of learning. In the words of Peter Kreeft: "Knowing everything would be more like Hell than Heaven for us. For one thing, we need progress and hope: we need to look forward to knowing something new tomorrow. Mystery is our mind's food. If we truly said, 'I have seen everything' [Ecclesiastes 1:14], we would conclude, as did the author of Ecclesiastes, 'all is vanity' [Ecclesiastes 12:8]. For another thing, the more knowledge, the more responsibility [James 3:1; Luke 12:48]. Only omnipotence can bear the burden of omniscience; only God's shoulders are strong enough to carry the burden of infinite knowledge without losing the joy."[1]

To begin with, we will never come to the end of exploring our Creator. God by nature is infinite, and we are limited. Thus, what we now merely apprehend about the Creator we will spend an eternity seeking to comprehend. Imagine finally beginning to get a handle on how God is one in nature and three in person. Or how Jesus Christ can at once be fully God and fully man. Imagine exploring the depths of God's love, wisdom, and holiness. Imagine forever growing in the capacity to fathom his immensity, immutability, and incomprehensibility. And to top it all off, the more we come to know him, the more of him there will be to know.

Furthermore, we will never come to an end of exploring the Creator's creative handiwork. The universe will literally be our playground. Even if we were capable of exhausting the "new heaven and new earth" (Revelation 21:1), God could create brand-new vistas for us to explore. I love the way A. A. Hodge puts it:

> Heaven, as the eternal home of the divine Man and of all the redeemed members of the human race, must necessarily be thoroughly human in its structure, conditions, and activities. Its joys and activities must all be rational, moral, emotional, voluntary and active. There must be the exercise of all the faculties, the gratification of all tastes, the development of all talent capacities, the realization of all ideals. The reason, the intellectual curiosity, the imagination, the aesthetic instincts, the holy affections, the social affinities, the inexhaustible resources of strength and power native to the human soul must all find in

heaven exercise and satisfaction. Then there must always be a goal of endeavor before us, ever future.[2]

Finally, we will never come to the end of exploring fellow Christians. Our ability to appreciate one another will be enhanced exponentially. In the words of B. H. Streeter, our love for one another will be of an "intenser quality, will lavish itself on a wide range of persons, and will always express itself more freely and in more diverse ways."[3] Imagine being able to love another human being without even a tinge of selfishness. Imagine appreciating, no, *reveling* in the exalted capacities and stations that God bestows on another without so much as a modicum of jealousy.

Will heaven be perfect? Absolutely. Will it be boring? Absolutely not! We will learn without error—but make no mistake about it, *we will learn, we will grow, and we will develop.* In heaven, "we remain like the tiny figures in a Chinese landscape: small subjects in an enormously larger objective world."[4] Far from being dead and dull, heaven will be an exhilarating, exciting experience that will never come to an end.

CHAPTER 13

ANIMALS

✢

Will God Raise Pets and Platypuses from the Dead?

I know every bird in the mountains, and the creatures of the field are mine.
—PSALM 50:11

Your kingdom is an everlasting kingdom, and your dominion endures through all generations. The LORD is faithful to all his promises and loving toward all he has made.

—PSALM 145:13

✢

Talk about a question that stirs up emotion! Joni Eareckson Tada (one of my heroes in the faith) found out firsthand when she suggested that pets would not be resurrected from the dead. In her words:

> I always thought I responded well to criticism. That is until my book *Heaven . . . Your Real Home* went to press. I received more critical letters over one paragraph on page fifty-five than all

totaled for anything I'd ever written. I penned it innocently enough: "[Animals] in heaven? Yes. I think animals are some of God's best and most avant-garde ideas; why would He throw out His greatest creative achievements? I'm not talking about my pet schnauzer, Scrappy, dying and going to heaven—Ecclesiastes 3:21 puts the brakes on that idea. I'm talking about new animals fit for a new order of things."[1]

Joni went on to explain that she is an animal lover from way back. Her bedroom shelves have been stacked with books from the *Black Stallion* to *Lassie,* and her pets have ranged from a tiny schnauzer to a towering Appaloosa. The mere suggestion that pets would not be resurrected from the dead, however, buried her in a deluge of angry letters. One person after the other questioned how she could possibly say that their pets would not be in heaven. As a result, Joni took a closer look at such Scripture passages as Ecclesiastes 3:21: "Who knows if the spirit of man rises upward and if the spirit of the animal goes down to the earth?" After sinking deeply into the words of Scripture, she wrote:

> If God brings our pets back to life, it wouldn't surprise me. It would be just like Him. It would be totally in keeping with His generous character. . . . Exorbitant. Excessive. Extravagant in grace after grace. Of all the dazzling discoveries and ecstatic pleasures heaven will hold for us, the potential of seeing Scrappy would be pure whimsy—utterly, joyfully, surprisingly superfluous. It's not that animals have souls or that God owes Scrappy anything, but that heaven is going to be a place that will refract and reflect in as many ways as possible the goodness and joy of our great God, who delights in lavishing love on His children. So will pets be in heaven? Who knows?![2]

Is Joni barking up the wrong tree, or is she right? As usual, I'd say she is right on. Scripture does not conclusively tell us whether our pets will make it to heaven. However, the Bible does provide us with some significant clues regarding whether animals will inhabit the new heaven and the new earth.

First, the Garden of Eden was populated by animals; thus, there is a precedent for believing that Eden restored will be populated by animals also. Joni has well said, "animals are some of God's best and most avant-garde ideas."[3] Thus, it would seem incredible that God would eliminate some of his most creative creations.

Furthermore, the Scriptures from first to last suggest that animals have souls. Both Moses in Genesis and John in Revelation communicate that the Creator endowed animals with souls (see Genesis 1:20, 24; Revelation 8:9).[4] However, because the soul of an animal is qualitatively different from the soul of a human, there is reasonable doubt that it can survive the death of its body. As noted in *Beyond Death*, Thomas Aquinas argued that "animal souls function in clear dependence on the animal body. For example, animals' functions are tied to sensory experiences, and these in turn depend upon the sense organs of sight, smell, and so on. However, the human soul gives evidence of being self-subsistent, of existing in its own right apart from the body."[5] It wasn't until the advent of seventeenth-century Enlightenment and the thought of Descartes and Hobbes that the existence of animal souls was even questioned in Western civilization.[6] "Throughout the history of the church, the classic understanding of living things has included the doctrine that animals, as well as humans, have souls."[7]

Finally, while we cannot say for certain that the pets we enjoy today will be "resurrected" in eternity, I, like Joni, am not willing to preclude the possibility. Some of the keenest thinkers from C. S. Lewis to Peter Kreeft[8] are not only convinced that animals in general but that pets in particular will be restored in the resurrection. Lewis, for one, argues that pets "may have an immortality, not in themselves, but in the immortality of their masters."[9] As Lewis explains, "very few animals indeed, in their wild state, attain to a 'self' or *ego*. But if any do, and if it is agreeable to the goodness of God that they should live again, their immortality would also be related to man—not, this time, to individual masters, but to humanity."[10]

Like Lewis, Dr. Peter Kreeft is convinced that animals will exist throughout eternity. "Are there animals in Heaven? The simplest answer is: Why not? How irrational is the prejudice that would allow plants (green fields and flowers) but not animals into Heaven! . . . Animals belong in the 'new earth' as much as trees."[11] Regarding pets, Kreeft writes: "Would the same animals be in Heaven as on earth? 'Is my dead cat in Heaven?' Again, why not? God can raise up the very grass; why not cats? Though the blessed have better things to do than play with pets, the better does not exclude the lesser. We were meant from the beginning to have stewardship over the animals; we have not fulfilled that divine plan yet on earth; therefore it seems likely that the right relationship with animals will be part of Heaven: proper 'pet-ship.' And what better place to begin than with already petted pets?"[12]

In the final analysis, one thing is certain: Scripture provides us with a sufficient precedent for suggesting that animals will continue to exist after the return of our Lord. Isaiah provides a particularly stirring image:

> *The wolf will live with the lamb,*
> *the leopard will lie down with the goat,*
> *the calf and the lion and the yearling together;*
> *and a little child will lead them.*
> *The cow will feed with the bear,*
> *their young will lie down together,*
> *and the lion will eat straw like the ox.*
> *The infant will play near the hole of the cobra,*
> *and the young child put his hand into the viper's nest.*
> *They will neither harm nor destroy*
> *on all my holy mountain,*
> *for the earth will be full of the knowledge of the LORD*
> *as the waters cover the sea.* (Isaiah 11:6–9)

CHAPTER 14

REINCARNATION

✛

Are Reincarnation and Resurrection Mutually Exclusive?

Just as man is destined to die once, and after that to face judgment, so Christ was sacrificed once to take away the sins of many people; and he will appear a second time, not to bear sin, but to bring salvation to those who are waiting for him.

—HEBREWS 9:27–28

✛

Reincarnation, literally, "rebirth in another body," has long been considered to be a universal law of life in the Eastern world. For multiplied millions of Buddhists, Hindus, Sikhs, and Jains, reincarnation is an inexorable reality, as predictable as the law of gravity. Conversely, resurrection, literally, "restoration in our present bodies," has traditionally been the predominant belief of the Western world. However, 1893 became a watershed date for a spiritual paradigm shift that had been previously initiated by theosophy. Buddhists, Baha'is, and Bhahti Yogis from the East arrived in Chicago to attend the inaugural World's

Parliament of Religions. Although their contingent was sizable, they were vastly outnumbered by Bible believers from the West. Despite the disparity in numbers, the impact of the Eastern contingent was monumental. Swami Vivekananda, a disciple of the self-proclaimed "godman" Sri Ramakrishna, skillfully used the Parliament to sow the seeds for a new global spirituality that supplanted the doctrine of resurrection with the dogma of reincarnation.

One hundred years later—at the centennial celebration of the original Parliament in August 1993—the impact of Vivekananda's message could be seen in living color. Buddhists outnumbered Baptists, and saffron robes were more common than Christian clerical clothing.[1] In like fashion, the swami's message of pantheism and reincarnation—cleverly repackaged for Western consumption—could be seen throughout the Western world through such media as music, manuscripts, and movies. In an article titled "I Was Beheaded in the 1700s," *Time* magazine documented the pervasive impact of reincarnation on Tinsel Town:

> Glenn Ford was a Christian martyr, eaten by a lion. Loretta Lynn was a Cherokee princess and a mistress of one of the King Georges, she is not sure which. Shirley MacLaine and Sylvester Stallone were both beheaded, she by Louis XV, he during the French Revolution. Stallone thinks he may have been a monkey in Guatemala, and MacLaine is sure she was a prostitute in a previous life. Many Hollywood stars and other celebrities are firm believers in reincarnation. With the aid of mediums and hypnotists, some of whom specialize in regressing people back to the distant past, they have tracked down what they say are some basic facts about previous lives. . . . Lynn is convinced she has lived at least six previous lives. Three of them she discovered on her own: Cherokee princess, an Irish woman and a rural American housewife. In 1980 a hypnotism session with two friends in Arizona brought memories of three more lives, as the

wife of a bedridden old man, a male restaurant employee in the 1920s and a maid in the royal household of one of the King Georges of England. She had an affair with the King, she says, and died because she attracted the amorous attention of a courtier. . . . Stallone thinks some of his talents hint at other past lives. "I can do American Indian dances, the eagle dance, for example," he says. "And I feel a very strong kinship with wolves. I won't bore you with wolf calls, but I've been able to go up to wolves in the wild and not have them dismember me." Unsurprisingly, Stallone wants to come back some day as a heavyweight boxing champion.[2]

Time cites a Gallup poll in evidence that reincarnation has become as prevalent on Main Street as it is on movie sets. Already two decades ago, a whopping 23 percent of Americans had begun to put their faith in reincarnation. One past-lives therapist said reincarnation had become so pervasive that "saying you have lived before is almost the equivalent of saying, 'You're a Leo; I'm a Scorpio.'"[3] The *Baker Encyclopedia of Christian Apologetics* notes that approximately "one in four Americans believe in reincarnation. Among college age young people the figure is nearly one in three. Surprisingly, about one in five who attend church regularly also believe in reincarnation, in spite of the fact that the Bible and orthodox Christian belief reject reincarnation."[4]

Even more tragically, an ever-growing number of people both in the church and in the culture have come to believe that reincarnation can be harmonized with a Christian world-view. In fact, multitudes have embraced the queer predilection that Scripture actually promotes reincarnation. The words of Jeremiah, John, and Jesus are typically cited as irrefutable evidence. In Jeremiah, God allegedly tells his prophet that he knew him as the result of a prior incarnation—"Before I formed you in the womb I knew you, before you were born I set you apart; I appointed you as a prophet to the nations" (Jeremiah 1:5).[5] In

John's Gospel, the disciples allegedly wonder whether a man born blind is paying off karmic debt for himself or for his parents (see John 9:1–2).[6] Additionally, Jesus himself is cited as suggesting that Elijah was reincarnated as John the Baptist (see Matthew 11:14).[7]

A quick look at the context of these Scripture passages, however, reveals that they have nothing whatsoever to do with reincarnation. First, in Jeremiah, God is not suggesting that his prophet had existed in a prior incarnation, but rather that he who has existed for all eternity preordained Jeremiah to a special task. Furthermore, John dispels the notion that the man born blind is paying off karmic debt by overtly stating that his blindness had nothing to do with either his sin or that of his parents (see John 9:3). If indeed the man was suffering for past indiscretions, Jesus would have violated the law of karma by healing him.[8] Finally, Jesus' alleged suggestion that Elijah had been reincarnated as John the Baptist is explicitly dismissed by Scripture itself. When the priests and Levites asked John if he was Elijah, he replied, "I am not" (John 1:21). In context, Elijah and John are not said to be two incarnations of the same *person*, but rather two separate people who functioned in a strikingly similar prophetic role.[9]

One thing is certain! Both the Bible and a biblical world-view make it crystal-clear that reincarnation and resurrection are mutually exclusive. To begin with, the writer of Hebrews emphatically states that human beings are "destined to die once, and after that to face judgment" (Hebrews 9:27).

One Death

At face value, the resurrectionist view of one death per person is mutually exclusive from the reincarnationist view of an ongoing cycle of death and rebirth. Scripture teaches that, upon death, the soul leaves the body and goes into the spirit world to await the resurrection. In his parable concerning the rich man and Lazarus, Jesus describes the horrors of judgment in the afterlife, rather than the horrors of karmic debt in another life (see Luke 16:19ff.). Likewise, the apostle Paul makes it clear that we await "the redemption of our bodies," rather than the reincarnation of our souls into different bodies (Romans 8:23). In sharp contrast to a world-view in which humanity perfects itself through an endless cycle of birth and rebirth, the Christian world-view maintains that we are vicariously perfected by the righteousness of Christ. Thus, salvation is not based on what we *do*, but rather on what Christ has *done*.

One Body

Furthermore, the biblical teaching of one body per person demonstrates that the gulf between reincarnation and resurrection can never be bridged. Rather than the *transmigration* of our souls into different bodies, the apostle Paul explains that Christ "will *transform* our lowly bodies" (Philippians 3:21; emphasis added). He explicitly says that the body that dies is the very body that rises. "The body that is sown is perishable, *it* is raised imperishable; it is sown in dishonor, *it* is raised in glory; it is sown in weakness, *it* is raised in power; it is sown a natural body, *it* is raised a spiritual body" (1 Corinthians 15:42–44; emphasis added). As Dr. Norman Geisler explains:

> Rather than a series of bodies that die, resurrection makes alive forever the same body that died. Rather than seeing personhood as a soul in a body, resurrection sees each human being as a soul-body unity. While reincarnation is a process of perfection, resurrection is a perfected state. Reincarnation is an intermediate state, while the soul longs to be disembodied and absorbed in God; but, resurrection is an ultimate state, in which the whole person, body and soul, enjoys the goodness of God.[10]

One Way

Finally, the Christian belief that there is only *one way* to God categorically demonstrates that resurrection and reincarnation can never be harmonized. As Christ himself put it, "I am *the* way and *the* truth and *the* life. No one comes to the Father except through me" (John 14:6; emphasis added). If Christ is truly God, his claim to be the only way has to be taken seriously. If, on the other hand, he is merely one more person in a pantheon of pretenders, his proclamations can easily be pushed aside. That is precisely why the resurrection is axiomatic to Christianity. Through the resurrection, Christ demonstrated that he does not stand in a line of peers with Buddha, Bahá'u'lláh, Krishna, or any other founder of a world religion. They died and are *still* dead, but Christ is risen. Ultimately, resurrection and reincarnation are mutually exclusive because the former is a historical fact, while the latter is but a Hindu fantasy.

CREMATION

✠

Is Cremation Commensurate with the Christian Concept of Resurrection?

Do you not know that your body is a temple of the Holy Spirit, who is in you, whom you have received from God? You are not your own; you were bought at a price. Therefore honor God with your body.

—1 CORINTHIANS 6:19–20

✠

Cremation has become an increasingly popular means for disposing of the dead. In fact, by the year 2010, it is estimated that 34 percent of all Americans will cremate their loved ones.[1] Those who opt for cremation often do so for emotional, economical, and ecological reasons. Emotionally, cremation is thought to bring immediate closure to the grieving process; economically, it is measured in hundreds rather than thousands of dollars; and ecologically, it is said to save valuable land for more productive purposes.[2]

The arguments for cremation from emotion, economics, and ecology are not particularly compelling. First, from an emotional perspective, cremation does not logically lead to a more satisfying sense of closure than does burial. "Much of the therapeutic value of any funerary ritual depends on cultural conditioning, prior understanding of the death experience, the circumstance of death itself, the relationship to the deceased, and the emotional make-up of the survivors."[3] Furthermore, economic considerations should not be valued more highly than ethical considerations—eternal values are ultimately more significant than economic values. Finally, the ecological argument is weak in that there is no warrant for suggesting that we will run out of suitable land for burial sites anytime soon.[4]

In sharp distinction to the arguments for cremation, the arguments for burial are incredibly persuasive. First, Scripture clearly favors burial over cremation. The Old Testament pattern was always burial, except in highly unusual circumstances. The exception that best proves the rule is the partial cremation of King Saul and his sons—and even in this case the bodies were burned, but the bones were buried (see 1 Samuel 31:12–13).

Likewise, the New Testament pattern is always burial. As well, Paul includes burial as an essential part of the gospel itself when he writes, "For what I received I passed on to you as of first importance: that Christ died for our sins according to the Scriptures, that *he was buried*, that he was raised on the third day according to the Scriptures" (1 Corinthians 15:3–4; emphasis added).[5] Additionally, Paul equates baptism with both burial and resurrection when he says that we were buried with Christ "through baptism into death in order that, just as Christ was raised from the dead through the glory of the Father, we too may live a new life" (Romans 6:4).

Furthermore, burial symbolizes the promise of resurrection by anticipating the preservation of the body. Cremation, however, symbolizes the pagan world-view of reincarnation.[6] As Dr. Norman Geisler puts it, "The Christian has escaped the judgment by fire presented in the Bible (Revelation 20:14). Cremation is the wrong picture to remind believers of *salvation in the body* by resurrection (cf.

Romans 8:11). . . . Cremation better symbolizes pantheism, which in its Eastern forms is usually associated with a *salvation from the body* by escaping the cycle of reincarnation."[7] Thus, while resurrectionists look forward to the restoration *of the body,* reincarnationists look forward to being relieved *from their bodies.*

Finally, burial highlights the sanctity of the body. In the Christian world-view, the body is incredibly significant, in that it has numerical identity to the resurrected body and is "uniquely designed to give expression to the image of God in man"[8] (see Genesis 1:27; 9:6; cf. 1 Corinthians 6:19–20). While God has no problem resurrecting the cremated, cremation does not point to the resurrection of God.[9] Ultimately, the hope of the believer rests in the one-to-one correspondence between the body that dies and the body that rises. In the immortal words of the apostle to the Gentiles:

> We will not all sleep, but we will all be changed—in a flash, in the twinkling of an eye, at the last trumpet. For the trumpet will sound, the dead will be raised imperishable, and we will be changed. For the perishable must clothe itself with the imperishable, and the mortal with immortality. When the perishable has been clothed with the imperishable, and the mortal with immortality, then the saying that is written will come true: "Death has been swallowed up in victory."
>
> "Where, O death, is your victory?
>
> Where, O death, is your sting?" (1 Corinthians 15:51–55)

CHAPTER 16

AGE

✛

Will We Be Resurrected at the Same Age That We Died?

Then will the eyes of the blind be opened and the ears of the deaf unstopped.
Then will the lame leap like a deer, and the mute tongue shout for joy.
Water will gush forth in the wilderness and streams in the desert.

—*ISAIAH 35:5–6*

✛

Answering this question requires a bit of sanctified speculation. First, when God created Adam and Eve in Eden, he created them with apparent age.[1] Additionally, Jesus apparently died and was resurrected at the prime of his physical development.[2]

Furthermore, our DNA is programmed in such a way that, at a particular point, we reach optimal development from a functional perspective. For the most part, it appears that we reach this stage somewhere in our twenties or thirties. Prior to this stage, the development of our bodies (anabolism) exceeds the devolution of our bodies (catabolism). From this point on, the rate of breakdown exceeds the rate of buildup, which eventually leads to physical death. With age, our muscles get shorter, our connective tissues degenerate, our hormone levels decline, our neurological functions break down, and so forth. As a golf fanatic, I can bear eloquent testimony to this reality. Twenty years ago, I could hit a golf ball a mile. Today, I can't even hit it in the same zip code as the "flat bellies." (That's precisely why the PGA now has the Seniors Tour—even Jack Nicklaus, arguably the greatest golfer who ever lived, can no longer compete with the likes of a Tiger Woods.) All of this is to say that if the blueprints for our glorified bodies are in the DNA, then it would stand to reason that our bodies will be resurrected at the optimal stage of development determined by our DNA.[3]

Finally, one thing can be stated with complete certainty: In the resurrection, there will be no deformities. You will be the perfect you, and I will be the perfect me. This point was amplified in an interview with Joni Eareckson Tada on the *Bible Answer Man* broadcast. Speaking from the perspective of a wheelchair, she exuded, "Some day in the not-too-distant future, I'm gonna pole-vault the pearly gates." Joni's hope echoes what the church has always believed. As Justin Martyr, a great apologist of the early second century, wrote, "All things which the Savior did, He did in the first place in order that what was spoken concerning Him in the prophets might be fulfilled, 'that the blind should receive sight, and the deaf hear' (Isaiah 35:5), and so on; but also to induce the belief that in the resurrection the flesh shall arise entire. For if on earth He healed the sicknesses of the flesh, and made the body whole, much more will He do this in the resurrection, so that the flesh shall rise perfect and entire."[4] Indeed, in heaven "there will be no more death or mourning or crying or pain, for the old order of things has passed away" (Revelation 21:4).

Peter Kreeft provides a poignant portrayal of how the body, tarnished by the Fall into a life of constant sin terminated by death, will be utterly transformed in the resurrection:

The Fall turned things upside down between soul and body. Before the Fall, the body was a transparent window, a totally malleable instrument, a perfectly obedient servant of the soul. The Resurrection restores this relationship. Once the perfected soul is perfectly subject to God, the perfected body can be perfectly subject to the soul, for the soul's authority over the body is a delegated and dependent authority. . . . Soul will no longer be frustrated by a semi-independent, recalcitrant body . . . and body will be a bright ray of light from soul, not an opaque object; it will be more subject, less object, more truly mine, truly me. No more will I crave ec-static out-of-the-body experiences, for the highest flights of mystic ecstasy will be *in* this new body.[5]

CHAPTER 17

SEX

✠

Will There Be Sex after the Resurrection?

How delightful is your love, my sister, my bride! How much more pleasing is your love than wine, and the fragrance of your perfume than any spice!

Your lips drop sweetness as the honeycomb, my bride; milk and honey are under your tongue. The fragrance of your garments is like that of Lebanon.

You are a garden locked up, my sister, my bride; you are a spring enclosed, a sealed fountain.

Your plants are an orchard of pomegranates with choice fruits, with henna and nard, nard and saffron, calamus and cinnamon, with every kind of incense tree, with myrrh and aloes and all the finest spices.

You are a garden fountain, a well of flowing water streaming down from Lebanon.

Awake, north wind, and come, south wind! Blow on my garden, that its fragrance may spread abroad. Let my lover come into his garden and taste its choice fruits.

—SONG OF SONGS 4:10–16

✠

What do you see in your mind's eye when the word *sex* is mentioned? An image of Madonna on MTV? A James Bond movie? *Cosmopolitan* magazine? Or does your mind immediately flash from sex to Scripture? Trust me: When it comes to sex, *Playboy* can't hold a candle to Scripture. If you think that's an overstatement, just read a few pages of the Song of Songs. As Phillip Yancey and Tim Stafford note, the average person is surprised to learn that Scripture contains a love song—complete with "erotic lyrics":

> But Song of Songs is exactly that. It shows no embarrassment about lovers enjoying each other's bodies, and talking about it. . . . These lovers love to look at each other. They love to tell each other what they feel. They revel in the sensuous: the beauty of nature, the scent of perfumes and spices. They are openly erotic.
>
> Their intoxication with love sounds quite up-to-date, not so different from what you hear on the radio. Yet Song of Songs conveys a very different atmosphere from most modern love songs. The explicit lyrics never become even slightly dirty. This love comes from the Garden of Eden, when both man and woman were naked and unashamed. It is tender, filled with delight, natural. You sense no shame or guilt; you feel that God is with the two as they love. The lovers act as equals. Both woman and man take the initiative in praising each other. They don't flirt or play games: they say what they mean.[1]

Sex may be the most commonly used word on Internet search engines, but it originated with God. In the beginning God created sex, and he called his creation "very good" (Genesis 1:31). And God did not just ordain sex for procreation; he originated sex for the purpose of pleasure (see Song of Songs 7). In *Pure Sex*, Dr. Edwin Young underscores the truth that sexual pleasure "was an intentional part of [God's] divine design, not a serendipitous by-product. He *meant* for sex to be a powerfully pleasurable experience. God could have made sex merely functional—but He did not. Instead, He made it to be a thrilling, passionate act—full of potential for physical delight."[2]

Tragically, what the Creator purposed to be pristine and pure, the creation has prostituted and perverted. But that is not where the story ends! God does not arbitrarily *remove* things—he *redeems* them. So will there be sex after the resurrection? Yes and no—it all depends on what you mean by *sex*.

Essence

First, by nature or essence we are sexual beings. Thus, sex is not just something you do. Sex is what you are! Philosopher Peter Kreeft drives this point home in memorable fashion:

> Suppose you saw a book with the title "The Sexual Life of a Nun." You would probably assume it was a scurrilous, gossipy sort of story about tunnels connecting convents and monasteries, clandestine rendezvous behind the high altar, and masking a pregnancy as a tumor. But it is a perfectly proper title: all nuns have a sexual life. They are women, not men. When a nun prays or acts charitably, she prays or acts, not he. Her celibacy forbids intercourse, but it cannot forbid her to be a woman. In everything she does her essence plays a part, and her sex is as much a part of her essence as her age, her race, and her sense of humor.[3]

Kreeft goes on to note that the phrase *having sex* is a counterfeit that has only recently been minted. A nun has sex because she is a female, not because she had a fling. This linguistic slight of mind has been used in our generation to trivialize sex as merely what we do, as opposed to treating sex as what we are. In our culture we have reduced having sex, or making love, to "a thing of surfaces and external feeling rather than of personality and internal feeling. Thus even masturbation is called 'having sex,' though it is exactly the opposite: a denial of real relationship with the other sex."[4]

The foremost reason we can say with certainty that sex will exist after the resurrection is that sex is not merely a word that describes an exotic experience; it is what we are by essence. In the beginning, God created us "male and female" (Genesis 1:27), and that is likely how it always will be.[5]

Enjoyment

Furthermore, we can safely surmise that there will be sexuality in heaven because heaven will personify enjoyment. Men and women will enjoy each other—not in a mere physical sense, but in a metaphysical sense. This reality is virtually impossible for a crass materialist to grasp. The materialist views sexual pleasure as a function of fitting body parts together. Christians, however, see humanity as a psychosomatic unity of both body and soul. Thus, we are not solely sexual somas (bodies); we are sexual souls as well. Indeed, sexuality pervades the entirety of our beings. In the resurrection, there will no doubt be "millions of more adequate ways to express love than the clumsy ecstasy of fitting two bodies together like pieces of a jigsaw puzzle."[6] Thus, we can rest assured that our temporary earthly passions are but a pale shadow of the pleasure we will experience in heaven when symbol is supplanted by substance. As C. S. Lewis explains, in heaven there will be something far greater to enjoy than physical sex:

> The letter and spirit of scripture, and of all Christianity, forbid us to suppose that life in the New Creation will be a sexual life; and this reduces our imagination to the withering alternative either of bodies which are hardly recognizable as human bodies at all or else of a perpetual fast. As regards the fast, I

think our present outlook might be like that of a small boy who, on being told that the sexual act was the highest bodily pleasure should immediately ask whether you ate chocolates at the same time. On receiving the answer "No," he might regard absence of chocolates as the chief characteristic of sexuality. In vain would you tell him that the reason why lovers in their carnal raptures don't bother about chocolates is that they have something better to think of. The boy knows chocolate: he does not know the positive thing that excludes it. We are in the same position. We know the sexual life; we do not know, except in glimpses, the other thing which, in Heaven, will leave no room for it. Hence where fullness awaits us we anticipate fasting. In denying that sexual life, as we now understand it, makes any part of the final beatitude, it is not of course necessary to suppose that the distinction of sexes will disappear.[7]

In heaven, the pleasure that the male and female sex will experience in one another will be infinitely magnified because in eternity our earthly conception of sex will have been eclipsed. In place of selfishness, we will take pleasure in selflessness. This is the principle of first and second things.[8] When the cart is put before the horse, the usefulness of both is compromised. Only in their proper sequence does the first thing retain its usefulness and enhance the usefulness of the second thing. I love the way Peter Kreeft applies this principle to enjoyment in heaven:

> The highest pleasure always comes in self-forgetfulness. Self always spoils its own pleasure. Pleasure is like light; if you grab at it, you miss it; if you try to bottle it, you get only darkness; if you let it pass, you catch the glory. The self has a built-in, God-imaging design of self-fulfillment by self-forgetfulness, pleasure through unselfishness, ecstasy by *ekstasis*, 'standing-outside-the-self.' This is not the self-conscious self-sacrifice of the do-gooder but the spontaneous, unconscious generosity of the lover.[9]

Eden

Finally, we can safely assume that there will be sex in eternity because God created sex in Eden *before* humanity's fall into a life of constant sin terminated by death. Thus, in Eden restored, we can rest assured that God will not *remove* our sexual nature; rather, he will *redeem* it. "God may unmake what *we* make, but He does not unmake what *He* makes. God made sex, and God makes no mistakes."[10] In the words of Thomas Aquinas, "grace does not destroy nature but perfects it."[11]

In the new heaven and new earth, sex will no longer be for the purpose of procreation. As Kreeft says, "Earth is the breeding colony; Heaven is the homeland."[12] Nor will it involve sexual intercourse—for "at the resurrection people will neither marry nor be given in marriage; they will be like the angels in heaven" (Matthew 22:30).[13] In heaven, we will experience a kind of spiritual intercourse that eludes our grasp on earth. In paradise, romance subverted will become romance sublime. It will be *agape* driven rather than animal driven. In Eden restored, our sexual bodies and sexual souls will fly full and free, unfettered by the stain of selfishness and sin.

Will there be sex after the resurrection? Again, yes and no. Yes, there will be sexuality in heaven in that *we* will be in heaven—and *we* by our very nature are sexual beings. And no, there is no warrant for believing there will be sex in heaven in terms of the physical act. As previously noted, we are presently in much the same state as the boy who wondered why spouses don't eat chocolates during sexual intercourse. "In vain would you tell him that the reason why lovers in their carnal raptures don't bother about chocolates is that they have something better to think of. The boy knows chocolate: he does not know the positive thing that excludes it. We are in the same position. We know the sexual life; we do not know, except in glimpses, the other thing which, in Heaven, will leave no room for it."[14]

CHAPTER 18

REWARDS

✛

What about Rewards in the Resurrection?

"Behold, I am coming soon! My reward is with me, and I will give to everyone according to what he has done. I am the Alpha and the Omega, the First and the Last, the Beginning and the End. Blessed are those who wash their robes, that they may have the right to the tree of life and may go through the gates into the city."

—REVELATION 22:12–14

✛

Not long ago, I had the opportunity to live out a lifelong fantasy: I received an invitation to play Cypress Point, arguably the most spectacular golf course on earth. A former president of the USGA devoutly referred to Cypress Point as "the Sistine Chapel of Golf." Playing its eighteen holes is said to be "something of a spiritual journey through a shadowed pine forest, over sparkling dunes, around beach grass, along the restless sea." It is an unparalleled collection of holes of which its architect Alister MacKenzie said, "I do not expect anyone will ever have the opportunity of constructing another course like Cypress Point . . . as I do not suppose anywhere in the world is there such a glorious combination of rocky coast, sand dunes, pine woods and cypress trees."[1]

While the invitation to play Cypress Point was freely given, I have seldom worked harder to prepare for anything in my life. For months, I beat my body into submission. I lifted weights, worked on stretching exercises, and pounded thousands of golf balls, all the while dreaming of the day I would physically experience walking the fairways of Cypress Point. I particularly set my sights on conquering "number sixteen"—the most photographed hole in golf.

In some cases reality does not live up to expectations, but this case was different. The real-life experience exceeded my wildest expectations. To this very day, I can still remember standing on the first tee, intoxicated by an overwhelming sense of nature's beauty in anticipation of playing an architectural masterpiece of precision and design. I savored each majestic hole until, finally, I stood on the bewilderingly beautiful sixteenth tee and prepared to hit a shot that I had seen a thousand times in my dreams. I will never forget the feeling of exhilaration as I watched my golf ball soar over the cobalt sea and land safely next to a flag surrounded by pounding waves.

The sensation I felt as my golf ball soared toward its intended target was worth all of the hard work. Without my strenuous preparation, I would have still experienced the same cliff-side vistas and breathtaking views. I would still have been able to smell the fragrance of the Monterey cypresses and feel the refreshing sting of the salt air upon my face. All the hard work, however, added immeasurably to the experience.

That is how I believe heaven will be. The work I do here and now will greatly enhance my hereafter. While we are saved by God's grace through faith in Jesus Christ alone, we are saved unto good works. My invitation to play Cypress Point was free. The hard work I put in ahead of time, however, was richly rewarded. As a master musician can appreciate Mozart more than can an average music lover, so too my strenuous training allowed me to more fully appreciate the architectural nuances MacKenzie had built into his golfing Mecca.[2]

As phenomenal as Cypress Point is, it pales by comparison to what paradise will be. I spent one day at a golf haven; I will spend an eternity in God's heaven. It stands to reason, therefore, that I would put a whole lot more effort into preparing for an eternity in heaven with God than I did for playing eighteen holes of golf. That is precisely the point Paul is driving at in one of his letters to the Corinthians. Pressing the analogy of athletics, he writes, "Do you not know that in a race all the runners run, but only one gets the prize? Run in such a way as to get the prize. Everyone who competes in the games goes into strict training. They do it to get a crown that will not last; but we do it to get a crown that will last forever" (1 Corinthians 9:24–25). Thus, says Paul, "I do not run like a man running aimlessly; I do not fight like a man beating the air. No, I beat my body and make it my slave so that after I have preached to others, I myself will not be disqualified for the prize" (vv. 26–27).

Crowns

Scripture frequently uses the majestic imagery of crowns to convey the concept of our eternal inheritance. Not only is the Redeemer portrayed as wearing many crowns (see Revelation 19:12), the redeemed are pictured wearing crowns as well. For Christ, the crowns are symbolic of royalty; for Christians, they are symbolic of our eternal reward. These are not perishable crowns like the wreaths awarded to those who win a mere athletic event on earth; rather, they are imperishable crowns that will reflect the glory of God throughout eternity.

In a letter to Timothy, Paul urges his young protégé to train himself for righteousness in the same way that a runner trains for a race. His portrayal conjures up images of a fatigued relay racer preparing to pass the baton. As he approaches the finish line, Paul exhorts young

Timothy to finish the race. You can almost hear Paul gasping for breath as he cries out, "I have fought the good fight, I have finished the race, I have kept the faith. Now there is in store for me the *crown of righteousness,* which the Lord, the righteous Judge, will award to me on that day—and not only to me, but also to all who have longed for his appearing" (2 Timothy 4:7–8; emphasis added).

Like Paul, Peter uses the imagery of crowns to portray the enduring reality of our eternal reward. He promises that when Jesus Christ returns we "will receive the *crown of glory* that will never fade away" (1 Peter 5:4; emphasis added). In sharp contrast to the fading character of a garland of leaflike gold awarded to the winner of a race, our reward will be a garland of grace that will never fade. It will be an enduring reminder that we are "a chosen people, a royal priesthood, a holy nation, a people belonging to God" (1 Peter 2:9).

As Peter urges us to live with an eternal perspective so that we will receive the crown of glory, James urges us to live with perseverance so that we may receive the crown of life. Says James, "Blessed is the man who perseveres under trial, because when he has stood the test, he will receive the *crown of life* that God has promised to those who love him" (James 1:12; emphasis added). Unlike Paul, who used the secular imagery of athletics to relate to a primarily Gentile audience, James uses spiritual imagery to relate to a primarily Jewish audience. Thus, the blessings he pronounces on those who persevere are reminiscent of those proclaimed by Jesus in the Beatitudes (see Matthew 5:11–12). In fact, the words of James mirror those of the Master, who said, "Do not be afraid of what you are about to suffer. I tell you, the devil will put some of you in prison to test you, and you will suffer persecution for ten days. Be faithful, even to the point of death, and I will give you the crown of life" (Revelation 2:10).

The enduring rewards of perseverance are the crown of righteousness, the crown of glory, and the crown of life. But there's more. Jesus explicitly points to *degrees* of reward that will be given for faithful service, self-sacrifice, and suffering. Such enduring rewards are not often the subject of contemporary sermons; they were, however, a constant theme in the sermons of Christ.

Christ

It is significant to note that in his most famous sermon, Christ repeatedly referred to rewards. In concluding the Beatitudes, he said, "Blessed are you when people insult you, persecute you and falsely say all kinds of evil against you because of me. Rejoice and be glad, because great is your *reward* in heaven" (Matthew 5:11–12; emphasis added). Christ continued his message by warning the crowd that if they did their acts of righteousness to be seen by men, they would not receive a reward in heaven:

> "Be careful not to do your 'acts of righteousness' before men, to be seen by them. If you do, you will have no reward from your Father in heaven.
>
> "So when you give to the needy, do not announce it with trumpets, as the hypocrites do in the synagogues and on the streets, to be honored by men. I tell you the truth, they have received their reward in full. But when you give to the needy, do not let your left hand know what your right hand is doing, so that your giving may be in secret. Then your Father, who sees what is done in secret, will reward you.
>
> "And when you pray, do not be like the hypocrites, for they love to pray standing in the synagogues and on the street corners to be seen by men. I tell you the truth, they have received their reward in full. But when you pray, go into your room, close the door and pray to your Father, who is unseen. Then your Father, who sees what is done in secret, will reward you. . . .
>
> "When you fast, do not look somber as the hypocrites do,

for they disfigure their faces to show men they are fasting. I tell you the truth, they have received their reward in full. But when you fast, put oil on your head and wash your face, so that it will not be obvious to men that you are fasting, but only to your Father, who is unseen; and your Father, who sees what is done in secret, will reward you." (Matthew 6:1–6, 16–18)

Christ's message is crystal-clear. Rather than fixate on earthly vanities, such as the admiration of men, we ought to focus on such eternal verities as the approval of the Master. He warned his followers not to store up for themselves "treasures on earth, where moth and rust destroy, and where thieves break in and steal" (Matthew 6:19). Instead, said Jesus, store up "treasures in heaven, where moth and rust do not destroy, and where thieves do not break in and steal" (v. 20).

Furthermore, Jesus made essentially the same point in his parables. In the parable of the talents, recorded in Matthew 25:14–30, Jesus tells the story of a man who entrusts his property to his servants before going on a long journey. Each servant received an amount commensurate with his abilities. To one he gave five talents, to another two talents, and to a third he gave one talent. The servant who received five talents doubled his money, as did the servant who had received two. The last servant, however, showed gross negligence and buried his master's money in the ground. When the master returned, he rewarded the faithful servants with the words, "Well done, good and faithful servant! You have been faithful with a few things; I will put you in charge of many things. Come and share your master's happiness!" (vv. 21, 23). The unfaithful servant not only forfeited his reward, but he was thrown into outer darkness, "where there will be weeping and gnashing of teeth" (v. 30).

Jesus not only uses this parable to point out that there will be rewards in eternity for our faithfulness, but he also uses it to underscore the fact that the judgment of our works will reveal whether our faith was genuine. If our faith is real, it will manifest itself in our works. Conversely, if we do not manifest good works, we demonstrate that our faith is not real. As James puts it, "What good is it, my brothers, if a man claims to have faith but has no deeds? Can such faith save him?" (James 2:14). The answer, of course, is no; such faith cannot save him. We are saved by the kind of faith that produces good works—not by mere intellectual assent.

James presses the point by adding, "Show me your faith without deeds, and I will show you my faith by what I do" (v. 18). As Anthony Hoekema explains, "The reason why the Bible teaches that the final judgment will be according to works, even though salvation comes through faith in Christ and is never earned by works, is the intimate connection between faith and works. Faith must reveal itself in works, and works, in turn, are the evidence of true faith. As John Calvin once put it, 'It is . . . faith alone which justifies, and yet the faith which justifies is not alone.'"[3] Hoekema further notes that our rewards are not only a function of enhanced spiritual capacities[4] but of enlarged responsibilities. He uses Christ's parable of the ten pounds (see Luke 19:12–27) to make his point:

> A nobleman went into a distant country to receive a kingdom and then to return. To each of his ten servants the nobleman gave one pound,[5] asking each one to trade with his pound in order to make a profit. When the nobleman returned, the first servant said to him, "Lord, your pound has made ten pounds more" (v. 16). And the nobleman said to him, "Well done, good servant! Because you have been faithful in a very little, you shall have authority over ten cities" (v. 17). The second servant told the nobleman that his pound had made five additional pounds. To this servant the nobleman said, "And you are to be over five cities" (v. 19). What is significant is that the variation in the reward bestowed is proportional to the variation in the number of pounds the servants earned over and above their original pound. The main point of the parable, to be sure, is that we must all be faithful in working with the gifts the Lord has given

us. But it would seem that the added detail about the five cities and the ten cities has at least some significance. It is also interesting to observe that the reward in this case seems to be a matter of increased responsibility rather than simply of increased enjoyment.[6]

Finally, Christ communicates the concept of rewards in his prophetic pronouncement in the very last chapter of the very last book of the Bible. Says Christ, "Behold, I am coming soon! My reward is with me, and I will give to everyone according to what he has done" (Revelation 22:12). And this is not a singular statement—in the Gospel of Matthew, the Savior says, "the Son of Man is going to come in his Father's glory with his angels, and then he will reward each person according to what he has done" (Matthew 16:27). Likewise, the apostle John records: "The dead, great and small, [were] standing before the throne, and books were opened. Another book was opened, which is the book of life. The dead were judged according to what they had done as recorded in the books. The sea gave up the dead that were in it, and death and Hades gave up the dead that were in them, and each person was judged according to what he had done. . . . If anyone's name was not found written in the book of life, he was thrown into the lake of fire" (Revelation 20:12–15).

Such passages confirm that the judgment of our works reveals both our redemption and our rewards. The judgment reveals our *redemption* in that our deeds demonstrate the *reality* of our faith. It reveals our *rewards* in that our deeds also demonstrate the *vitality* of our faith. Thus, at the Great White Throne Judgment, both *the book of mercy* and *the books of merit* will be opened. The *book of mercy* (book of life) reveals those who had a genuine faith in Jesus Christ.[7] As our Lord himself puts it, "those who have done good will rise to live, and those who have done evil will rise to be condemned" (John 5:29). Conversely, the *books of merit* contain a record of our deeds. These books suggest that what we do during our earthly sojourn counts and will impact what we do throughout eternity.

Canon

In addition to the words of Christ, the canon of Scripture is replete
with references to rewards. The basis of our salvation is the finished
work of Christ, but Christians can erect a building of rewards upon
that foundation. As Paul puts it:

> No one can lay any foundation other than the one already
> laid, which is Jesus Christ. If any man builds on this founda-
> tion using gold, silver, costly stones, wood, hay or straw, his
> work will be shown for what it is, because the Day will bring it
> to light. It will be revealed with fire, and the fire will test the
> quality of each man's work. If what he has built survives, he
> will receive his reward. If it is burned up, he will suffer loss; he
> himself will be saved, but only as one escaping through the
> flames. (1 Corinthians 3:11–15)

In this text, Paul illustrates the sober reality that some Christians will
be resurrected with precious little to show for the time they spent on
earth—they "will be saved, but only as one escaping through the flames"
(v. 15). This conjures up images of people escaping burning buildings
with little more than the charred clothes upon their backs. Likewise,
Christ, whose eyes are "like blazing fire" (Revelation 1:14) will incinerate
the work of those who built monuments to themselves using "wood, hay
or straw" (1 Corinthians 3:12). This will be the lot of even the most visible Christian leaders whose motives were selfish rather than selfless.

Conversely, those who build selflessly upon the foundation of Christ
using "gold, silver and costly stones" (v. 12) will receive enduring
rewards. Indeed, a selfless Christian layman who labors in virtual
obscurity will hear the words he has longed for throughout his life:
"Well done, good and faithful servant! You have been faithful with a
few things; I will put you in charge of many things. Come and share
your master's happiness!" (Matthew 25:21).

Those who perform such acts of selfless service will scarcely remember their deeds of righteousness. When the Lord rewards them for feeding and clothing the starving, ministering to strangers, and visiting shut-ins, they will respond in bewilderment: "Lord, when did we see you hungry and feed you, or thirsty and give you something to drink? When did we see you a stranger and invite you in, or needing clothes and clothe you? When did we see you sick or in prison and go to visit you?" (Matthew 25:37–39). While deeds are our duty, not the smallest act of kindness will go without its reward. Of this we can be certain—our redemption is a free gift (see Ephesians 2:8–9), but our rewards are the result of our works in grace and are earned (see 1 Corinthians 3:14).

Paul further amplifies the reality of rewards in his letter to the Christians at Colosse, in which he writes, "Whatever you do, work at it with all your heart, as working for the Lord, not for men, since you know that you will receive an inheritance from the Lord as a reward" (Colossians 3:23–24).⁸ Paul's point is that what we do now counts for all eternity. It's not our bank statement on earth that counts; it's the one in heaven! If our hope is fixed on the account we have down here, we are bankrupt—no matter how many digits we can count next to our names. Paul specifically warns "those who are rich in this present world not to be arrogant nor to put their hope in wealth, which is so uncertain, but to put their hope in God, who richly provides us with everything for our enjoyment" (1 Timothy 6:17). He goes on to exhort believers "to do good, to be rich in good deeds, and to be generous and willing to share" (v. 18). In so doing, says Paul, true believers "will lay up treasure for themselves as a firm foundation for the coming age, so that they may take hold of the life that is truly life" (v. 19). Thus, Paul urges us to live as responsible servants because on Judgment Day it is God himself who will richly reward us.

Finally, the epistle to the Hebrews, like Paul's letter to Colosse, clearly underscores the reality of rewards. Hebrews 11 is a classic example. There we see that Abraham was willing to live like a stranger in a foreign country because he was "looking forward to the city with foundations, whose architect and builder is God" (v. 10). Like the other great saints in the Faith Hall of Fame, he realized that he was an alien and stranger on earth (see v. 13), and so he was "longing for a better country—a heavenly one" (v. 16). Like a host of others in the Faith Hall of Fame, Abraham had his eyes firmly fixed on a heavenly reward. As noted in *The Student Bible*, the heroes of faith in Hebrews 11 not only did not receive their promised rewards here and now, they instead suffered pain and persecution. Many of them died horrifying deaths. Their earthly sojourn resembled a lengthy marathon in which the runner fixed his gaze on the prize and refused to give up until he finished the race: "'Throw off everything that hinders,' Hebrews coaches (12:1). 'Strengthen your feeble arms and weak knees' (12:12). . . . Why do people punish their bodies to run a grueling marathon race? Most runners name two reasons: the sense of personal reward they get and the physical benefits of the exercise. The same two rewards apply in the spiritual realm: great prizes await those who persevere, and the very process of living by faith builds strong character. In this race, no one loses. If you finish, you get the reward."[9]

The characteristics necessary for induction into the Faith Hall of Fame are exemplified by Job as he persevered in the midst of affliction and steadfastly trusted God despite the whirlwind that blew his life into oblivion. Indeed, Job is the personification of perseverance in the midst of life's storms.

This same perseverance is manifested in the life of the apostle Paul, who not only fought the good fight, but finished the race and kept his faith. Paul's faith, like that of Job, was fixed not on the temporary circumstances of life, but on the "author and perfecter" of his faith— Jesus Christ himself (Hebrews 12:2). The Faith Hall of Fame is replete with men and women who willingly gave their lives in loving service of the Master. Those like Gideon, Barak, Samson, Jepthah, David, Samuel, and the prophets, who through faith conquered kingdoms; who were tortured, jeered, and flogged; who had been chained and put in prison; stoned and put to death; destitute; persecuted and mis-treated; yet were commended for their faith—because their faith was not fixed on circumstances, but on God. These who were inducted into the Faith Hall of Fame blazed a trail of faith for all of us to follow. They were the examples for Joni Eareckson Tada, who learned that true faith does not necessarily equip you to arise from a wheelchair, but rather prepares you to use adversity as a means of bringing men and women into the kingdom of God.

Like Joni, we would do well to realize that the real tragedy is not being a quadriplegic or even dying young; the real tragedy is living a long, robust life and failing to use it for the glory of God. Joni has endured tragedy and pain for a season, but through her suffering she has been privileged to influence the eternal destiny of multitudes. She exhorts us to put on spiritual spectacles as well:

I'm constructing with an eye toward eternity, and so can you. Every day we have the opportunity to roll up our spiritual sleeves and apply our spiritual energies toward building some-thing that lasts, in our lives and the lives of others. . . . We will bring to the judgment seat of Christ all that we are and all that we've done. One look from the Lord will scrutinize the quality of what we've built, and selfish service will be consumed in a fiery flash. Although its true that no child of God will be scolded, some will walk away scalded from the heat; their only reward will be their eternal salvation.

This is sobering. I can't help but see myself coming away a little singed on the edges. Don't get me wrong, I believe I will bask in God's approval for my service on earth, but pride and impure motives have probably sullied a lot of it. Burnt away will be those times I gave the gospel out of puffed-up pride. Up in flames will go any service I performed for "performance's sake." Reduced to charcoal will be manipulative behavior and lies-dressed-up-like-truth.

But hey, even if a lot of people survive the judgment seat by the skin of their teeth, keeping only their crown of salvation, that's plenty of cause for rejoicing. Look at all the people who trusted Christ on their deathbed with barely time to say yes to Jesus, let alone build anything for eternity. Think of being snatched from the jaws of hell seconds before one dies. Such joy would be hard to beat.

One look from the Lord will consume worthless service. But it will illuminate God-honoring service. Like gold and precious stones, pure service will easily survive the test. It is *this* for which we shall be commended. . . . I want to put to death every selfish motive and prideful pretense so that when the Lord's eyes scan my service, what I have built will stand the test. I want to be careful how I build, and realize that every smile, prayer, or ounce of muscle or money sacrificed is a golden girder, brick, or two-by-four. I want everything I do here to be an eternal investment, a way of building something bright and beautiful there. That's how much things down here count.

And no one will be left out. Each will receive his reward.[10]

EPILOGUE

✛

I began this book with my granddaughter Elise transitioning from the womb to the world. I was enthralled as I saw her emerge from the security of a water wonderland and take her first breath on Planet Earth. Two years earlier, I watched my father transition from this world to the next. He took one final breath and entered an unexplored existence just waiting to be experienced. Exactly forty years before taking that final breath, my father was lying in another hospital room, fighting for his life. For all intents and purposes, the doctors had given up on him. My mother had been advised that, apart from a miracle, her husband was going to die.

Years later, my father shared with me how he had pleaded with the Lord to spare his life—not because he was not ready to die, but because he was convinced that he had not yet accomplished the purpose for which he had been created. For years he had known that God was calling him to be a pastor, yet he had never responded to the call. On his deathbed, he pleaded for one more chance at life—one more chance to make his life count for eternity. The Lord saw my father's tears. He heard his prayers. And he healed him.

Not long after he regained his strength, Dad began making changes. He resigned a comfortable position as a design draftsman engineer, sold his home in a Canadian suburb, moved his family to an inner-city neighborhood in the United States, and began studying to be a pastor. For the next four decades, he served the Lord with purpose and passion. He pastored the hurting, prayed for the sick, and preached from the Scriptures. And each day he would rise early in the morning and pray for a son who had little interest in the things of God.

While I had grown up in a Christian home, I had been unwilling to become a disciple of Christ. Deep inside, I knew that to surrender to Christ meant to submit to his lordship, and I was unwilling to do so. And so for twenty-nine years I chose rebellion over repentance. Before he died, however, my father realized the answer to his prayers—I surrendered my life to Christ and to his calling. I'll never forget the day Dad told me how proud he was of what God had done in my life. With a twinkle in his eye, he said, "And I had a part in that." And so he did. Not only am I a product of his prayers, but throughout the forty years that God added to my father's life, Dad modeled what it meant to be a fearless defender of the faith.

Not everyone gets a second chance to make his or her life count in this world; however, everyone will have another life in the world to come. On the last day, the trump shall resound and the resurrected Christ shall descend. This time he will not come as a suffering servant lying prostrate in the pool of his own blood, but as King of kings and Lord of lords. At the sound of his voice, the dead will be resurrected to give an accounting of their lives.

Not everyone has been called to be a pastor, but everyone has been called to serve the Master. Whatever our calling, we are to invest our time, talents, and treasures in those things that will last for all eternity. Of one thing I am certain—if twenty-first-century Christians would grasp the significance of resurrection like the first-century Christians did, our lives would be radically revolutionized. Rather than being microcosms of the culture, we would become change agents. Like a small band of seemingly insignificant believers who succeeded in turning an empire upside down, we would leave a lasting mark on society. In the end, it all depends on whether we only *say* we believe in resurrection or whether we *really* believe!

This Jesus of Nazareth, without money and arms, conquered more millions than Alexander, Caesar, Mohammed, and Napoleon; without science and learning, He shed more light on things human and divine than all philosophers and scholars combined; without the eloquence of schools, He spoke such words of life as were never spoken before or since, and produced effects which lie beyond the reach of orator or poet; without writing a single line, He set more pens in motion, and furnished themes for more sermons, orations, discussions, learned volumes, works of art, and songs of praise than the whole army of great men of ancient and modern times.[1]

APPENDIX A

✛

Receiving the Resurrected Redeemer[1]

By now you have finished reading *Resurrection,* and one thing should be crystal-clear. Every single person who has ever lived on Planet Earth *will* be resurrected—some to eternal life and some to eternal torment. In the Lord's own words, "Do not be amazed at this, for a time is coming when all who are in their graves will hear his voice and come out— those who have done good will rise to live, and those who have done evil will rise to be condemned" (John 5:28–29).

Everyone reading these words is in one of these two categories. If you are a Christian, the next few pages will provide you with an overview on how to communicate the good news of the gospel. If you are not yet a Christian, the greatest gift you can receive is the resurrected Redeemer. Here's how. You need to realize that Christianity is not merely a religion; rather, it is a relationship.

Relationship

The distinction between *religion* and *relationship* makes all the difference in the world. Religion is merely man's attempt to reach up and become acceptable to God through his own efforts—living a good life, attempting to obey the Ten Commandments, or following the golden rule. Some religions even teach that this cannot be accomplished in one lifetime. Thus, you are reincarnated over and over again until you finally become one with nirvana or one with the universe.

The problem with the answer provided by *religion* is that the Bible says that if we are ever to become acceptable to God, we must be absolutely perfect! As Jesus put it in his Sermon on the Mount—one of the most famous literary masterpieces in the history of humanity—"Be perfect, therefore, as your heavenly Father is perfect" (Matthew 5:48). Obviously no one is perfect; therefore, if we are ever going to know the resurrected Redeemer here and now, as well as rule and reign with him throughout the eons of time, there has to be another way. And that way is found in a *relationship.*

Relationship is what the Christian faith is all about. It is not primarily a set of dos and don'ts. It's a personal relationship with God. That relationship does not depend on our ability to reach up and touch God through our own good works, but rather on God's willingness to reach down and touch us through his love.

By way of illustration, if I wanted to have a relationship with an ant, the only way I could do so is to become one. Obviously I can't become an ant, but God did become a man. The Bible says that God in the person of Jesus Christ "became flesh" and lived for a while "among us" (John 1:14). He came into time and space to restore a relationship with man that was severed by sin.

It is crucial that you understand the problem of sin. If you do not recognize that you are sinner, you will also not realize your need for a Savior.

Sin

Sin is not just murder, rape, or robbery. Sin is failing to do the things we should and doing those things we should not. In short, *sin* is a word that describes anything that fails to meet God's standard of perfection.

Thus, sin is the barrier between you and a satisfying relationship with God. As Scripture puts it, "Your iniquities [sins] have separated you from your God" (Isaiah 59:2).

Just as light and dark cannot exist together, neither can God and sin. And each day we are further separated from God as we add to the account of our sin. But that's not the only problem. Sin also separates us from others. You need only read the newspaper or listen to a news report to see how true this really is. Locally, we read of murder, robbery, and fraud. Nationally, we hear of corruption in politics, racial tension, and an escalating rate of suicide. Internationally, we constantly see wars and hear rumors of war. We live in a time when terrorism abounds and when the world as we know it can be instantly obliterated by nuclear aggression.

All of these things are symbolic of sin. The Bible says that we "all have sinned and fall short of the glory of God" (Romans 3:23).[2] There are no exceptions to the rule. The problem is further compounded when we begin to understand who God is. Virtually every heresy begins with a misconception of the nature of God.

God

On one hand, God is the perfect Father. We all have had earthly fathers, but no matter how good—or bad, as the case may be—none are perfect. God, however, is the perfect Father. And as the perfect Father, he desires an intimate personal relationship with us. In his Word, God says, "I have loved you with an everlasting love" (Jeremiah 31:3).

Yet the same Bible that tells us that God loves us and wants a relationship with us as our heavenly Father also tells us that he is the perfect Judge. As the perfect Judge, God is absolutely just, righteous, and holy. The Bible says of God, "Your eyes are too pure to look on evil; you cannot tolerate wrong" (Habakkuk 1:13).

Herein lies the dilemma. On the one hand, we see that God is the perfect Father. He loves us and wants to have a personal relationship with us. On the other hand, he is the perfect Judge, whose very nature is too pure to tolerate our sin. This dilemma is brought into sharper focus by a story I heard many years ago.

A young man was caught driving under the influence of alcohol after having committed several crimes. He was brought before a judge nicknamed the "hanging judge." Although the judge's integrity was beyond question, he always handed out the stiffest penalty allowable by law (to wit the nickname, "hanging judge"). It turns out that the judge was the young man's father. As you can imagine, everyone in the courthouse that day waited with bated breath to see how the judge would treat his own son. Would he show him favoritism as a father, or would he, as always, hand out the stiffest penalty allowable by law?

As the spellbound courtroom full of spectators looked on, the judge, without hesitation, issued the maximum financial penalty allowable by law. Then he took off his judicial robes, walked over to where his son stood, and paid the penalty his son could not pay. In that one act, he satisfied the justice of the law and yet demonstrated extraordinary love.

That, however, is but a faint glimpse of what God the Father did for us through his Son, Jesus Christ. You see, Jesus Christ—God himself—came to earth to be our Savior and to be our Lord.

Through his resurrection, Jesus demonstrated that he does not stand in a line of peers with Buddha, Mohammed, or any other founders of world religions. They died and are still dead, but Christ had the power to lay down his life and to take it up again.

Jesus Christ

As our Savior, Jesus lived the perfect life we cannot live. Earlier I pointed out that Scripture says in order to be acceptable to God we need to be perfect. Well, Jesus Christ came into time and space to be perfection for us. As the Bible puts it, "God made him [Jesus Christ] who had no sin to be sin for us, so that in him we might become the righteousness of God" (2 Corinthians 5:21).

This is the great exchange over which all of the Bible was written. God took our sins and placed them on Jesus Christ, who suffered and died to pay the debt we could not pay. Then, wonder of wonders, he gave us the perfect life of Jesus Christ. He took our sins and gave us his perfection as an absolutely free gift. We cannot earn it or deserve it; we can only live a life of gratitude for this gift that God freely offers us. But that's not all. Jesus not only died to be our Savior; he also lives to be our Lord.

As our Lord, Jesus Christ gives our lives meaning, purpose, and fulfillment. This is a particularly exciting thought when you stop to realize that the one who wants to be your Lord is the very one who spoke and the universe leaped into existence. He not only made this universe and everything in it, but he made *you*. He knows all about you, he loves you, and he wants you to have a satisfying life here and now and an eternity of joy with him in heaven forever.

The Bible says, "If you confess with your mouth, 'Jesus is Lord,' and believe in your heart God raised him from the dead, you will be saved" (Romans 10:9). As we saw in Part One, the resurrection of Jesus Christ is an undeniable fact of history. Through the immutable fact of the resurrection, God the Father vindicated Christ's claims to deity,[3] thus demonstrating that Jesus was God in human flesh. To receive Jesus Christ as Savior and Lord, one need only take two steps. The one step is *repent,* the other is *receive.*

Two Steps

The first step involves *repentance. Repentance* is an old English word that describes a willingness to turn from sin toward Jesus Christ. It literally means a complete U-turn on the road of life—a change of heart and a change of mind. It means a willingness to follow Jesus Christ and receive him as Savior and Lord. In the words of Christ, "The time has come. . . . The kingdom of God is near. Repent and believe the good news!" (Mark 1:15).

The second step is *receive*. To demonstrate true belief means to be willing to receive God's free gift. To truly receive God's gift is to trust in and depend on Jesus Christ alone to be the Lord of our lives here and now and our Savior for all eternity.

Receiving God's free gift takes more than knowledge. (The devil knows about Jesus and trembles.) It takes more than agreeing that the knowledge is accurate. (The devil agrees that Jesus is Lord.) True saving faith entails not only knowledge and agreement, but trust. By way of illustration, when you are sick you can know a particular medicine can cure you. You can even agree that it's cured thousands of others. But until you trust it enough to take it, it cannot cure *you*. In like manner, you can know about Jesus Christ, and you can agree that he has saved others, but until you personally place your trust in him, you will not be saved. The requirements for eternal life are not based on what *you can do* but on what *Jesus Christ has done*. He stands ready to exchange his perfection for your imperfection.

To those who have never received him as Savior and Lord, Jesus says, "Here I am! I stand at the door and knock. If anyone hears my voice and opens the door, I will come in" (Revelation 3:20).⁴ Jesus knocks on the door of the human heart, and the question he asks is, Are you ready *now* to receive me as Savior and Lord?

According to Jesus Christ, those who repent and receive him as Savior and Lord are "born again" (John 3:3)—not physically, but spiritually. And with this spiritual birth must come spiritual growth.

Growth

First, no relationship can flourish without constant, heartfelt communication. This is true not only in human relationships, but also in our relationship with God. If we are to nurture a strong relationship with our Savior, we must be in constant communication with him. The way to do that is through prayer.

Prayer is the way we talk with God. You do not need a special vocabulary to pray. You can simply speak to God as you would to your best friend. The more time you spend with God in prayer, the more intimate your relationship will be. And remember, there is no problem great or small that God cannot handle. If it's important to you, it's important to him.

Furthermore, in addition to prayer, it is crucial that new believers spend time reading God's written revelation of himself—the Bible. The Bible not only forms the foundation of an effective prayer life, but it is foundational to every other aspect of Christian living. While prayer is our primary way of communicating with God, the Bible is God's primary way of communicating with us. Nothing should take precedence over getting into the Word and getting the Word into us.

If we fail to eat well-balanced meals on a regular basis, we will eventually suffer the physical consequences. What is true of the outer man is also true of the inner man. If we do not regularly feed on the Word of God, we will starve spiritually.

I generally recommend that new believers begin by reading one chapter from the Gospel of John each day. As you do, you will experience the joy of having God speak to you directly through his Word. As Jesus put it, "I am the bread of life. He who comes to me will never go hungry, and he who believes in me will never be thirsty" (John 6:35).

Finally, it is crucial for new believers to become active participants in a healthy, well-balanced church. In Scripture, the church is referred to as the body of Christ. Just as our body is one and yet has many parts, so the body of Christ is one but is composed of many members. Those who receive Christ as the Savior and Lord of their lives are already a part of the church universal. It is crucial, however, that all Christians become vital, reproducing members of a local body of believers as well.

Scripture exhorts us not to neglect the gathering of ourselves together, as is the custom of some (see Hebrews 10:25). It is in the local church where God is worshiped through prayer, praise, and proclamation; where believers experience fellowship with one another; and where they are equipped to reach others through the testimony of their love, their lips, and their lives.

Application

I began by pointing out that Christianity is not merely a religion; rather, it is a relationship with the resurrected Redeemer. You can know *of* him through historical evidences, but you can *know* him only by the Spirit of God. Even now, if God's Spirit is moving upon your heart, you can receive the resurrected Christ as your personal Savior and Lord. Simply pray this prayer—and remember, there is no magic in the words; God is looking at the intent of your heart.

> Heavenly Father,
> I thank you that you have provided a way for me to have a
>   relationship with you;
> I *realize* that I am a sinner;
> I thank you that you are my perfect Father;
> I thank you for sending Jesus to be my Savior and Lord;
> I *repent* and *receive* his perfection in exchange for my sin;
> In Jesus' name, I pray. Amen.

Assurance

The assurance of eternal life is found in these words from the resurrected Redeemer: "I tell you the truth, whoever hears my word and believes him who sent me has eternal life and will not be condemned; he has crossed over from death to life" (John 5:24).

APPENDIX B

✠

Resurrection of Christ[1]

Fatal Torment

Psalm 22:14–18 I am poured out like water, and all my bones are out of joint. My heart has turned to wax; it has melted away within me. My strength is dried up like a potsherd, and my tongue sticks to the roof of my mouth; you lay me in the dust of death. Dogs have surrounded me; a band of evil men has encircled me, they have pierced my hands and my feet. I can count all my bones; people stare and gloat over me. They divide my garments among them and cast lots for my clothing.

Isaiah 52:13–15 See, my servant will act wisely; he will be raised and lifted up and highly exalted. Just as there were many who were appalled at him—his appearance was so disfigured beyond that of any man and his form marred beyond human likeness—so will he sprinkle many nations, and kings will shut their mouths because of him. For what they were not told, they will see, and what they have not heard, they will understand.

Isaiah 53:1–12 Who has believed our message and to whom has the arm of the LORD been revealed? He grew up before him like a tender shoot, and like a root out of dry ground. He had no beauty or majesty to attract us to him, nothing in his appearance that we should desire him. He was despised and rejected by men, a man of sorrows, and familiar with suffering. Like one from whom men hide their faces he was despised, and we esteemed him not. Surely he took up our infirmities and carried our sorrows, yet we considered him stricken by God, smitten by him, and afflicted. But he was pierced for our transgressions, he was crushed for our iniquities; the punishment that brought us peace was upon him, and by his wounds we are healed. We all, like sheep, have gone astray, each of us has turned to his own way; and the LORD has laid on him the iniquity of us all. He was oppressed and afflicted, yet he did not open his mouth; he was led like a lamb to the slaughter, and as a sheep before her shearers is silent, so he did not open his mouth. By oppression and judgment he was taken away. And who can speak of his descendants? For he was cut off from the land of the living; for the transgression of my people he was stricken. He was assigned a grave with the wicked, and with the rich in his death, though he had done no violence, nor was any deceit in his mouth. Yet it was the LORD's will to crush him and cause him to suffer, and though the LORD makes his life a guilt offering, he will see his offspring and prolong his days, and the will of the LORD will prosper in his hand. After the suffering of his soul, he will see the light of life and be satisfied; by his knowledge my righteous servant will justify many, and he will bear their iniquities. Therefore I will give him a portion among the great, and he will divide the spoils with the strong, because he poured out his life unto death, and was numbered with the transgressors. For he bore the sin of many, and made intercession for the transgressors.

Zechariah 12:10 They will look on me, the one they have pierced, and they will mourn for him as one mourns for an only child, and grieve bitterly for him as one grieves for a firstborn son.

Luke 18:31–33 Jesus took the Twelve aside and told them, "We are going up to Jerusalem, and everything that is written by the prophets about the Son of Man will be fulfilled. He will be handed over to the Gentiles. They will mock him, insult him, spit on him, flog him and kill him. On the third day he will rise again." The disciples did not understand any of this. Its meaning was hidden from them, and they did not know what he was talking about.
(Cf. Matthew 20:17–19; Mark 10:32–34.)

John 2:19–22 Jesus answered them, "Destroy this temple, and I will raise it again in three days." The Jews replied, "It has taken forty-six years to build this temple, and you are going to raise it in three days?" But the temple he had spoken of was his body. After he was raised from the dead, his disciples recalled what he had said. Then they believed the Scripture and the words that Jesus had spoken.

John 3:14–15 "Just as Moses lifted up the snake in the desert, so the Son of Man must be lifted up, that everyone who believes in him may have eternal life."

John 12:32–33 "But I, when I am lifted up from the earth, will draw all men to myself." He said this to show the kind of death he was going to die.

Mark 15:12–37 "What shall I do, then, with the one you call the king of the Jews?" Pilate asked them. "Crucify him!" they shouted. "Why? What crime has he committed?" asked Pilate. But they shouted all the louder, "Crucify him!" Wanting to satisfy the crowd, Pilate released Barabbas to them. He had Jesus flogged, and handed him over to be crucified. The soldiers led Jesus away into the palace (that is, the Praetorium) and called together the whole company of soldiers. They put a purple robe on him, then twisted together a crown of thorns and set it on him. And they began to call out to him, "Hail, king of the Jews!" Again and again they struck him on the head with a staff and spit on him. Falling on their knees, they paid homage to him. And when they had mocked him, they took off the purple robe and put his own clothes on him. Then they led him out to crucify him. A certain man from Cyrene, Simon, the father of Alexander and Rufus, was passing by on his way in from the country, and they forced him to carry the cross. They brought Jesus to the place called Golgotha (which means The Place of the Skull). Then they offered him wine mixed with myrrh, but he did not take it. And they crucified him. Dividing up his clothes, they cast lots to see what each would get. It was the third hour when they crucified him. The written notice of the charge against him read: THE KING OF THE JEWS. They crucified two robbers with him, one on his right and one on his left. Those who passed by hurled insults at him, shaking their heads and saying, "So! You who are going to destroy the temple and build it in three days, come down from the cross and save yourself!" In the same way the chief priests and the teachers of the law mocked him among themselves. "He saved others," they said, "but he can't save himself! Let this Christ, this King of Israel, come down now from the cross, that we may see and believe." Those crucified with him also heaped insults on him. At the sixth hour darkness came over the whole land until the ninth hour. And at the ninth hour Jesus cried out in a loud voice, "Eloi, Eloi, lama sabachthani?"—which means, "My God, my God, why have you forsaken me?" When some of those standing near heard this, they said, "Listen, he's calling Elijah." One man ran, filled a sponge with wine vinegar, put it on a stick, and offered it to Jesus to drink. "Now leave him alone. Let's see if Elijah comes to take him down," he said. With a loud cry, Jesus breathed his last.

(Cf. Matthew 27:26–50; Luke 23:18–46.)

John 19:14–37 It was the day of Preparation of Passover Week, about the sixth hour. "Here is your king," Pilate said to the Jews. But they shouted, "Take him away! Take him away! Crucify him!"

"Shall I crucify your king?" Pilate asked. "We have no king but Caesar," the chief priests answered. Finally Pilate handed him over to them to be crucified. So the soldiers took charge of Jesus. Carrying his own cross, he went out to the place of the Skull (which in Aramaic is called Golgotha). Here they crucified him, and with him two others—one on each side and Jesus in the middle. Pilate had a notice prepared and fastened to the cross. It read: JESUS OF NAZARETH, THE KING OF JEWS. Many of the Jews read this sign, for the place where Jesus was crucified was near the city, and the sign was written in Aramaic, Latin and Greek. The chief priests of the Jews protested to Pilate, "Do not write 'The King of the Jews,' but that this man claimed to be king of the Jews." Pilate answered, "What I have written, I have written." When the soldiers crucified Jesus, they took his clothes, dividing them into four shares, one for each of them, with the undergarment remaining. This garment was seamless, woven in one piece from top to bottom. "Let's not tear it," they said to one another. "Let's decide by lot who will get it." This happened that the scripture might be fulfilled which said, "They divided my garments among them and cast lots for my clothing." So this is what the soldiers did. Near the cross of Jesus stood his mother, his mother's sister, Mary the wife of Clopas, and Mary Magdalene. When Jesus saw his mother there, and the disciple whom he loved standing nearby, he said to his mother, "Dear woman, here is your son," and to the disciple, "Here is your mother." From that time on, this disciple took her into his home. Later, knowing that all was now completed, and so that the Scripture would be fulfilled, Jesus said, "I am thirsty." A jar of wine vinegar was there, so they soaked a sponge in it, put the sponge on a stalk of the hyssop plant, and lifted it to Jesus' lips. When he had received the drink, Jesus said, "It is finished." With that, he bowed his head and gave up his spirit. Now it was the day of Preparation, and the next day was to be a special Sabbath. Because the Jews did not want the bodies left on the crosses during the Sabbath, they asked Pilate to have the legs broken and the bodies taken down. The soldiers therefore came and broke the legs of the first man who had been crucified with Jesus, and then those of the other. But when they came to Jesus and found that he was already dead, they did not break his legs. Instead, one of the soldiers pierced Jesus' side with a spear, bringing a sudden flow of blood and water. The man who saw it has given testimony, and his testimony is true. He knows that he tells the truth, and he testifies so that you also may believe. These things happened so that the scripture would be fulfilled: "Not one of his bones will be broken," and, as another scripture says, "They will look on the one they have pierced."

Acts 2:23 "This man was handed over to you by God's set purpose and foreknowledge; and you, with the help of wicked men, put him to death by nailing him to the cross."

1 Corinthians 15:3 For what I received I passed on to you as of first importance: that Christ died for our sins according to the Scriptures . . .

(Cf. Acts 8:30–35; 13:28–29; 17:3; 1 Corinthians 1:23; 2:2; 11:26–29; Galatians 3:1; Philippians 2:8; 1 Peter 2:24.)

Empty Tomb

Matthew 28:1–10 After the Sabbath, at dawn on the first day of the week, Mary Magdalene and the other Mary went to look at the tomb. There was a violent earthquake, for an angel of the Lord came down from heaven and, going to the tomb, rolled back the stone and sat on it. His appearance was like lightning, and his clothes were white as snow. The guards were so afraid of him that they shook and became like dead men. The angel said to the women, "Do not be afraid, for I know that you are looking for Jesus, who was crucified. He is not here; he has risen, just as he said. Come and see the place where he lay. Then go quickly and tell his disciples: 'He has risen from the dead and is going ahead of you into Galilee. There you will see him.' Now I have told you." So the women hurried away from the tomb, afraid yet filled with joy, and ran to tell his disciples. Suddenly Jesus met them. "Greetings," he said. They came to him, clasped his feet and worshiped him. Then Jesus said to them, "Do not be afraid. Go and tell my brothers to go to Galilee; there they will see me."

Mark 16:1–8 When the Sabbath was over, Mary Magdalene, Mary the mother of James, and Salome bought spices so that they might go to anoint Jesus' body. Very early on the first day of the week, just after sunrise, they were on their way to the tomb and they asked each other, "Who will roll the stone away from the entrance of the tomb?" But when they looked up, they saw that the stone, which was very large, had been rolled away. As they entered the tomb, they saw a young man dressed in a white robe sitting on the right side, and they were alarmed. "Don't be alarmed," he said. "You are looking for Jesus the Nazarene, who was crucified. He has risen! He is not here. See the place where they laid him. But go, tell his disciples and Peter, 'He is going ahead of you into Galilee. There you will see him, just as he told you.'" Trembling and bewildered, the women went out and fled from the tomb. They said nothing to anyone, because they were afraid.

Luke 24:1–12 On the first day of the week, very early in the morning, the women took the spices they had prepared and went to the tomb. They found the stone rolled away from the tomb, but when they entered, they did not find the body of the Lord Jesus. While they were wondering about this, suddenly two men in clothes that gleamed like lightning stood beside them. In their fright the women bowed down with their faces to the ground, but the men said to them, "Why do you look for the living among the dead? He is not here; he has risen! Remember how he told you, while he was still with you in Galilee: 'The Son of Man must be delivered into the hands of sinful men, be crucified and on the third day be raised again.'" Then they remembered his words. When they came back from the tomb, they told all these things to the Eleven and to all the others. It was Mary Magdalene, Joanna, Mary the mother of James, and the others with them who told this to the apostles. But they did not believe the women, because their words seemed to them like nonsense. Peter, however, got up and ran to the tomb. Bending over, he saw the strips of linen lying by themselves, and he went away, wondering to himself what had happened.

John 20:1–18 Early on the first day of the week, while it was still dark, Mary Magdalene went to the tomb and saw that the stone had been removed from the entrance. So she came running to Simon Peter and the other disciple, the one Jesus loved, and said, "They have taken the Lord out of the tomb, and we don't know where they have put him!" So Peter and the other disciple started for the tomb. Both were running, but the other disciple outran Peter and reached the tomb first. He bent over and looked in at the strips of linen lying there but did not go in. Then Simon Peter, who was behind him, arrived and went into the tomb. He saw the strips of linen lying there, as well as the burial cloth that had been around Jesus' head. The cloth was folded up by itself, separate from the linen. Finally the other disciple, who had reached the tomb first, also went inside. He saw and believed. (They still did not understand from Scripture that Jesus had to rise from the dead.) Then the disciples went back to their homes, but Mary stood outside the tomb crying. As she wept, she bent over to look into the tomb and saw two angels in white, seated where Jesus' body had been, one at the head and the other at the foot. They asked her, "Woman, why are you crying?" "They have taken my Lord away," she said, "and I don't know where they have put him." At this, she turned around and saw Jesus standing there, but she did not realize that it was Jesus. "Woman," he said, "why are you crying? Who is it you are looking for?" Thinking he was the gardener, she said, "Sir, if you have carried him away, tell me where you have put him, and I will get him." Jesus said to her, "Mary." She turned toward him and cried out in Aramaic, "Rabboni!" (which means Teacher). Jesus said, "Do not hold on to me, for I have not yet returned to the Father. Go instead to my brothers and tell them, 'I am returning to my Father and your Father, to my God and your God.'" Mary Magdalene went to the disciples with the news: "I have seen the Lord!" And she told them that he had said these things to her.

Matthew 28:11–15 While the women were on their way, some of the guards went into the city and reported to the chief priests everything that had happened. When the chief priests had met with the elders and devised a plan, they gave the soldiers a large sum of money, telling them, "You are to say, 'His disciples came during the night and stole him away while we were asleep.' If this report gets to the governor, we will satisfy him and keep you out of trouble." So the soldiers took the money and did as they were instructed. And this story has been widely circulated among the Jews to this very day.

Acts 2:29–32 "Brothers, I can tell you confidently that the patriarch David died and was buried, and his tomb is here to this day. But he was a prophet and knew that God had promised him on oath that he would place one of his descendants on his throne. Seeing what was ahead, he spoke of the resurrection of the Christ, that he was not abandoned to the grave, nor did his body see decay. God has raised this Jesus to life, and we are all witnesses of the fact."

Acts 13:29–30, 35–37 "The people of Jerusalem and their rulers did not recognize Jesus, yet in condemning him they fulfilled the words of the prophets that are read every Sabbath. Though they found no proper ground for a death sentence, they asked Pilate to have him executed. When they had carried out all that was written about him, they took him down from the tree and laid him in a tomb. But God raised him from the dead. . . . So it is stated elsewhere: 'You will not let your Holy One see decay.' For when David had served God's purpose in his own generation, he fell asleep; he was buried with his fathers and his body decayed. But the one whom God raised from the dead did not see decay."

Acts 26:25–27 "What I am saying is true and reasonable. The king is familiar with these things, and I can speak freely to him. I am convinced that none of this has escaped his notice, because it was not done in a corner. King Agrippa, do you believe the prophets? I know you do."

1 Corinthians 15:3–4 For what I received I passed on to you as of first importance: that Christ died for our sins according to the Scriptures, that he was buried, that he was raised on the third day according to the Scriptures.

Appearances of Christ

Matthew 28:8–10, 16–20 So the women hurried away from the tomb, afraid yet filled with joy, and ran to tell his disciples. Suddenly Jesus met them. "Greetings," he said. They came to him, clasped his feet and worshiped him. Then Jesus said to them, "Do not be afraid. Go and tell my brothers to go to Galilee; there they will see me." . . . Then the eleven disciples went to Galilee, to the mountain where Jesus had told them to go. When they saw him, they worshiped him; but some doubted. Then Jesus came to them and said, "All authority in heaven and on earth has been given to me. Therefore go and make disciples of all nations, baptizing them in the name of the Father and of the Son and of the Holy Spirit, and teaching them to obey everything I have commanded you. And surely I am with you always, to the very end of the age."

Mark 16:6–8 "Don't be alarmed," he said. "You are looking for Jesus the Nazarene, who was crucified. He has risen! He is not here. See the place where they laid him. But go, tell his disciples and Peter, 'He is going ahead of you into Galilee. There you will see him, just as he told you.'" Trembling and bewildered, the women went out and fled from the tomb. They said nothing to anyone, because they were afraid.

Luke 24:13–49 Now that same day two of them were going to a village called Emmaus, about seven miles from Jerusalem. They were talking with each other about everything that had happened. As they talked and discussed these things with each other, Jesus himself came up and walked along with them; but they were kept from recognizing him. He asked them, "What are you discussing together as you walk along?" They stood still, their faces downcast. One of them, named Cleopas, asked him, "Are you only a visitor to Jerusalem and do not know the things that have happened there in these days?" "What things?" he asked. "About Jesus of Nazareth," they replied. "He was a prophet, powerful in word and deed before God and all the people. The chief priests and our rulers handed him over to be sentenced to death, and they crucified him; but we had hoped that he was the one who was going to redeem Israel. And what is more, it is the third day since all this took place. In addition, some of our women amazed us. They went to the tomb early this morning but didn't find his body. They came and told us that they had seen a vision of angels, who said he was alive. Then some of our companions went to the tomb and found it just as the women had said, but him they did not see." He said to them, "How foolish you are, and how slow of heart to believe all that the prophets have spoken! Did not the Christ have to suffer these things and then enter his glory?" And beginning with Moses and all the Prophets, he explained to them what was said in all the Scriptures concerning himself. As they approached the village to which they were going, Jesus acted as if he were going farther. But they urged him strongly, "Stay with us, for it is nearly evening; the day is almost over." So he went in to stay with them. When he was at the table with them, he took bread, gave thanks, broke it and began to give it to them. Then their eyes were opened and they recognized him, and he disappeared from their sight. They asked each other, "Were not our hearts burning within us while he talked with us on the road and opened the Scriptures to us?" They got up and returned at once to Jerusalem. There they found the Eleven and those with them, assembled together and saying, "It is true! The Lord has risen and has appeared to Simon." Then the two told what had happened on the way, and how Jesus was recognized by them when he broke the bread. While they were still talking about this, Jesus himself stood among them and said to them, "Peace be with you." They were startled and frightened, thinking they saw a ghost. He said to them, "Why are you troubled, and why do doubts rise in your minds? Look at my hands and my feet. It is I myself! Touch me and see; a ghost does not have flesh and bones, as you see I have." When he had said this, he showed them his hands and feet. And while they still did not believe it because of joy and amazement, he asked them, "Do you have anything here to eat?" They gave him a piece of broiled fish, and he took it and ate it in their presence. He said to them, "This is what I told you while I was still with you: Everything must be fulfilled that is written about me in the Law of Moses, the Prophets and the Psalm." Then he opened their minds so they could understand the Scriptures. He told them, "This is what is written: The Christ will suffer and rise from the dead on the third day, and repentance and forgiveness of sins will be preached in his name to all nations, beginning at Jerusalem. You are witnesses of these things. I am going to send you what my Father has promised; but stay in the city until you have been clothed with power from on high."

John 20:10–21:25 Then the disciples went back to their homes, but Mary stood outside the tomb crying. As she wept, she bent over to look into the tomb and saw two angels in white, seated where Jesus' body had been, one at the head and the other at the foot. They asked her, "Woman, why are you crying?" "They have taken my Lord away," she said, "and I don't know where they have put him." At this, she turned around and saw Jesus standing there, but she did not realize that it was Jesus. "Woman," he said, "why are you crying? Who is it you are looking for?" Thinking he was the gardener, she said, "Sir, if you have carried him away, tell me where you have put him, and I will get him." Jesus said to her, "Mary." She turned toward him and cried out in Aramaic, "Rabboni!" (which means Teacher). Jesus said, "Do not hold on to me, for I have not yet returned to the Father. Go instead to my brothers and tell them, 'I am returning to my Father and your Father, to my God and your God.'" Mary Magdalene went to the disciples with the news: "I have seen the Lord!" And she told them that he had said these things to her. On the evening of that first day of the week, when the disciples were together, with the doors locked for fear of the Jews, Jesus came and stood among them and said, "Peace be with you!" After he said this, he showed them his hands and side. The disciples were overjoyed when they saw the Lord. Again Jesus said, "Peace be with you! As the Father has sent me, I am sending you." And with that he breathed on them and said, "Receive the Holy Spirit. If you forgive anyone his sins, they are forgiven; if you do not forgive them, they are not forgiven." Now Thomas (called Didymus), one of the Twelve, was not with the disciples when Jesus came. So the other disciples told him, "We have seen the Lord!" But he said to them, "Unless I see the nail marks in his hands and put my finger where the nails were, and put my hand into his side, I will not believe it." A week later his disciples were in the house again, and Thomas was with them. Though the doors were locked, Jesus came and stood among them and said, "Peace be with you!" Then he said to Thomas, "Put your finger here; see my hands. Reach out your hand and put it into my side. Stop doubting and believe." Thomas said to him, "My Lord and my God!" Then Jesus told him, "Because you have seen me, you have believed; blessed are those who have not seen and yet have believed." Jesus did many other miraculous signs in the presence of his disciples, which are not recorded in this book. But these are written that you may believe that Jesus is the Christ, the Son of God, and that by believing you may have life in his name. Afterward Jesus appeared again to his disciples, by the Sea of Tiberias. It happened this way: Simon Peter, Thomas (called Didymus), Nathanael from Cana in Galilee, the sons of Zebedee, and two other disciples were together. "I'm going out to fish," Simon Peter told them, and they said, "We'll go with you." So they went out and got into the boat, but that night they caught nothing. Early in the morning, Jesus stood on the shore, but the disciples did not realize that it was Jesus. He called out to them, "Friends, haven't you any fish?" "No," they answered. He said, "Throw your net on the right side of the boat and you will find some." When they did, they were unable to haul the net in because of the large number of fish. Then the disciple whom Jesus loved said to Peter, "It is the Lord!" As soon as Simon Peter heard him say, "It is the Lord," he wrapped his outer garment around him (for he had taken it off) and jumped into the water. The other disciples followed in the boat, towing the net full of fish, for they were not far from shore, about a hundred yards. When they landed, they saw a fire of burning coals there with fish on it, and some bread. Jesus said to them, "Bring some of the fish you have just caught." Simon Peter climbed aboard and dragged the net ashore. It was full of large fish, 153, but even with so many the net was not torn. Jesus said to them, "Come and have breakfast." None of the disciples dared ask him, "Who are you?" They knew it was the Lord. Jesus came, took the bread and gave it to them, and did the same with the fish. This was now the third time Jesus appeared to his disciples after he was raised from the dead. When they had finished eating, Jesus said to Simon Peter, "Simon son of John, do you truly love me more than these?" "Yes, Lord," he said, "you know that I love you." Jesus said, "Feed my lambs." Again Jesus said, "Simon son of John, do you truly love me?" He answered, "Yes, Lord, you know that I love you." Jesus said, "Take care of my sheep." The third time he said to him, "Simon son of

John, do you love me?" Peter was hurt because Jesus asked him the third time, "Do you love me?" He said, "Lord, you know all things; you know that I love you." Jesus said, "Feed my sheep. I tell you the truth, when you were younger you dressed yourself and went where you wanted; but when you are old you will stretch out your hands, and someone else will dress you and lead you where you do not want to go." Jesus said this to indicate the kind of death by which Peter would glorify God. Then he said to him, "Follow me!" Peter turned and saw that the disciple whom Jesus loved was following them. (This was the one who had leaned back against Jesus at the supper and had said, "Lord, who is going to betray you?") When Peter saw him, he asked, "Lord, what about him?" Jesus answered, "If I want him to remain alive until I return, what is that to you? You must follow me." Because of this, the rumor spread among the brothers that this disciple would not die. But Jesus did not say that he would not die; he only said, "If I want him to remain alive until I return, what is that to you?" This is the disciple who testifies to these things and who wrote them down. We know that his testimony is true. Jesus did many other things as well. If every one of them were written down, I suppose that even the whole world would not have room for the books that would be written.

Acts 1:1–8 In my former book, Theophilus, I wrote about all that Jesus began to do and to teach until the day he was taken up to heaven, after giving instructions through the Holy Spirit to the apostles he had chosen. After his suffering, he showed himself to these men and gave many convincing proofs that he was alive. He appeared to them over a period of forty days and spoke about the kingdom of God. On one occasion, while he was eating with them, he gave them this command: "Do not leave Jerusalem, but wait for the gift my Father promised, which you have heard me speak about. For John baptized with water, but in a few days you will be baptized with the Holy Spirit." So when they met together, they asked him, "Lord, are you at this time going to restore the kingdom to Israel?" He said to them: "It is not for you to know the times or dates the Father has set by his own authority. But you will receive power when the Holy Spirit comes on you; and you will be my witnesses in Jerusalem, and in all Judea and Samaria, and to the ends of the earth."

Acts 1:21–22 "Therefore it is necessary to choose one of the men who have been with us the whole time the Lord Jesus went in and out among us, beginning from John's baptism to the time when Jesus was taken up from us. For one of these must become a witness with us of his resurrection."

Acts 2:31–32 "Seeing what was ahead, he spoke of the resurrection of the Christ, that he was not abandoned to the grave, nor did his body see decay. God has raised this Jesus to life, and we are all witnesses of the fact."

Acts 3:15 "You killed the author of life, but God raised him from the dead. We are witnesses of this."

Acts 5:30–32 "The God of our fathers raised Jesus from the dead—whom you had killed by hanging him on a tree. God exalted him to his own right hand as Prince and Savior that he might give repentance and forgiveness of sins to Israel. We are witnesses of these things, and so is the Holy Spirit, whom God has given to those who obey him."

Acts 9:1–19 Meanwhile, Saul was still breathing out murderous threats against the Lord's disciples. He went to the high priest and asked him for letters to the synagogues in Damascus, so that if he found any there who belonged to the Way, whether men or women, he might take them as prisoners to Jerusalem. As he neared Damascus on his journey, suddenly a light from heaven flashed around him. He fell to the ground and heard a voice say to him, "Saul, Saul, why do you persecute me?" "Who are you, Lord?" Saul asked. "I am Jesus, whom you are persecuting," he replied. "Now get up and go into the city, and you will be told what you must do." The men traveling with Saul stood there speechless; they heard the sound but did not see anyone. Saul got up from the ground, but when he opened his eyes he could see nothing. So they led him by the hand into Damascus. For three days he was blind, and did not eat or drink anything. In Damascus there was a disciple named Ananias. The Lord called to him in a vision, "Ananias!" "Yes, Lord," he answered. The Lord told him, "Go to the house of Judas on Straight Street and ask for a man from Tarsus named Saul, for he is praying. In a vision he has seen a man named Ananias come and place his hands on him to restore his sight." "Lord," Ananias answered, "I have heard many reports about this man and all the harm he has done to your saints in Jerusalem. And he has come here with authority from the chief priests to arrest all who call on your name." But the Lord said to Ananias, "Go! This man is my chosen instrument to carry my name before the Gentiles and their kings and before the people of Israel. I will show him how much he must suffer for my name." Then Ananias went to the house and entered it. Placing his hands on Saul, he said, "Brother Saul, the Lord—Jesus, who appeared to you on the road as you were coming here—has sent me so that you may see again and be filled with the Holy Spirit." Immediately, something like scales fell from Saul's eyes, and he could see again. He got up and was baptized, and after taking some food, he regained his strength. Saul spent several days with the disciples in Damascus.

(Cf. Acts 22:3–16; 26:9–18; 1 Corinthians 9:1.)

Acts 10:39–43 "We are witnesses of everything he did in the country of the Jews and in Jerusalem. They killed him by hanging him on a tree, but God raised him from the dead on the third day and caused him to be seen. He was not seen by all the people, but by witnesses whom God had already chosen—by us who ate and drank with him after he rose from the dead. He commanded us to preach to the people and to testify that he is the one whom God appointed as judge of the living and the dead. All the prophets testify about him that everyone who believes in him receives forgiveness of sins through his name."

Acts 13:29–31 "When they had carried out all that was written about him, they took him down from the tree and laid him in a tomb. But God raised him from the dead, and for many days he was seen by those who had traveled with him from Galilee to Jerusalem. They are now his witnesses to our people."

1 Corinthians 9:1 Am I not an apostle? Have I not seen Jesus our Lord?

1 Corinthians 15:3–8 For what I received I passed on to you as of first importance: that Christ died for our sins according to the Scriptures, that he was buried, that he was raised on the third day according to the Scriptures, and that he appeared to Peter, and then to the Twelve. After that, he appeared to more than five hundred of the brothers at the same time, most of whom are still living, though some have fallen asleep. Then he appeared to James, then to all the apostles, and last of all he appeared to me also, as to one abnormally born.

1 John 1:1–3 That which was from the beginning, which we have heard, which we have seen with our eyes, which we have looked at and our hands have touched—this we proclaim concerning the Word of life. The life appeared; we have seen it and testify to it, and we proclaim to you the eternal life, which was with the Father and has appeared to us. We proclaim to you what we have seen and heard, so that you also may have fellowship with us. And our fellowship is with the Father and with his Son, Jesus Christ.

Transformation

Twelve

Acts 2:14, 22–24, 38–41 Then Peter stood up with the Eleven, raised his voice and addressed the crowd. . . . "Men of Israel, listen to this: Jesus of Nazareth was a man accredited by God to you by miracles, wonders and signs, which God did among you through him, as you yourselves know. This man was handed over to you by God's set purpose and foreknowledge; and you, with the help of wicked men, put him to death by nailing him to the cross. But God raised him from the dead, freeing him from the agony of death, because it was impossible for death to keep its hold on him. . . . Peter replied, "Repent and be baptized, every one of you, in the name of Jesus Christ for the forgiveness of your sins. And you will receive the gift of the Holy Spirit. The promise is for you and your children and for all who are far off—for all whom the Lord our God will call." With many other words he warned them; and he pleaded with them, "Save yourselves from this corrupt generation." Those who accepted his message were baptized, and about three thousand were added to their number that day.

Acts 4:1–31 The priests and the captain of the temple guard and the Sadducees came up to Peter and John while they were speaking to the people. They were greatly disturbed because the apostles were teaching the people and proclaiming in Jesus the resurrection of the dead. They seized Peter and John, and because it was evening, they put them in jail until the next day. But many who heard the message believed, and the number of men grew to about five thousand. The next day the rulers, elders and teachers of the law met in Jerusalem. Annas the high priest was there, and so were Caiaphas, John, Alexander and the other men of the high priest's family. They had Peter and John brought before them and began to question them: "By what power or what name did you do this?" Then Peter, filled with the Holy Spirit, said to them: "Rulers and elders of the people! If we are being called to account today for an act of kindness shown to a cripple and are asked how he was healed, then know this, you and all the people of Israel: It is by the name of Jesus Christ of Nazareth, whom you crucified but whom God raised from the dead, that this man stands before you healed. He is 'the stone you builders rejected, which has become the capstone.' Salvation is found in no one else, for there is no other name under heaven given to men by which we must be saved." When they saw the courage of Peter and John and realized that they were unschooled, ordinary men, they were astonished and they took note that these men had been with Jesus. But since they could see the man who had been healed standing there with them, there was nothing they could say. So they ordered them to withdraw from the Sanhedrin and then conferred together. "What are we going to do with these men?" they asked. "Everybody living in Jerusalem knows they have done an outstanding miracle, and we cannot deny it. But to stop this thing from spreading any further among the people, we must warn these men to speak no longer to anyone in this name." Then they called them in again and commanded them not to speak or teach at all in the name of Jesus. But Peter and John replied, "Judge for yourselves whether it is right in God's sight to obey you rather than God. For we cannot help speaking about what we have seen and heard." After further threats they let them go. They could not decide how to punish them, because all the people were praising God for what had happened. For the man who was miraculously healed was over forty years old. On their release, Peter and John went back to their own people and reported all that the chief priests and elders had said to them. When they heard this, they raised their voices together in prayer to God. "Sovereign Lord," they said, "you made the heaven and the earth and the sea, and everything in them. You spoke by the Holy Spirit through the mouth of your servant, our father David: 'Why do the nations rage and the peoples plot in vain? The kings of the earth take their stand and the rulers gather together against the Lord and against his Anointed One.' Indeed Herod and Pontius Pilate met together with the Gentiles and the people of Israel in this city to conspire against your holy servant Jesus, whom you anointed. They did what your power and will had decided beforehand should happen. Now, Lord, consider their threats and enable your servants to speak your word with great boldness. Stretch out your hand to heal and perform miraculous signs and wonders through the name of your holy servant Jesus." After they prayed, the place where they were meeting was shaken. And they were all filled with the Holy Spirit and spoke the word of God boldly.

(See also Acts 12:1–5.)

Acts 7:54–60 When they heard this, they were furious and gnashed their teeth at him. But Stephen, full of the Holy Spirit, looked up to heaven and saw the glory of God, and Jesus standing at the right hand of God. "Look," he said, "I see heaven open and the Son of Man standing at the right hand of God." At this they covered their ears and, yelling at the top of their voices, they all rushed at him, dragged him out of the city and began to stone him. Meanwhile, the witnesses laid their clothes at the feet of a young man named Saul. While they were stoning him, Stephen prayed, "Lord Jesus, receive my spirit." Then he fell on his knees and cried out, "Lord, do not hold this sin against them." When he had said this, he fell asleep.

Acts 12:1–2 It was about this time that King Herod arrested some who belonged to the church, intending to persecute them. He had James, the brother of John, put to death with the sword.

Acts 14:1–3, 19 At Iconium Paul and Barnabas went as usual into the Jewish synagogue. There they spoke so effectively that a great number of Jews and Gentiles believed. But the Jews who refused to believe stirred up the Gentiles and poisoned their minds against the brothers. So Paul and Barnabas spent considerable time there, speaking boldly for the Lord, who confirmed the message of his grace by enabling them to do miraculous signs and wonders. . . . Then some Jews came from Antioch and Iconium and won the crowd over. They stoned Paul and dragged him outside the city, thinking he was dead.

Acts 16:19–24 When the owners of the slave girl realized that their hope of making money was gone, they seized Paul and Silas and dragged them into the marketplace to face the authorities. They brought them before the magistrates and said, "These men are Jews, and are throwing our city into an uproar by advocating customs unlawful for us Romans to accept or practice." The crowd joined in the attack against Paul and Silas, and the magistrates ordered them to be stripped and beaten. After they had been severely flogged, they were thrown into prison, and the jailer was commanded to guard them carefully. Upon receiving such orders, he put them in the inner cell and fastened their feet in the stocks. **(See also Acts 17:14–34; 19:13–41; 23:1–10; 24:1–23.)**

Acts 22:2–5 Then Paul said: "I am a Jew, born in Tarsus of Cilicia, but brought up in this city. Under Gamaliel I was thoroughly trained in the law of our fathers and was just as zealous for God as any of you are today. I persecuted the followers of this Way to their death, arresting both men and women and throwing them into prison, as also the high priest and all the Council can testify. I even obtained letters from them to their brothers in Damascus, and went there to bring these people as prisoners to Jerusalem to be punished."

2 Corinthians 11:23–31 Are they servants of Christ? (I am out of my mind to talk like this.) I am more. I have worked much harder, been in prison more frequently, been flogged more severely, and been exposed to death again and again. Five times I received from the Jews the forty lashes minus one. Three times I was beaten with rods, once I was stoned, three times I was shipwrecked, I spent a night and a day in the open sea, I have been constantly on the move. I have been in danger from rivers, in danger from bandits, in danger from my own countrymen, in danger from Gentiles; in danger in the city, in danger in the country, in danger at sea; and in danger from false brothers. I have labored and toiled and have often gone without sleep; I have known hunger and thirst and have often gone without food; I have been cold and naked. Besides everything else, I face daily the pressure of my concern for all the churches. Who is weak, and I do not feel weak? Who is led into sin, and I do not inwardly burn? If I must boast, I will boast of the things that show my weakness. The God and Father of the Lord Jesus, who is to be praised forever, knows that I am not lying.

Galatians 1:13 For you have heard of my previous way of life in Judaism, how intensely I persecuted the church of God and tried to destroy it.

Philippians 3:4–11 If anyone else thinks he has reasons to put confidence in the flesh, I have more: circumcised on the eighth day, of the people of Israel, of the tribe of Benjamin, a Hebrew of Hebrews; in regard to the law, a Pharisee; as for zeal, persecuting the church; as for legalistic righteousness, faultless. But whatever was to my profit I now consider loss for the sake of Christ. What is more, I consider everything a loss compared to the surpassing greatness of knowing Christ Jesus my Lord, for whose sake I have lost all things. I consider them rubbish, that I may gain Christ and be found in him, not having a righteousness of my own that comes from the law, but that which is through faith in Christ—the righteousness that comes from God and is by faith. I want to know Christ and the power of his resurrection and the fellowship of sharing in his sufferings, becoming like him in his death, and so, somehow, to attain to the resurrection from the dead.

1 Thessalonians 2:2 We had previously suffered and been insulted in Philippi, as you know, but with the help of our God we dared to tell you his gospel in spite of strong opposition.

1 Timothy 1:13–16 Even though I was once a blasphemer and a persecutor and a violent man, I was shown mercy because I acted in ignorance and unbelief. The grace of our Lord was poured out on me abundantly, along with the faith and love that are in Christ Jesus. Here is a trustworthy saying that deserves full acceptance: Christ Jesus came into the world to save sinners—of whom I am the worst. But for that very reason I was shown mercy so that in me, the worst of sinners, Christ Jesus might display his unlimited patience as an example for those who would believe on him and receive eternal life.

2 Timothy 1:8–12 So do not be ashamed to testify about our Lord, or ashamed of me his prisoner. But join with me in suffering for the gospel, by the power of God, who has saved us and called us to a holy life—not because of anything we have done but because of his own purpose and grace. This grace was given us in Christ Jesus before the beginning of time, but it has now been revealed through the appearing of our Savior, Christ Jesus, who has destroyed death and has brought life and immortality to light through the gospel. And of this gospel I was appointed a herald and an apostle and a teacher. That is why I am suffering as I am. Yet I am not ashamed, because I know whom I have believed, and am convinced that he is able to guard what I have entrusted to him for that day.

2 Timothy 2:8–9 Remember Jesus Christ, raised from the dead, descended from David. This is my gospel, for which I am suffering even to the point of being chained like a criminal. But God's word is not chained.

Revelation 2:12–13 These are the words of him who has the sharp, double-edged sword. I know where you live—where Satan has his throne. Yet you remain true to my name. You did not renounce your faith in me, even in the days of Antipas, my faithful witness, who was put to death in your city—where Satan lives.

Revelation 6:9–11 When he opened the fifth seal, I saw under the altar the souls of those who had been slain because of the word of God and the testimony they had maintained. They called out in a loud voice, "How long, Sovereign Lord, holy and true, until you judge the inhabitants of the earth and avenge our blood?" Then each of them was given a white robe, and they were told to wait a little longer, until the number of their fellow servants and brothers who were to be killed as they had been was completed.

Traditions

Sabbath

Matthew 12:8 "For the Son of Man is Lord of the Sabbath."

Matthew 28:1 After the Sabbath, at dawn on the first day of the week, Mary Magdalene and the other Mary went to look at the tomb. **(Cf. Mark 16:1; Luke 24:1; John 20:1; see also 1 Corinthians 15:4.)**

Mark 2:27 Then he said to them, "The Sabbath was made for man, not man for the Sabbath. So the Son of Man is Lord even of the Sabbath."

John 20:26 A week later [on the first day of the week] his disciples were in the house again, and Thomas was with them. Though the doors were locked, Jesus came and stood among them and said, "Peace be with you!"

Acts 2:1–4 When the day of Pentecost came [on the first day of the week], they were all together in one place. Suddenly a sound like the blowing of a violent wind came from heaven and filled the whole house where they were sitting. They saw what seemed to be tongues of fire that separated and came to rest on each of them. All of them were filled with the Holy Spirit and began to speak in other tongues as the Spirit enabled them.

Acts 20:7 On the first day of the week we came together to break bread.

Romans 6:14 For sin shall not be your master, because you are not under law, but under grace.

1 Corinthians 16:1–2 Now about the collection for God's people: Do what I told the Galatian churches to do. On the first day of every week, each one of you should set aside a sum of money in keeping with his income, saving it up, so that when I come no collections will have to be made.

Galatians 3:24–25 So the law was put in charge to lead us to Christ that we might be justified by faith. Now that faith has come, we are no longer under the supervision of the law.

Colossians 2:16–17 Therefore do not let anyone judge you by what you eat or drink, or with regard to a religious festival, a New Moon celebration or a Sabbath day. These are a shadow of the things that were to come; the reality, however, is found in Christ.

Hebrews 4:1–11 Therefore, since the promise of entering his rest still stands, let us be careful that none of you be found to have fallen short of it. For we also have had the gospel preached to us, just as they did; but the message they heard was of no value to them, because those who heard did not combine it with faith. Now we who have believed enter that rest, just as God has said, "So I declared on oath in my anger, 'They shall never enter my rest.'" And yet his work has been finished since the creation of the world. For somewhere he has spoken about the seventh day in these words: "And on the seventh day God rested from all his work." And again in the passage above he says, "They shall never enter my rest." It still remains that some will enter that rest, and those who formerly had the gospel preached to them did not go in, because of their disobedience. Therefore God again set a certain day, calling it Today, when a long time later he spoke through David, as was said before: "Today, if you hear his voice, do not harden your hearts." For if Joshua had given them rest, God would not have spoken later about another day. There remains, then, a Sabbath-rest for the people of God; for anyone who enters God's rest also rests from his own work, just as God did from his. Let us, therefore, make every effort to enter that rest, so that no one will fall by following their example of disobedience.

Revelation 1:9–11 I, John, your brother and companion in the suffering and kingdom and patient endurance that are ours in Jesus, was on the island of Patmos because of the word of God and the testimony of Jesus. On the Lord's Day I was in the Spirit, and I heard behind me a loud voice like a trumpet, which said: "Write on a scroll what you see and send it to the seven churches: to Ephesus, Smyrna, Pergamum, Thyatira, Sardis, Philadelphia and Laodicea."

Sacrifices

Matthew 27:50–51 And when Jesus had cried out again in a loud voice, he gave up his spirit. At that moment the curtain of the temple was torn in two from top to bottom.
(Cf. Mark 15:38; Luke 23:45.)

Romans 3:25 God presented him as a sacrifice of atonement, through faith in his blood. He did this to demonstrate his justice.

Ephesians 5:1–2 Be imitators of God, therefore, as dearly loved children and live a life of love, just as Christ loved us and gave himself up for us as a fragrant offering and sacrifice to God.

Hebrews 7:23–28 Now there have been many of those priests, since death prevented them from continuing in office; but because Jesus lives forever, he has a permanent priesthood. Therefore he is able to save completely those who come to God through him, because he always lives to intercede for them. Such a high priest meets our need—one who is holy, blameless, pure, set apart from sinners, exalted above the heavens. Unlike the other high priests, he does not need to offer sacrifices day after day, first for his own sins, and then for the sins of the people. He sacrificed for their sins once for all when he offered himself. For the law appoints as high priests men who are weak; but the oath, which came after the law, appointed the Son, who has been made perfect forever.

Hebrews 9:1–28 Now the first covenant had regulations for worship and also an earthly sanctuary. A tabernacle was set up. In its first room were the lampstand, the table and the consecrated bread; this was called the Holy Place. Behind the second curtain was a room called the Most Holy Place, which had the golden altar of incense and the gold-covered ark of the covenant. This ark contained the gold jar of manna, Aaron's staff that had budded, and the stone tablets of the covenant. Above the ark were the cherubim of the Glory, overshadowing the atonement cover. But we cannot discuss these things in detail now.

When everything had been arranged like this, the priests entered regularly into the outer room to carry on their ministry. But only the high priest entered the inner room, and that only once a year, and never without blood, which he offered for himself and for the sins the people had committed in ignorance. The Holy Spirit was showing by this that the way into the Most Holy Place had not yet been disclosed as long as the first tabernacle was still standing. This is an illustration for the present time, indicating that the gifts and sacrifices being offered were not able to clear the conscience of the worshiper. They are only a matter of food and drink and various ceremonial washings—external regulations applying until the time of the new order.

When Christ came as high priest of the good things that are already here, he went through the greater and more perfect tabernacle that is not man-made, that is to say, not a part of this creation. He did not enter by means of the blood of goats and calves; but he entered the Most Holy Place once for all by his own blood, having obtained eternal redemption. The blood of goats and bulls and the ashes of a heifer sprinkled on those who are ceremonially unclean sanctify them so that they are outwardly clean. How much more, then, will the blood of Christ, who through the eternal Spirit offered himself unblemished to God, cleanse our consciences from acts that lead to death, so that we may serve the living God! For this reason Christ is the mediator of a new covenant, that those who are called may receive the promised eternal inheritance—now that he has died as a ransom to set them free from the sins committed under the first covenant.

In the case of a will, it is necessary to prove the death of the one who made it, because a will is in force only when somebody has died; it never takes effect while the one who made it is living. This is why even the first covenant was not put into effect without blood. When Moses had proclaimed every commandment of the law to all the people, he took the blood of calves, together with water, scarlet wool and branches of hyssop, and sprinkled the scroll and all the people. He said, "This is the blood of the covenant, which God has commanded you to keep." In the same way, he sprinkled with the blood both the tabernacle and everything used in its ceremonies. In fact, the law requires that nearly everything be cleansed with blood, and without the shedding of blood there is no forgiveness.

It was necessary, then, for the copies of the heavenly things to be purified with these sacrifices, but the heavenly things themselves with better sacrifices than these. For Christ did not enter a man-made sanctuary that was only a copy of the true one; he entered heaven itself, now to appear for us in God's presence. Nor did he enter heaven to offer himself again and again, the way the high priest enters the Most Holy Place every year with blood that is not his own. Then Christ would have had to suffer many times since the creation of the world. But now he has appeared once for all at the end of the ages to do away with sin by the sacrifice of himself. Just as man is destined to die once, and after that to face judgment, so Christ was sacrificed once to take away the sins of many people; and he will appear a second time, not to bear sin, but to bring salvation to those who are waiting for him.

Hebrews 10:1–4 The law is only a shadow of the good things that are coming—not the realities themselves. For this reason it can never, by the same sacrifices repeated endlessly year after year, make perfect those who draw near to worship. If it could, would they not have stopped being offered? For the worshipers would have been cleansed once for all, and would no longer have felt guilty for their sins. But those sacrifices are an annual reminder of sins, because it is impossible for the blood of bulls and goats to take away sins.

Hebrews 10:8–22 First he said, "Sacrifices and offerings, burnt offerings and sin offerings you did not desire, nor were you pleased with them" (although the law required them to be made). Then he said, "Here I am, I have come to do your will." He sets aside the first to establish the second. And by that will, we have been made holy through the sacrifice of the body of Jesus Christ once for all. Day after day every priest stands and performs his religious duties; again and again he offers the same sacrifices, which can never take away sins. But when this priest had offered for all time one sacrifice for sins, he sat down at the right hand of God. Since that time he waits for his enemies to be made his footstool, because by one sacrifice he has made perfect forever those who are being made holy. The Holy Spirit also testifies to us about this. First he says: "This is the covenant I will make with them after that time, says the Lord. I will put my laws in their hearts, and I will write them on their minds." Then he adds: "Their sins and lawless acts I will remember no more." And where these have been forgiven, there is no longer any sacrifice for sin. Therefore, brothers, since we have confidence to enter the Most Holy Place by the blood of Jesus, by a new and living way opened for us through the curtain, that is, his body, and since we have a great priest over the house of God, let us draw near to God with a sincere heart in full assurance of faith, having our hearts sprinkled to cleanse us from a guilty conscience and having our bodies washed with pure water.

1 John 2:2 He is the atoning sacrifice for our sins, and not only for ours but also for the sins of the whole world.

1 John 4:10 This is love: not that we loved God, but that he loved us and sent his Son as an atoning sacrifice for our sins.

Sacraments

Baptism

Matthew 28:18–20 Then Jesus came to them and said, "All authority in heaven and on earth has been given to me. Therefore go and make disciples of all nations, baptizing them in the name of the Father and of the Son and of the Holy Spirit, and teaching them to obey everything I have commanded you. And surely I am with you always, to the very end of the age."

Acts 2:38 Peter replied, "Repent and be baptized, every one of you, in the name of Jesus Christ for the forgiveness of your sins. And you will receive the gift of the Holy Spirit."

Acts 8:15–16 When they arrived, they prayed for them that they might receive the Holy Spirit, because the Holy Spirit had not yet come upon any of them; they had simply been baptized into the name of the Lord Jesus.

Acts 10:46–48 Then Peter said, "Can anyone keep these people from being baptized with water? They have received the Holy Spirit just as we have." So he ordered that they be baptized in the name of Jesus Christ.

Acts 19:4–6 Paul said, "John's baptism was a baptism of repentance. He told the people to believe in the one coming after him, that is, in Jesus." On hearing this, they were baptized into the name of the Lord Jesus. When Paul placed his hands on them, the Holy Spirit came on them, and they spoke in tongues and prophesied.

Romans 6:3–5 Or don't you know that all of us who were baptized into Christ Jesus were baptized into his death? We were therefore buried with him through baptism into death in order that, just as Christ was raised from the dead through the glory of the Father, we too may live a new life. If we have been united with him like this in his death, we will certainly also be united with him in his resurrection.

1 Corinthians 6:11 And that is what some of you were. But you were washed, you were sanctified, you were justified in the name of the Lord Jesus Christ and by the Spirit of our God.

Lord's Supper

Exodus 12:12–28 "On that same night I will pass through Egypt and strike down every firstborn—both men and animals—and I will bring judgment on all the gods of Egypt. I am the LORD. The blood will be a sign for you on the houses where you are; and when I see the blood, I will pass over you. No destructive plague will touch you when I strike Egypt.

"This is a day you are to commemorate; for the generations to come you shall celebrate it as a festival to the LORD—a lasting ordinance. For seven days you are to eat bread made without yeast. On the first day remove the yeast from your houses, for whoever eats anything with yeast in it from the first day through the seventh must be cut off from Israel. On the first day hold a sacred assembly, and another one on the seventh day. Do no work at all on these days, except to prepare food for everyone to eat—that is all you may do.

"Celebrate the Feast of Unleavened Bread, because it was on this very day that I brought your divisions out of Egypt. Celebrate this day as a lasting ordinance for the generations to come. In the first month you are to eat bread made without yeast, from the evening of the fourteenth day until the evening of the twenty-first day. For seven days no yeast is to be found in your houses. And whoever eats anything with yeast in it must be cut off from the community of Israel, whether he is an alien or native-born. Eat nothing made with yeast. Wherever you live, you must eat unleavened bread."

Then Moses summoned all the elders of Israel and said to them, "Go at once and select the animals for your families and slaughter the Passover lamb. Take a bunch of hyssop, dip it into the blood in the basin and put some of the blood on the top and on both sides of the doorframe. Not one of you shall go out the door of his house until morning. When the LORD goes through the land to strike down the Egyptians, he will see the blood on the top and sides of the doorframe and will pass over that doorway, and he will not permit the destroyer to enter your houses and strike you down. Obey these instructions as a lasting ordinance for you and your descendants. When you enter the land that the LORD will give you as he promised, observe this ceremony. And when your children ask you, 'What does this ceremony mean to you?' then tell them, 'It is the Passover sacrifice to the LORD, who passed over the houses of the Israelites in Egypt and spared our homes when he struck down the Egyptians.'" Then the people bowed down and worshiped. The Israelites did just what the LORD commanded Moses and Aaron.

Matthew 26:26–29 While they were eating, Jesus took bread, gave thanks and broke it, and gave it to his disciples, saying, "Take and eat; this is my body." Then he took the cup, gave thanks and offered it to them, saying, "Drink from it, all of you. This is my blood of the covenant, which is poured out for many for the forgiveness of sins. I tell you, I will not drink of this fruit of the vine from now on until that day when I drink it anew with you in my Father's kingdom."

Mark 14:22–25 While they were eating, Jesus took bread, gave thanks and broke it, and gave it to his disciples, saying, "Take it; this is my body." Then he took the cup, gave thanks and offered it to them, and they all drank from it. "This is my blood of the covenant, which is poured out for many, . . . I tell you the truth, I will not drink again of the fruit of the vine until that day when I drink it anew in the kingdom of God."

Luke 22:17–20 After taking the cup, he gave thanks and said, "Take this and divide it among you. For I tell you I will not drink again of the fruit of the vine until the kingdom of God comes." And he took bread, gave thanks and broke it, and gave it to them, saying, "This is my body given for you; do this in remembrance of me." In the same way, after the supper he took the cup, saying, "This cup is the new covenant in my blood, which is poured out for you."

1 Corinthians 10:16 Is not the cup of thanksgiving for which we give thanks a participation in the blood of Christ? And is not the bread that we break a participation in the body of Christ?

1 Corinthians 11:23–26 For I received from the Lord what I also passed on to you: The Lord Jesus, on the night he was betrayed, took bread, and when he had given thanks, he broke it and said, "This is my body, which is for you; do this in remembrance of me." In the same way, after supper he took the cup, saying, "This cup is the new covenant in my blood; do this, whenever you drink it, in remembrance of me." For whenever you eat this bread and drink this cup, you proclaim the Lord's death until he comes.

APPENDIX C

✛

Resurrection of Creation[1]

Physical Resurrection of Believers to Eternal Life

Job 19:25–27 I know that my Redeemer lives, and that in the end he will stand upon the earth; And after my skin has been destroyed, yet in my flesh I will see God; I myself will see him with my own eyes—I, and not another. How my heart yearns within me!

Psalm 16:9–11 Therefore my heart is glad and my tongue rejoices; my body also will rest secure, because you will not abandon me to the grave, nor will you let your Holy One see decay. You have made known to me the path of life; you will fill me with joy in your presence, with eternal pleasures at your right hand.

Psalm 17:15 And I—in righteousness I will see your face; when I awake, I will be satisfied with seeing your likeness.

Psalm 49:15 But God will redeem my life from the grave; he will surely take me to himself.

Psalm 71:20 Though you have made me see troubles, many and bitter, you will restore my life again; from the depths of the earth you will again bring me up.

Isaiah 26:19 But your dead will live; their bodies will rise. You who dwell in the dust, wake up and shout for joy. Your dew is like the dew of the morning; the earth will give birth to her dead.

Daniel 12:2 Multitudes who sleep in the dust of the earth will awake: some to everlasting life, others to shame and everlasting contempt.

Daniel 12:13 "As for you, go your way till the end. You will rest, and then at the end of the days you will rise to receive your allotted inheritance."

Hosea 13:14 "I will ransom them from the power of the grave; I will redeem them from death. Where, O death, are your plagues? Where, O grave, is your destruction?"

Matthew 8:10–11 When Jesus heard this, he was astonished and said to those following him, "I tell you the truth, I have not found anyone in Israel with such great faith. I say to you that many will come from the east and the west, and will take their places at the feast with Abraham, Isaac and Jacob in the kingdom of heaven."

Matthew 19:28–29 Jesus said to them, "I tell you the truth, at the renewal of all things, when the Son of Man sits on his glorious throne, you who have followed me will also sit on twelve thrones, judging the twelve tribes of Israel. And everyone who has left houses or brothers or sisters or father or mother or children or fields for my sake will receive a hundred times as much and will inherit eternal life."

Mark 12:26–27 "Now about the dead rising—have you not read in the book of Moses, in the account of the bush, how God said to him, 'I am the God of Abraham, the God of Isaac, and the God of Jacob'? He is not the God of the dead, but of the living."
(Cf. Matthew 22:31–32; Luke 20:37–38.)

Luke 14:12–14 Then Jesus said to his host, "When you give a luncheon or dinner, do not invite your friends, your brothers or relatives, or your rich neighbors; if you do, they may invite you back and so you will be repaid. But when you give a banquet, invite the poor, the crippled, the lame, the blind, and you will be blessed. Although they cannot repay you, you will be repaid at the resurrection of the righteous."

John 5:21–29 "For just as the Father raises the dead and gives them life, even so the Son gives life to whom he is pleased to give it. Moreover, the Father judges no one, but has entrusted all judgment to the Son, that all may honor the Son just as they honor the Father. He who does not honor the Son does not honor the Father, who sent him. I tell you the truth, whoever hears my word and believes him who sent me has eternal life and will not be condemned; he has crossed over from death to life. I tell you the truth, a time is coming and has now come when the dead will hear the voice of the Son of God and those who hear will live. For as the Father has life in himself, so he has granted the Son to have life in himself. And he has given him authority to judge because he is the Son of Man. Do not be amazed at this, for a time is coming when all who are in their graves will hear his voice and come out—those who have done good will rise to live, and those who have done evil will rise to be condemned."

John 6:39–40 "And this is the will of him who sent me, that I shall lose none of all that he has given me, but raise them up at the last day. For my Father's will is that everyone who looks to the Son and believes in him shall have eternal life, and I will raise him up at the last day."

John 11:21–26 "Lord," Martha said to Jesus, "if you had been here, my brother would not have died. But I know that even now God will give you whatever you ask." Jesus said to her, "Your brother will rise again." Martha answered, "I know he will rise again in the resurrection at the last day." Jesus said to her, "I am the resurrection and the life. He who believes in me will live, even though he dies; and whoever lives and believes in me will never die. Do you believe this?"

John 14:3 "And if I go and prepare a place for you, I will come back and take you to be with me that you also may be where I am."

John 17:24 "Father, I want those you have given me to be with me where I am, and to see my glory, the glory you have given me because you loved me before the creation of the world."

Acts 24:14–15 "However, I admit that I worship the God of our fathers as a follower of the Way, which they call a sect. I believe everything that agrees with the Law and that is written in the Prophets, and I have the same hope in God as these men, that there will be a resurrection of both the righteous and the wicked."

Romans 4:17 As it is written: "I have made you a father of many nations." He is our father in the sight of God, in whom he believed—the God who gives life to the dead and calls things that are not as though they were.

Romans 8:11 And if the Spirit of him who raised Jesus from the dead is living in you, he who raised Christ from the dead will also give life to your mortal bodies through his Spirit, who lives in you.

1 Corinthians 15:12–23 But if it is preached that Christ has been raised from the dead, how can some of you say that there is no resurrection of the dead? If there is no resurrection of the dead, then not even Christ has been raised. And if Christ has not been raised, our preaching is useless and so is your faith. More than that, we are then found to be false witnesses about God, for we have testified about God that he raised Christ from the dead. But he did not raise him if in fact the dead are not raised. For if the dead are not raised, then Christ has not been raised either. And if Christ has not been raised, your faith is futile; you are still in your sins. Then those also who have fallen asleep in Christ are lost. If only for this life we have hope in Christ, we are to be pitied more than all men. But Christ has indeed been raised from the dead, the firstfruits of those who have fallen asleep. For since death came through a man, the resurrection of the dead comes also through a man. For as in Adam all die, so in Christ all will be made alive. But each in his own turn: Christ, the firstfruits; then, when he comes, those who belong to him.

1 Corinthians 15:35–56 But someone may ask, "How are the dead raised? With what kind of body will they come?" How foolish! What you sow does not come to life unless it dies. When you sow, you do not plant the body that will be, but just a seed, perhaps of wheat or of something else. But God gives it a body as he has determined, and to each kind of seed he gives its own body. All flesh is not the same: Men have one kind of flesh, animals have another, birds another and fish another. There are also heavenly bodies and there are earthly bodies; but the splendor of the heavenly bodies is one kind, and the splendor of the earthly bodies is another. The sun has one kind of splendor, the moon another and the stars another; and star differs from star in splendor. So will it be with the resurrection of the dead. The body that is sown is perishable, it is raised imperishable; it is sown in dishonor, it is raised in glory; it is sown in weakness, it is raised in power; it is sown a natural body, it is raised a spiritual body. If there is a natural body, there is also a spiritual body. So it is written: "The first man Adam became a living being"; the last Adam, a life-giving spirit. The spiritual did not come first, but the natural, and after that the spiritual. The first man was of the dust of the earth, the second man from heaven. As was the earthly man, so are those who are of the earth; and as is the man from heaven, so also are those who are of heaven. And just as we have borne the likeness of the earthly man, so shall we bear the likeness of the man from heaven. I declare to you, brothers, that flesh and blood cannot inherit the kingdom of God, nor does the perishable inherit the imperishable. Listen, I tell you a mystery: We will not all sleep, but we will all be changed—in a flash, in the twinkling of an eye, at the last trumpet. For the trumpet will sound, the dead will be raised imperishable, and we will be changed. For the perishable must clothe itself with the imperishable, and the mortal with immortality. When the perishable has been clothed with the imperishable, and the mortal with immortality, then the saying that is written will come true: "Death has been swallowed up in victory. Where, O death, is your victory? Where, O death, is your sting?" The sting of death is sin, and the power of sin is the law. But thanks be to God! He gives us the victory through our Lord Jesus Christ.

2 Corinthians 4:14 . . . because we know that the one who raised the Lord Jesus from the dead will also raise us with Jesus and present us with you in his presence.

2 Corinthians 5:1–10 Now we know that if the earthly tent we live in is destroyed, we have a building from God, an eternal house in heaven, not built by human hands. Meanwhile we groan, longing to be clothed with our heavenly dwelling, because when we are clothed, we will not be found naked. For while we are in this tent, we groan and are burdened, because we do not wish to be unclothed but to be clothed with our heavenly dwelling, so that what is mortal may be swallowed up by life. Now it is God who has made us for this very purpose and has given us the Spirit as a deposit, guaranteeing what is to come. Therefore we are always confident and know that as long as we are at home in the body we are away from the Lord. We live by faith, not by sight. We are confident, I say, and would prefer to be away from the body and at home with the Lord. So we make it our goal to please him, whether we are at home in the body or away from it. For we must all appear before the judgment seat of Christ, that each one may receive what is due him for the things done while in the body, whether good or bad.

Philippians 3:20–21 But our citizenship is in heaven. And we eagerly await a Savior from there, the Lord Jesus Christ, who, by the power that enables him to bring everything under his control, will transform our lowly bodies so that they will be like his glorious body.

1 Thessalonians 4:14–17 We believe that Jesus died and rose again and so we believe that God will bring with Jesus those who have fallen asleep in him. According to the Lord's own word, we tell you that we who are still alive, who are left till the coming of the Lord, will certainly not precede those who have fallen asleep. For the Lord himself will come down from heaven, with a loud command, with the voice of the archangel and with the trumpet call of God, and the dead in Christ will rise first. After that, we who are still alive and are left will be caught up together with them in the clouds to meet the Lord in the air. And so we will be with the Lord forever.

2 Timothy 1:9–10 This grace was given us in Christ Jesus before the beginning of time, but it has now been revealed through the appearing of our Savior, Christ Jesus, who has destroyed death and has brought life and immortality to light through the gospel.

1 Peter 1:3–4 Praise be to the God and Father of our Lord Jesus Christ! In his great mercy he has given us new birth into a living hope through the resurrection of Jesus Christ from the dead, and into an inheritance that can never perish, spoil or fade—kept in heaven for you.

1 John 5:11–13 And this is the testimony: God has given us eternal life, and this life is in his Son. He who has the Son has life; he who does not have the Son of God does not have life. I write these things to you who believe in the name of the Son of God so that you may know that you have eternal life.

Jude 21 Keep yourselves in God's love as you wait for the mercy of our Lord Jesus Christ to bring you to eternal life.

Revelation 21:5–7 He who was seated on the throne said, "I am making everything new!" Then he said, "Write this down, for these words are trustworthy and true." He said to me: "It is done. I am the Alpha and the Omega, the Beginning and the End. To him who is thirsty I will give to drink without cost from the spring of the water of life. He who overcomes will inherit all this, and I will be his God and he will be my son."

Revelation 22:14 "Blessed are those who wash their robes, that they may have the right to the tree of life and may go through the gates into the city."

Physical Resurrection of Unbelievers to Eternal Torment

Isaiah 66:22–24 "As the new heavens and the new earth that I make will endure before me," declares the LORD, "so will your name and descendants endure. From one New Moon to another and from one Sabbath to another, all mankind will come and bow down before me," says the LORD. "And they will go out and look upon the dead bodies of those who rebelled against me; their worm will not die, nor will their fire be quenched, and they will be loathsome to all mankind."

Daniel 12:2 Multitudes who sleep in the dust of the earth will awake: some to everlasting life, others to shame and everlasting contempt.

Matthew 3:10, 12 "The ax is already at the root of the trees, and every tree that does not produce good fruit will be cut down and thrown into the fire. . . . His winnowing fork is in his hand, and he will clear his threshing floor, gathering his wheat into the barn and burning up the chaff with unquenchable fire."
(Cf. Luke 3:17.)

Matthew 5:22 "But I tell you that anyone who is angry with his brother will be subject to judgment. Again, anyone who says to his brother, 'Raca,' is answerable to the Sanhedrin. But anyone who says, 'You fool!' will be in danger of the fire of hell."

Matthew 5:29–30 "If your right eye causes you to sin, gouge it out and throw it away. It is better for you to lose one part of your body than for your whole body to be thrown into hell. And if your right hand causes you to sin, cut it off and throw it away. It is better for you to lose one part of your body than for your whole body to go into hell."

Matthew 7:13 "Enter through the narrow gate. For wide is the gate and broad is the road that leads to destruction, and many enter through it."

Matthew 7:19, 21–23 "Every tree that does not bear good fruit is cut down and thrown into the fire. . . . Not everyone who says to me, 'Lord, Lord,' will enter the kingdom of heaven, but only he who does the will of my Father who is in heaven. Many will say to me on that day, 'Lord, Lord, did we not prophesy in your name, and in your name drive out demons and perform many miracles?' Then I will tell them plainly, 'I never knew you. Away from me, you evildoers!'"

Matthew 8:10–12 When Jesus heard this, he was astonished and said to those following him, "I tell you the truth, I have not found anyone in Israel with such great faith. I say to you that many will come from the east and the west, and will take their places at the feast with Abraham, Isaac and Jacob in the kingdom of heaven. But the subjects of the kingdom will be thrown outside, into the darkness, where there will be weeping and gnashing of teeth."

Matthew 10:28 Do not be afraid of those who kill the body but cannot kill the soul. Rather, be afraid of the One who can destroy both soul and body in hell.

Matthew 12:32 Anyone who speaks a word against the Son of Man will be forgiven, but anyone who speaks against the Holy Spirit will not be forgiven, either in this age or in the age to come.

Matthew 13:24–30 Jesus told them another parable: "The kingdom of heaven is like a man who sowed good seed in his field. But while everyone was sleeping, his enemy came and sowed weeds among the wheat, and went away. When the wheat sprouted and formed heads, then the weeds also appeared. The owner's servants came to him and said, 'Sir, didn't you sow good seed in your field? Where then did the weeds come from?' 'An enemy did this,' he replied. The servants asked him, 'Do you want us to go and pull them up?' 'No,' he answered, 'because while you are pulling the weeds, you may root up the wheat with them. Let both grow together until the harvest. At that time I will tell the harvesters: First collect the weeds and tie them in bundles to be burned; then gather the wheat and bring it into my barn.'"

Matthew 13:38, 40–42 "The field is the world, and the good seed stands for the sons of the kingdom. The weeds are the sons of the evil one. . . . As the weeds are pulled up and burned in the fire, so it will be at the end of the age. The Son of Man will send out his angels, and they will weed out of his kingdom everything that causes sin and all who do evil. They will throw them into the fiery furnace, where there will be weeping and gnashing of teeth."

Matthew 13:47–50 "Once again, the kingdom of heaven is like a net that was let down into the lake and caught all kinds of fish. When it was full, the fishermen pulled it up on the shore. Then they sat down and collected the good fish in baskets, but threw the bad away. This is how it will be at the end of the age. The angels will come and separate the wicked from the righteous and throw them into the fiery furnace, where there will be weeping and gnashing of teeth."

Matthew 18:8–9 "If your hand or your foot causes you to sin, cut it off and throw it away. It is better for you to enter life maimed or crippled than to have two hands or two feet and be thrown into eternal fire. And if your eye causes you to sin, gouge it out and throw it away. It is better for you to enter life with one eye than to have two eyes and be thrown into the fire of hell."

Matthew 22:13 "Then the king told the attendants, 'Tie him hand and foot, and throw him outside, into the darkness, where there will be weeping and gnashing of teeth.'"

Matthew 23:33 "You snakes! You brood of vipers! How will you escape being condemned to hell?"

Matthew 25:29–33, 41–46 "'For everyone who has will be given more, and he will have an abundance. Whoever does not have, even what he has will be taken from him. And throw that worthless servant outside, into the darkness, where there will be weeping and gnashing of teeth.' When the Son of Man comes in his glory, and all the angels with him, he will sit on his throne in heavenly glory. All the nations will be gathered before him, and he will separate the people one from another as a shepherd separates the sheep from the goats. He will put the sheep on his right and the goats on his left. . . . Then he will say to those on his left, 'Depart from me, you who are cursed, into the eternal fire prepared for the devil and his angels. For I was hungry and you gave me nothing to eat, I was thirsty and you gave me nothing to drink, I was a stranger and you did not invite me in, I needed clothes and you did not clothe me, I was sick and in prison and you did not look after me.' They also will answer, 'Lord, when did we see you hungry or thirsty or a stranger or needing clothes or sick or in prison, and did not help you?' He will reply, 'I tell you the truth, whatever you did not do for one of the least of these, you did not do for me.' Then they will go away to eternal punishment, but the righteous to eternal life."

Mark 9:43–48 "If your hand causes you to sin, cut it off. It is better for you to enter life maimed than with two hands to go into hell, where the fire never goes out. And if your foot causes you to sin, cut it off. It is better for you to enter life crippled than to have two feet and be thrown into hell. And if your eye causes you to sin, pluck it out. It is better for you to enter the kingdom of God with one eye than to have two eyes and be thrown into hell, where 'their worm does not die, and the fire is not quenched.'"

Luke 16:19–31 "There was a rich man who was dressed in purple and fine linen and lived in luxury every day. At his gate was laid a beggar named Lazarus, covered with sores and longing to eat what fell from the rich man's table. Even the dogs came and licked his sores. The time came when the beggar died and the angels carried him to Abraham's side. The rich man also died and was buried. In hell, where he was in torment, he looked up and saw Abraham far away, with Lazarus by his side. So he called to him, 'Father Abraham, have pity on me and send Lazarus to dip the tip of his finger in water and cool my tongue, because I am in agony in this fire.' But Abraham replied, 'Son, remember that in your lifetime you received your good things, while Lazarus received bad things, but now he is comforted here and you are in agony. And besides all this, between us and you a great chasm has been fixed, so that those who want to go from here to you cannot, nor can anyone cross over from there to us.' He answered, 'Then I beg you, father, send Lazarus to my father's house, for I have five brothers. Let him warn them, so that they will not also come to this place of torment.' Abraham replied, 'They have Moses and the Prophets; let them listen to them.' 'No, father Abraham,' he said, 'but if someone from the dead goes to them, they will repent.' He said to him, 'If they do not listen to Moses and the Prophets, they will not be convinced even if someone rises from the dead.'"

John 3:36 Whoever believes in the Son has eternal life, but whoever rejects the Son will not see life, for God's wrath remains on him.

John 5:28–29 "Do not be amazed at this, for a time is coming when all who are in their graves will hear his voice and come out—those who have done good will rise to live, and those who have done evil will rise to be condemned."

Acts 24:14–15 "However, I admit that I worship the God of our fathers as a follower of the Way, which they call a sect. I believe everything that agrees with the Law and that is written in the Prophets, and I have the same hope in God as these men, that there will be a resurrection of both the righteous and the wicked."

Galatians 5:19–21 The acts of the sinful nature are obvious: sexual immorality, impurity and debauchery; idolatry and witchcraft; hatred, discord, jealousy, fits of rage, selfish ambition, dissensions, factions and envy; drunkenness, orgies, and the like. I warn you, as I did before, that those who live like this will not inherit the kingdom of God.

(Cf. 1 Corinthians 6:9–10; Ephesians 5:5-6.)

2 Thessalonians 1:8–9 He will punish those who do not know God and do not obey the gospel of our Lord Jesus. They will be punished with everlasting destruction and shut out from the presence of the Lord and from the majesty of his power.

Hebrews 10:26–27 If we deliberately keep on sinning after we have received the knowledge of the truth, no sacrifice for sins is left, but only a fearful expectation of judgment and of raging fire that will consume the enemies of God.

Hebrews 10:30–31 For we know him who said, "It is mine to avenge; I will repay," and again, "The Lord will judge his people." It is a dreadful thing to fall into the hands of the living God.

2 Peter 2:4–9 For if God did not spare angels when they sinned, but sent them to hell, putting them into gloomy dungeons to be held for judgment; if he did not spare the ancient world when he brought the flood on its ungodly people, but protected Noah, a preacher of righteousness, and seven others; if he condemned the cities of Sodom and Gomorrah by burning them to ashes, and made them an example of what is going to happen to the ungodly; and if he rescued Lot, a righteous man, who was distressed by the filthy lives of lawless men (for that righteous man, living among them day after day, was tormented in his righteous soul by the lawless deeds he saw and heard)—if this is so, then the Lord knows how to rescue godly men from trials and to hold the unrighteous for the day of judgment, while continuing their punishment.

Jude 4–7, 11–15 For certain men whose condemnation was written about long ago have secretly slipped in among you. They are godless men, who change the grace of our God into a license for immorality and deny Jesus Christ our only Sovereign and Lord. Though you already know all this, I want to remind you that the Lord delivered his people out of Egypt, but later destroyed those who did not believe. And the angels who did not keep their positions of authority but abandoned their own home—these he has kept in darkness, bound with everlasting chains for judgment on the great Day. In a similar way, Sodom and Gomorrah and the surrounding towns gave themselves up to sexual immorality and perversion. They serve as an example of those who suffer the punishment of eternal fire. . . . Woe to them! They have taken the way of Cain; they have rushed for profit into Balaam's error; they have been destroyed in Korah's rebellion. These men are blemishes at your love feasts, eating with you without the slightest qualm—shepherds who feed only themselves. They are clouds without rain, blown along by the wind; autumn trees, without fruit and uprooted—twice dead. They are wild waves of the sea, foaming up their shame; wandering stars, for whom blackest darkness has been reserved forever. Enoch, the seventh from Adam, prophesied about these men: "See, the Lord is coming with thousands upon thousands of his holy ones to judge everyone, and to convict all the ungodly of all the ungodly acts they have done in the ungodly way, and of all the harsh words ungodly sinners have spoken against him."

Revelation 14:9–11 A third angel followed them and said in a loud voice: "If anyone worships the beast and his image and receives his mark on the forehead or on the hand, he, too, will drink of the wine of God's fury, which has been poured full strength into the cup of his wrath. He will be tormented with burning sulfur in the presence of the holy angels and of the Lamb. And the smoke of their torment rises for ever and ever. There is no rest day or night for those who worship the beast and his image, or for anyone who receives the mark of his name."

Revelation 19:20 But the beast was captured, and with him the false prophet who had performed the miraculous signs on his behalf. With these signs he had deluded those who had received the mark of the beast and worshiped his image. The two of them were thrown alive into the fiery lake of burning sulfur.

Revelation 20:5, 10–15 (The rest of the dead did not come to life until the thousand years were ended.) . . . And the devil, who deceived them, was thrown into the lake of burning sulfur, where the beast and the false prophet had been thrown. They will be tormented day and night for ever and ever. Then I saw a great white throne and him who was seated on it. Earth and sky fled from his presence, and there was no place for them. And I saw the dead, great and small, standing before the throne, and books were opened. Another book was opened, which is the book of life. The dead were judged according to what they had done as recorded in the books. The sea gave up the dead that were in it, and death and Hades gave up the dead that were in them, and each person was judged according to what he had done. Then death and Hades were thrown into the lake of fire. The lake of fire is the second death. If anyone's name was not found written in the book of life, he was thrown into the lake of fire.

Revelation 21:8 "But the cowardly, the unbelieving, the vile, the murderers, the sexually immoral, those who practice magic arts, the idolaters and all liars—their place will be in the fiery lake of burning sulfur. This is the second death."

Revelation 22:14–15 "Blessed are those who wash their robes, that they may have the right to the tree of life and may go through the gates into the city. Outside are the dogs, those who practice magic arts, the sexually immoral, the murderers, the idolaters and everyone who loves and practices falsehood."

Physical "Resurrection" of the Cosmos

Isaiah 25:7–8 On this mountain he will destroy the shroud that enfolds all peoples, the sheet that covers all nations; he will swallow up death forever. The Sovereign LORD will wipe away the tears from all faces; he will remove the disgrace of his people from all the earth. The LORD has spoken.

Isaiah 33:24 No one living in Zion will say, "I am ill"; and the sins of those who dwell there will be forgiven.

Isaiah 60:19–20 The sun will no more be your light by day, nor will the brightness of the moon shine on you, for the LORD will be your everlasting light, and your God will be your glory. Your sun will never set again, and your moon will wane no more; the LORD will be your everlasting light, and your days of sorrow will end.

Isaiah 65:17–25 "Behold, I will create new heavens and a new earth. The former things will not be remembered, nor will they come to mind. But be glad and rejoice forever in what I will create, for I will create Jerusalem to be a delight and its people a joy. I will rejoice over Jerusalem and take delight in my people; the sound of weeping and of crying will be heard in it no more. Never again will there be in it an infant who lives but a few days, or an old man who does not live out his years; he who dies at a hundred will be thought a mere youth; he who fails to reach a hundred will be considered accursed. They will build houses and dwell in them; they will plant vineyards and eat their fruit. No longer will they build houses and others live in them, or plant and others eat. For as the days of a tree, so will be the days of my people; my chosen ones will long enjoy the works of their hands. They will not toil in vain or bear children doomed to misfortune; for they will be a people blessed by the LORD, they and their descendants with them. Before they call I will answer; while they are still speaking I will hear. The wolf and the lamb will feed together, and the lion will eat straw like the ox, but dust will be the serpent's food. They will neither harm nor destroy on all my holy mountain," says the LORD.

Isaiah 66:22–24 "As the new heavens and the new earth that I make will endure before me," declares the LORD, "so will your name and descendants endure. From one New Moon to another and from one Sabbath to another, all mankind will come and bow down before me," says the LORD. "And they will go out and look upon the dead bodies of those who rebelled against me; their worm will not die, nor will their fire be quenched, and they will be loathsome to all mankind."

Matthew 19:28 Jesus said to them, "I tell you the truth, at the renewal of all things, when the Son of Man sits on his glorious throne, you who have followed me will also sit on twelve thrones, judging the twelve tribes of Israel."

Acts 3:19–21 Repent, then, and turn to God, so that your sins may be wiped out, that times of refreshing may come from the Lord, and that he may send the Christ, who has been appointed for you—even Jesus. He must remain in heaven until the time comes for God to restore everything, as he promised long ago through his holy prophets.

Romans 8:19–24 The creation waits in eager expectation for the sons of God to be revealed. For the creation was subjected to frustration, not by its own choice, but by the will of the one who subjected it, in hope that the creation itself will be liberated from its bondage to decay and brought into the glorious freedom of the children of God. We know that the whole creation has been groaning as in the pains of childbirth right up to the present time. Not only so, but we ourselves, who have the firstfruits of the Spirit, groan inwardly as we wait eagerly for our adoption as sons, the redemption of our bodies. For in this hope we were saved.

Ephesians 1:9–10 And he made known to us the mystery of his will according to his good pleasure, which he purposed in Christ, to be put into effect when the times will have reached their fulfillment—to bring all things in heaven and on earth together under one head, even Christ.

Hebrews 1:10–12 He also says, "In the beginning, O Lord, you laid the foundations of the earth, and the heavens are the work of your hands. They will perish, but you remain; they will all wear out like a garment. You will roll them up like a robe; like a garment they will be changed. But you remain the same, and your years will never end." **(Cf. Psalm 102:25–27.)**

Hebrews 11:13–16 All these people were still living by faith when they died. They did not receive the things promised; they only saw them and welcomed them from a distance. And they admitted that they were aliens and strangers on earth. People who say such things show that they are looking for a country of their own. If they had been thinking of the country they had left, they would have had opportunity to return. Instead, they were longing for a better country—a heavenly one. Therefore God is not ashamed to be called their God, for he has prepared a city for them.

Hebrews 12:22 But you have come to Mount Zion, to the heavenly Jerusalem, the city of the living God. You have come to thousands upon thousands of angels in joyful assembly.

2 Peter 3:7–13 By the same word the present heavens and earth are reserved for fire, being kept for the day of judgment and destruction of ungodly men. But do not forget this one thing, dear friends: With the Lord a day is like a thousand years, and a thousand years are like a day. The Lord is not slow in keeping his promise, as some understand slowness. He is patient with you, not wanting anyone to perish, but everyone to come to repentance. But the day of the Lord will come like a thief. The heavens will disappear with a roar; the elements will be destroyed by fire, and the earth and everything in it will be laid bare. Since everything will be destroyed in this way, what kind of people ought you to be? You ought to live holy and godly lives as you look forward to the day of God and speed its coming. That day will bring about the destruction of the heavens by fire, and the elements will melt in the heat. But in keeping with his promise we are looking forward to a new heaven and a new earth, the home of righteousness.

Revelation 3:11–12 I am coming soon. Hold on to what you have, so that no one will take your crown. Him who overcomes I will make a pillar in the temple of my God. Never again will he leave it. I will write on him the name of my God and the name of the city of my God, the new Jerusalem, which is coming down out of heaven from my God; and I will also write on him my new name.

Revelation 21:1–27 Then I saw a new heaven and a new earth, for the first heaven and the first earth had passed away, and there was no longer any sea. I saw the Holy City, the new Jerusalem, coming down out of heaven from God, prepared as a bride beautifully dressed for her husband. And I heard a loud voice from the throne saying, "Now the dwelling of God is with men, and he will live with them. They will be his people, and God himself will be with them and be their God. He will wipe every tear from their eyes. There will be no more death or mourning or crying or pain, for the old order of things has passed away." He who was seated on the throne said, "I am making everything new!" Then he said, "Write this down, for these words are trustworthy and true." He said to me: "It is done. I am the Alpha and the Omega, the Beginning and the End. To him who is thirsty I will give to drink without cost from the spring of the water of life. He who overcomes will inherit all this, and I will be his God and he will be my son. But the cowardly, the unbelieving, the vile, the murderers, the sexually immoral, those who practice magic arts, the idolaters and all liars—their place will be in the fiery lake of burning sulfur. This is the second death." One of the seven angels who had the seven bowls full of the seven last plagues came and said to me, "Come, I will show you the bride, the wife of the Lamb." And he carried me away in the Spirit to a mountain great and high, and showed me the Holy City, Jerusalem, coming down out of heaven from God. It shone with the glory of God, and its brilliance was like that of a very precious jewel, like a jasper, clear as crystal. It had a great, high wall with twelve gates, and with twelve angels at the gates. On the gates were written the names of the twelve tribes of Israel. There were three gates on the east, three on the north, three on the south and three on the west. The wall of the city had twelve foundations, and on them were the names of the twelve apostles of the Lamb. The angel who talked with me had a measuring rod of gold to measure the city, its gates and its walls. The city was laid out like a square, as long as it was wide. He measured the city with the rod and found it to be 12,000 stadia in length, and as wide and high as it is long. He measured its wall and it was 144 cubits thick, by man's measurement, which the angel was using. The wall was made of jasper, and the city of pure gold, as pure as glass. The foundations of the city walls were decorated with every kind of precious stone. The first foundation was jasper, the second sapphire, the third chalcedony, the fourth emerald, the fifth sardonyx, the sixth carnelian, the seventh chrysolite, the eighth beryl, the ninth topaz, the tenth chrysoprase, the eleventh jacinth, and the twelfth amethyst. The twelve gates were twelve pearls, each gate made of a single pearl. The great street of the city was of pure gold, like transparent glass. I did not see a temple in the city, because the Lord God Almighty and the Lamb are its temple. The city does not need the sun or the moon to shine on it, for the glory of God gives it light, and the Lamb is its lamp. The nations will walk by its light, and the kings of the earth will bring their splendor into it. On no day will its gates ever be shut, for there will be no night there. The glory and honor of the nations will be brought into it. Nothing impure will ever enter it, nor will anyone who does what is shameful or deceitful, but only those whose names are written in the Lamb's book of life.

Revelation 22:1–5 Then the angel showed me the river of the water of life, as clear as crystal, flowing from the throne of God and of the Lamb down the middle of the great street of the city. On each side of the river stood the tree of life, bearing twelve crops of fruit, yielding its fruit every month. And the leaves of the tree are for the healing of the nations. No longer will there be any curse. The throne of God and of the Lamb will be in the city, and his servants will serve him. They will see his face, and his name will be on their foreheads. There will be no more night. They will not need the light of a lamp or the light of the sun, for the Lord God will give them light. And they will reign for ever and ever.

ENDNOTES

✛

Chapter 1. Mythologies

1. Hugh J. Schonfield, *The Passover Plot: A New Interpretation of the Life and Death of Jesus* (New York: Bernard Geis Associates, 1965).
2. Ibid., inside front cover flap.
3. Ibid., inside back cover flap.
4. Ibid., back cover.
5. Ibid.
6. Ibid., 13.
7. Lee Strobel, *The Case for Christ* (Grand Rapids: Zondervan, 1998), 192–93.
8. Gary R. Habermas, *The Historical Jesus: Ancient Evidence for the Life of Christ* (Joplin, Mo.: College Press Publishing Co., 1996), 73; J. P. Moreland, *Scaling the Secular City: A Defense of Christianity* (Grand Rapids: Baker Book House, 1987), 171.
9. D. H. Lawrence, *Love among the Haystacks and Other Stories* (New York: Penguin, 1960), 125, as cited in Strobel, *The Case for Christ*, 192.

10. Donovan Joyce, *The Jesus Scroll* (New York: New American Library, 1972), as cited in Strobel, *The Case for Christ,* 192. In addition to citing the swoon hypotheses of D. H. Lawrence, Donovan Joyce, and Barbara Thiering, Strobel also cites Baigent, Leigh, and Lincoln's *Holy Blood, Holy Grail* (New York: Delacorte, 1982), 372, in which Pontius Pilate was allegedly bribed to allow Jesus to be taken down from the cross before he died.

11. Habermas, *The Historical Jesus,* 90–91.

12. Barbara Thiering, *Jesus and the Riddle of the Dead Sea Scrolls: Unlocking the Secrets of His Life Story* (San Francisco: HarperSanFrancisco, 1992).

13. Michael J. Wilkins and J. P. Moreland, eds., *Jesus Under Fire: Modern Scholarship Reinvents the Historical Jesus* (Grand Rapids: Zondervan, 1995), 210.

14. The swoon hypothesis and the twin theory are just two of many naturalistic accounts for the biblical data surrounding the resurrection of Christ. But all naturalistic accounts begin with a bias against the supernatural. Naturalistic accounts grow out of the antisupernatural environment fostered by the influential work of philosopher David Hume (1711–1776) in his famous arguments against miracles. An excellent presentation and refutation of Hume's position can be found in R. Douglas Geivett and Gary R. Habermas, *In Defense of Miracles: A Comprehensive Case for God's Actions in History* (Downer's Grove, Ill.: InterVarsity Press, 1997).

15. Spelling for this name is uncertain—derived from audiotape (see note 16).

16. William Lane Craig and Robert Greg Cavin, "Dead or Alive? A Debate on the Resurrection of Jesus" (Anaheim, Calif.: Simon Greenleaf University, 1995), audiotape.

17. See Qur'an 4:157–9.

18. Norman L. Geisler and Abdul Saleeb, *Answering Islam: The Crescent in Light of the Cross* (Grand Rapids: Baker Book House, 1993), 65.

19. Ibid., 65.

20. Ibid. *The Gospel of Barnabas* purports to be another first-century record of the life of Christ but is actually a late medieval invention with no bearing on the historical Jesus (see Ibid., 295–299).

21. Ibid., 65–66 (see 64–67).

22. For an excellent presentation of the doctrines of the Jehovah's Witnesses and a refutation of them in light of historic biblical Christianity, see Walter Martin, *The Kingdom of the Cults*, Revised, Updated, Expanded Anniversary Edition (Minneapolis: Bethany House Publishers, 1997), chap. 5.

23. Concerning Christ's identity as Michael the archangel, Jehovah's Witnesses not only claim that "the Scriptures identify the Word (Jesus in his prehuman existence) as God's first creation, his first-born Son," but they also assert that "the name Michael applies to God's Son before he left heaven to become Jesus Christ and also after his return. Michael is the only one said to be the 'archangel,' meaning 'chief angel' or 'principal angel.'" Rather than being the creator of all things, Jesus is reduced to the status of a junior partner and creator of all *other* things. (In Colossians 1:15ff of the *New World Translation*, the Watchtower inserts the word *other* four times to press this point.) (*Aid to Bible Understanding* [Brooklyn: Watchtower Bible and Tract Society, 1971], 918, 1152.) For a defense of the deity of Christ and the biblical doctrine of the Trinity against cultic constructs, see James R. White, *The Forgotten Trinity* (Minneapolis: Bethany House Publishers, 1998).

24. *Let God Be True* (Brooklyn: Watchtower Bible and Tract Society, rev. ed. 1952), 138.

25. Ibid., 41.

26. *Things in Which It Is Impossible for God to Lie* (Brooklyn: Watchtower Bible and Tract Society, 1965), 354.

27. Ibid., 355.

28. *Studies in the Scriptures*, Series II (Allegheny, Penn.: Watchtower Bible and Tract Society, 1908), 129.

29. *The Kingdom Is at Hand* (Brooklyn: Watchtower Bible and Tract

Society, 1944), 259. Cf. *Reasoning from the Scriptures* (Brooklyn: Watchtower Bible and Tract Society, 1985), 334.

30. *From Paradise Lost to Paradise Regained* (Brooklyn: Watchtower Bible and Tract Society, 1958), 144.

31. Josh McDowell, *The New Evidence That Demands a Verdict* (Nashville: Thomas Nelson Publishers, 1999), 203.

32. Wilbur M. Smith, *Therefore Stand: Christian Apologetics* (Grand Rapids: Baker Book House, 1965), 369–70; as quoted in McDowell, *The New Evidence That Demands a Verdict*, 206–7.

33. Ibid., 207.

34. Ibid.

Chapter 2. Fatal Torment

1. See Habermas, *The Historical Jesus*, 143–70 (see esp. 158); Paul Copan, ed., *Will the Real Jesus Please Stand Up? A Debate between William Lane Craig and John Dominic Crossan* (Grand Rapids: Baker Book House, 1998), 26–27

2. Except as noted, all following medical data and descriptions concerning Christ's suffering adapted from C. Truman Davis, "The Crucifixion of Jesus: The Passion of Christ from a Medical Point of View," *Arizona Medicine* (March 1965): 183–87; and William D. Edwards, Wesley J. Gabel, and Floyd E. Hosmer, "On the Physical Death of Jesus Christ," *The Journal of the American Medical Association* (21 March 1986): 1455–63.

3. Strobel, *The Case for Christ*, 197–8.

4. More specifically, the spikes were driven through Christ's wrists, which in Jewish understanding were part of the hands.

5. Strobel, *The Case for Christ*, 202.

6. Habermas, *The Historical Jesus*, 74. See Davis, "The Crucifixion of Jesus: The Passion of Christ from a Medical Point of View," 183–87; and Edwards, Gabel, and Hosmer, "On the Physical Death of Jesus Christ," 1455–63.

7. Habermas, *The Historical Jesus*, 72–73.

8. Ibid., 73.

9. Ibid., 73–74.

10. Ibid., 71.

11. A helpful response to those who think that the Bible has been corrupted over time is found in the following illustration: Suppose you wrote an essay and asked five friends each to produce a handwritten copy of it. Imagine further that each of them asked five more friends to do the same. The first five people to copy it would make mistakes, and those who copy from them would add additional errors. By the "fifth generation" you would have approximately four thousand flawed manuscripts. Sounds pretty grim, right?

    But think with me for a moment. Your five friends might have made mistakes, but they wouldn't all have made the *same* mistakes. If you compared the copies, you would find that one group contained the same mistake, while the other four did not. This, of course, would make it easy to tell the copies from the original. Not only that, but most of the mistakes would be obvious—such as misspelled words or words accidentally omitted. Thus, even if you lost the original, as long as you had access to the copies, it would be a rather simple matter to reproduce the original essay. That's essentially the situation with the New Testament. We've got thousands of copies of which have been classified by scholars into groups and thus can determine with great precision what the autographs actually said. While it can be argued that there are differences in style and spelling among the various manuscripts, it cannot be asserted that there are differences in substance.

12. The New Testament was originally written in Greek. Nearly all of these extant Greek manuscripts or fragments predate the invention of the printing press, and some eight hundred manuscripts predate A.D. 1000. Lee Strobel, interviewing Dr. Bruce Metzger of Princeton Theological Seminary, writes: "'While papyrus manuscripts represent the earliest copies of the New Testament, there are also ancient copies written on parchment, which was made

from the skins of cattle, sheep, goats and antelope.

"'We have what are called uncial manuscripts, which are written in all-capital Greek letters,' Metzger explained. 'Today we have 306 of these, several dating back as early as the third century. The most important are *Codex Sinaiticus*, which is the only complete New Testament in uncial letters, and *Codex Vaticanus*, which is not quite complete. Both date to about A.D. 350.

"'A new style of writing, more cursive in nature, emerged in roughly A.D. 800. It's called minuscule, and we have 2,856 of these manuscripts. Then there are also lectionaries, which contain New Testament Scripture in the sequence it was to be read in the early churches at appropriate times during the year. A total of 2,403 of these have been cataloged. That puts the grand total of Greek manuscripts at 5,664'" (Strobel, *The Case for Christ*, 62–63). According to Michael Welte of the *Institut Für Neutestamentliche Textforschung*, the latest total of Greek manuscripts of the New Testament is 5,686 (copy of personal letter received 31 August 1998).

The acronym LUMP can be used as a memory aid so as not to *lump* all manuscripts together—*L*ectionaries, *U*ncials, *M*iniscules, and *P*apyri.

13. See Carsten Peter Thiede and Mathew d'Ancona, *Eyewitness to Jesus* (New York: Doubleday, 1996), 29–31, chap. 5; Philip Wesley Comfort, ed., *The Origin of the Bible* (Wheaton: Tyndale House Publishers, 1992), 179–207.

14. See William M. Ramsay, *The Bearing of Recent Discovery on the Trustworthiness of the New Testament*, reprint ed. (Grand Rapids: Baker Book House, 1953); *St. Paul the Traveller and The Roman Citizen* (Grand Rapids: Baker Book House, 1962).

15. Jeffrey L. Sheler, "Is the Bible True?" *U.S. News and World Report*, 25 October 1999, 58; reprinted from Jeffrey L. Sheler, *Is the Bible True?* (San Francisco: HarperSanFrancisco, 1999).

16. Sheler, "Is the Bible True?" 58–59.

17. Ibid., 59. Sheler discusses other archaeological and historical

insights of recent years, including the House of David inscription at Dan, which affirms the historicity of King David (54–58).

18. While archaeology, in principle, cannot prove the Bible, it offers overall support for biblical historicity (see, e.g., Alfred J. Hoerth, *Archaeology and the Old Testament* [Grand Rapids: Baker Book House, 1998]).

19. The Bible was written over a span of sixteen hundred years by forty authors in three languages (Hebrew, Aramaic, and Greek) on hundreds of subjects. And yet there is one consistent, noncontradictory theme that runs through it all: *God's redemption of humankind.* Clearly, statistical probability concerning biblical prophecy is a powerful indicator of the trustworthiness of Scripture.

Chapter 3. Empty Tomb

1. Wilkins and Moreland, *Jesus Under Fire*, 2.
2. Robert W. Funk, *Honest to Jesus* (San Francisco: HarperSanFrancisco, 1996), 305.
3. Interview by Mary Rourke, "Cross Examination," *Los Angeles Times,* 24 February 1994, E1, E5, as quoted in Wilkins and Moreland, *Jesus Under Fire*, 2.
4. Richard N. Ostling, "Jesus Christ, Plain and Simple," *Time,* 10 January 1994, from the *Time* Web site at http://cgi.pathfinder.com/time/magazine/archive/1994/940110/940110.religion.html. Cf. Wilkins and Moreland, *Jesus Under Fire*, 2.
5. "Facts About the Jesus Seminar and Founder Robert W. Funk," Answers in Action Web site at www.answers.org/Apologetics/jesuseminar.html (retrieved 17 December 1999).
6. Ostling, "Jesus Christ, Plain and Simple"; cf. Wilkins and Moreland, *Jesus Under Fire*, 142.
7. Strobel, *The Case for Christ*, 114; cf. Gregory A. Boyd, *Cynic Sage or Son of God?* (Wheaton: BridgePoint, 1995), 59–62. Bob and Gretchen Passantino explain that the methodology used by the Jesus Seminar for determining what is and is not "authentic"

includes the following unjustified presuppositions: a direct quote must be short and "punchy"; a thought must run against the religious grain of the day; an action must be in the style of contemporary "wise men" of the day; parables must not have explicit applications; a word or passage must not contain Old Testament quotations; a passage must not contain contextual connections; any prophecy is immediately deemed invalid; and any miracle is immediately deemed invalid ("Facts About the Jesus Seminar," Answers in Action at www.answers.org/Apologetics/jesuseminar.html).

8. Boyd, *Cynic Sage or Son of God?* 62.

9. Robert W. Funk, Roy W. Hoover, and THE JESUS SEMINAR, *The Five Gospels* (New York: Macmillan Publishing Co., 1993), x.

10. Gospel of Thomas, 114, in Funk, Hoover, and THE JESUS SEMINAR, *The Five Gospels*, 532.

11. James R. White, "The Jesus Seminar and the Gospel of Thomas: Courting the Media at the Cost of Truth," *Christian Research Journal* (Winter 1998): 51, available on CRI Web site at www.equip.org.

12. See Gospel of Thomas, 114, cited above. As well, Dr. Gregory Boyd writes, "It is difficult to escape the conclusion that the talk about the 'the kingdom of God' or 'the kingdom of the Father' in GosThom [Gospel of Thomas] is often attributable to a gnostic-tending reworking of the canonical material. In GosThom, this phrase is taken to indicate 'the present secret religious knowledge of a heavenly world.' Hence, for example, the Jesus of GosThom says, 'The Kingdom is inside of you, and it is outside of you. When you come to know yourselves, then you will become known, and you will realize that it is you who are the sons of the living Father. But if you will not know yourselves, you dwell in poverty and it is you who are that poverty' (GosThom, 3)" (Boyd, *Cynic Sage or Son of God?* 135).

13. The Jesus Seminar is influenced by the view that the Gospel of Thomas does not depend on the canonical Gospels (Matthew, Mark, Luke, and John) and, in fact, predates Matthew and Luke in the first century. However, Dr. Gregory Boyd writes: "Numerous

scholars . . . have argued that such a position is untenable. For example, ever since the 1964 landmark study of Wolfgang Schrage, much of German scholarship has been convinced that Thomas is largely dependent upon the canonical Gospels, or at least upon traditions that stem from the canonical Gospels. Indeed, many international scholars, representing a wide variety of methodological persuasions and theological interests, have come to similar conclusions: Thomas does not represent much in the way of reliable independent early church traditions. The summary statement of Klyne Snodgrass helps to nuance this general opinion.

"The dependence of *Thomas* on the canonical Gospels is not . . . a direct literary dependence. Rather, it is an indirect dependence, probably at some distance and apparently mediated through oral tradition that had shaped and harmonized the Gospels. The author of *Thomas* has also continued the redaction of the sayings. No doubt there is independent tradition in *Thomas* as well, but the bulk of the material seems to have its origin in the canonical Gospels.

"Such conclusions, of course, have a direct bearing on the *date* of Thomas and the traditions it contains. Once it is recognized that Thomas is significantly dependent upon the canonical Gospels, the recent post-Bultmannian push for an early date (A.D. 50–70) for its content is no longer feasible. In fact, most of the scholars who did the pioneering work on GosThom date it around A.D. 140. Among other considerations, we have no independent attestation of the existence of this work until the early third century when it is cited by Hippolytus and Origen—an unexpected silence if this is, in fact, a first-century work. What is more, GosThom reflects a distinct gnosticizing tendency which renders a second-century dating most feasible" (Boyd, *Cynic Sage or Son of God?* 134).

14. Wilkins and Moreland, *Jesus Under Fire*, 142.

15. John A. T. Robinson, *The Human Face of God* (Philadelphia: Westminster, 1973), 131, as quoted in Copan, *Will the Real Jesus Please Stand Up?* 27. And as scholar D. H. Van Daalen has noted,

"It is extremely difficult to object to the empty tomb on historical grounds; those who deny it do so on the basis of theological or philosophical assumptions" (William Lane Craig, "Contemporary Scholarship and the Historical Evidence for the Resurrection of Jesus Christ," *Truth* 1 (1985): 89–95, from the Leadership University Web site at http://www.leaderu.com/truth/1truth22. html; see D. H. Van Daalen, *The Real Resurrection* (London: Collins, 1970), 41, cited in Wilkins and Moreland, *Jesus Under Fire*, 152).

16. Wilkins and Moreland, *Jesus Under Fire*, 148.

17. Ibid., 149.

18. Ibid., 148, 152.

19. Ibid., 147–8; See also Craig, "Contemporary Scholarship and the Historical Evidence." For arguments establishing early dates for the writing of Mark, see John Wehham, *Redating Matthew, Mark & Luke* (Downers Grove: Ill.: InterVarsity Press, 1992), chaps. 6–8; Boyd, *Cynic Sage or Son of God?* chap. 11.

20. Wilkins and Moreland, *Jesus Under Fire*, 147. In an interview with investigative journalist Lee Strobel, Craig notes that the confession used by Paul is incredibly early and therefore trustworthy. Craig goes on to point out that "essentially, it's a four-line formula. The first line refers to the Crucifixion, the second to the burial, the third to the Resurrection, and the fourth to Jesus' appearances. . . . This creed is actually a summary that corresponds line for line with what the gospels teach. When we turn to the gospels, we find multiple, independent attestation of this burial story, and Joseph of Arimathea is specifically named in all four accounts. On top of that, the burial story in Mark is so extremely early that it's simply not possible for it to have been subject to legendary corruption" (Strobel, *The Case for Christ*, 209). See pp. 38–40 for a discussion of the pre-Pauline creed in 1 Corinthians 15:3–7; see Habermas, *The Historical Jesus*, chap. 7.

21. Strobel, *The Case for Christ*, 217.

22. Ibid., 218.

23. William Lane Craig, *Reasonable Faith* (Wheaton: Crossway Books, 1994), 276.

24. Ibid.

25. Ronald F. Youngblood, gen. ed., *Nelson's New Illustrated Bible Dictionary* (Nashville: Thomas Nelson Publishers, 1995), 1318. It is in part because of first-century Jewish attitudes toward women that liberal scholars dated the Gospels so late, even into the second century, believing that the Gospel accounts of the women's testimony must have been made up. Indeed, if the women's testimony had not been so overwhelmingly persuasive, it would have been dismissed.

26. Craig S. Keener, *The IVP Bible Background Commentary: New Testament* (Downers Grove, Ill.: InterVarsity Press, 1993), 210. See Luke 8:1–3.

27. Youngblood, *Nelson's New Illustrated Bible Dictionary*, 1318.

28. Paragraph adapted from Wilkins and Moreland, *Jesus Under Fire*, 152.

29. Paragraph adapted from Habermas, *The Historical Jesus*, 205–6.

30. Paragraph adapted from Wilkins and Moreland, *Jesus Under Fire*, 146–47.

Chapter 4. Appearances of Christ

1. Wilkins and Moreland, *Jesus Under Fire*, 147.

2. Habermas, *The Historical Jesus*, 154; cf. Wilkins and Moreland, *Jesus Under Fire*, 42–43, 147.

3. Habermas, *The Historical Jesus*, 153–54.

4. Gary R. Habermas and Antony G. N. Flew, *Did Jesus Rise from the Dead?* (San Francisco: Harper and Row, 1987), 86.

5. Strobel, *The Case for Christ*, 230. See Joachim Jeremias, "Easter: The Earliest Tradition and the Earliest Interpretation," *New Testament Theology: The Proclamation of Jesus*, trans. by John Bowden (New York: Scribner's, 1971), 306; Ulrich Wilckens, *Resurrection* (Atlanta: John Knox Press, 1978), 2.

6. Craig, *Reasonable Faith*, 285; see A. N. Sherwin-White, *Roman Society and Roman Law in the New Testament* (Oxford: Clarendon, 1963), 188–91.

7. Adapted from Craig, *Reasonable Faith*, 285.

8. Herodotus (c. 484–424 B.C.) was an important Greek historian.

9. Craig, *Reasonable Faith*, 285.

10. Julius Müller, *The Theory of Myths, in Its Application to the Gospel History Examined and Confuted* (London: John Chapman, 1844), 26; as quoted in Craig, *Reasonable Faith*, 285.

11. Craig, *Reasonable Faith*, 285 (emphasis added).

12. Strobel, *The Case for Christ*, 233.

13. See 1 Corinthians 15:6. Paul received this creed from the believing community (v. 3), perhaps from Peter and James in Jerusalem (see Galatians 1:18–19), if not sooner (see Habermas, *The Historical Jesus*, 155).

14. C. H. Dodd, "The Appearances of the Risen Christ: A Study in the Form Criticism of the Gospels," in *More New Testament Studies* (Manchester: University of Manchester, 1968), 128; as quoted in Craig, *Reasonable Faith*, 282.

15. Craig, *Reasonable Faith*, 282.

16. Youngblood, *Nelson's New Illustrated Bible Dictionary*, 955.

17. Discussion adapted from Craig, *Reasonable Faith*, 281–83.

18. Ibid., 281–282 (emphasis in original).

19. Ibid., 283. See Josephus, *Antiquities of the Jews*, 20:200.

20. Adapted from Craig, *Reasonable Faith*, 283.

21. Ibid. See Hans Grass, *Ostergeschehen und Osterberichte*, 4th ed. (Gottingen: Vandenhoeck & Ruprecht, 1974), 80.

22. Michael Martin, *The Case Against Christianity* (Philadelphia: Temple University Press, 1991), 94.

23. Ibid., 94–95.

24. Rick Joyner, "The Heart of David: Worship and Warfare," Conference Report (April 1996), audiotape.

25. Ibid.

26. Ibid.

27. Habermas and Flew, *Did Jesus Rise from the Dead*, 50. (Habermas cites personal correspondence from Dr. Collins, 21 February 1977.)

28. Ibid., 51. Habermas also cites J. P. Brady, "The Veridicality of Hypnotic, Visual Hallucinations," in Wolfram Keup, *Origin and*

Mechanisms of Hallucinations, (New York: Plenum Press, 1970), 181; Weston La Barre, "Anthropological Perspectives on Hallucination and Hallucinogens," in *Hallucinations: Behavior, Experience and Theory*, ed. R. K. Siegel and L. J. West (New York: John Wiley and Sons, 1975), 9–10.

29. Strobel, *The Case for Christ*, 239.

30. Craig, *Reasonable Faith*, 292 .

31. Ibid., 292–93. In Jewish thought, the resurrection was only general, after the end of the world, and void of any conception of an isolated resurrection for Messiah (Ibid., 290–91).

32. E.g., Atheist Morton Smith wrote an entire book trying to show that Jesus employed hypnosis and other sociopsychological manipulation tactics to dupe his devotees (see Morton Smith, *Jesus the Magician* [San Francisco: Harper and Row, 1978]).

33. Charles T. Tart, "Transpersonal Potentialities of Deep Hypnosis," *Journal of Transpersonal Psychology*, no. 1 (1970): 37.

34. See Hank Hanegraaff, *Counterfeit Revival: Looking for God in all the Wrong Places* (Dallas: Word Publishing, 1997), Part 5. Discussion adapted from Hanegraaff, *Counterfeit Revival*, 221, 239.

35. Robert W. Marks, *The Story of Hypnotism* (Grand Rapids: Prentice-Hall, 1947), 190.

36. Ibid., 191.

37. Ibid., 193.

38. Ibid., 195.

39. Charles Baudouin, *Suggestion and Autosuggestion* (London: George Allen and Unwin, 1954), 82.

40. Discussion adapted from Hanegraaff, *Counterfeit Revival*, 235–36.

41. Marks, *Story of Hypnotism*, 150.

42. Ibid.

43. Baghwan Shree Rajneesh, *Fear Is the Master*, Jeremiah Films, 1986, video.

44. Carl Braaten, *History and Hermeneutics*, vol. 2 of *New Directions in Theology Today*, ed. William Hordern (Philadelphia: Westminster

Press, 1966), 78; as quoted in Habermas and Flew, *Did Jesus Rise from the Dead?* 24.

45. Elizabeth L. Hillstrom, *Testing the Spirits* (Downers Grove, Ill.: InterVarsity Press, 1995), 79. An all-too-prevalent notion in our culture is that Christians are, by nature, hypersuggestible. Critics put forth the argument that if Christians in the twenty-first century fall for the selling of fear, sloppy journalism, sophistry, and sensationalism surrounding, for example, the so-called "Millennium Bug," then it is just as likely that the first-century followers of Christ were hypersuggestible as well.

46. Gradations of hypnotizability range from zero (almost no hypnotizability) to five (extremely hypnotizable). See Jon Trott, "The Grade Five Syndrome," *Cornerstone*, vol. 20, no. 96. Discussion adapted from Hanegraaff, *Counterfeit Revival*, 237–38.

47. This information was summarized from a variety of sources, including Dr. George Ganaway, "Historical Versus Narrative Truth," *Journal of Dissociation* II, no. 4 (December 1989): 205–20; and Steven Jay Lynn and Judith W. Rhue, "Fantasy Proneness," *American Psychologist* (January 1988): 35–44.

48. Judith W. Rhue and Steven Jay Lynn, "Fantasy Proneness, Hypnotizability, and Multiple Personality" in *Human Suggestibility*, ed. John F. Schumaker (New York: Routledge, 1991), 201.

49. Trott, "The Grade Five Syndrome," 16. Trott writes, "One out of twelve Americans is susceptible to creating a memory out of thin air, then believing it."

50. Habermas and Flew, *Did Jesus Rise from the Dead?* 22.

51. Norman Perrin, *The Resurrection according to Matthew, Mark, and Luke* (Philadelphia: Fortress, 1977), 80, as quoted in Paul Copan, *Will the Real Jesus Please Stand Up?* 28 (emphasis added).

Chapter 5. Transformation

1. Source unknown.

2. Simon Greenleaf, *The Testimony of the Evangelists: The Gospels*

Examined by the Rules of Evidence (Grand Rapids: Kregel Classics, 1995; originally published 1874), 31–32.

3. See 1 Corinthians 15:5, in which the original apostles, minus Judas, are referred to as the Twelve (cf. John 20:24).

4. See Clement of Rome (c. A.D. 30–100), *First Epistle to the Corinthians*, chap. V; Tertullian (c. 160–225), *On Prescription Against Heretics*, chap. XXXVI; Eusebius (c. 260–340), *History of the Church*, Book II: XXV.

5. See Eusebius, *History of the Church*, Book III: I, where Eusebius quotes Origen (c. 185–254) concerning Peter's crucifixion.

6. Kenneth Barker, gen. ed., *The NIV Study Bible* (Grand Rapids: Zondervan, 1985), 1879.

7. Eusebius, Bk. II: XXIII. Cf. Josephus, *Antiquities*, 20:9:1; see John P. Meier, *A Marginal Jew: Rethinking the Historical Jesus*, vol. 1 (New York: Doubleday, 1991), 57–59.

8. Strobel, *The Case for Christ*, 251.

9. Norman Geisler and Thomas Howe, *When Critics Ask* (Wheaton: Victor Books, 1992), 78. See Matthew 28:1–10; John 20:26ff; Acts 2:1; 20:7; 1 Corinthians 16:2.

10. Discussion adapted from Lee Strobel, *The Case for Christ*, 251, 253.

11. "Proselytes entering Judaism were expected to strip themselves of their former clothing, submit to circumcision, and bathe themselves completely, after which they were reckoned members of the Jewish community. The rite was acknowledgment of defilement and of the acceptance of the law as a purifying agent." (Carl F. H. Henry, ed., *Basic Christian Doctrines* [Grand Rapids: Baker Book House, 1971], 256.)

12. See also Matthew 28:19; Acts 8:16; 10:48; 19:5; Romans 6:3–5; 1 Corinthians 6:11.

13. Adapted from Strobel, *The Case for Christ*, 253.

Chapter 6. Physical Resurrection of Believers to Eternal Life

1. Adapted from Peter Kreeft, *Everything You Ever Wanted to Know about Heaven . . . But Never Dreamed of Asking* (San Francisco: Ignatius Press, 1990), 84–85.

2. Joni Eareckson Tada, *Heaven . . . Your Real Home* (Grand Rapids: Zondervan, 1995), 33.

3. Ibid., 33–34.

4. Ibid., 34.

5. Norman L. Geisler, *The Battle for the Resurrection* (Nashville: Thomas Nelson Publishers, 1992), 63 (emphasis in original).

6. Ibid. (emphasis in original).

7. Eareckson Tada, *Heaven . . . Your Real Home*, 36–37.

8. DNA provides one possible means for explaining the blueprint for the resurrection body.

9. Scripture makes it clear, however, that graves will be emptied (see Matthew 28:6; John 5:28–29; cf. Matthew 27:52–53). It is possible that God will use new particles, in part, in resurrecting our bodies, but most assuredly he will utilize those particles from our current bodies that are *available* (e.g., bones). Cf. Ezekiel 37:1–14.

10. Peter Kreeft describes continuity as follows:

    "Body is form. Even now what makes our bodies our bodies is not atoms but structure. The atoms change every seven years; yet it is the same body because of its continuity of form. ('Continuity' does not mean 'unchangingness,' of course.)

    " . . . My body is its form, not its atoms. This form is not just outer shape but life, animating principle. The Greek word often translated 'form,' *logos*, comes from *legein*, which means to collect, gather, or make one. Once the form (soul) departs, this unity departs: the atoms, molecules, tissues, and organs of the body begin to disintegrate and scatter" (*Everything You Ever Wanted to Know about Heaven*, 95–96).

11. Norman L. Geisler, *Baker Encyclopedia of Christian Apologetics* (Grand Rapids: Baker Book House, 1999), 658.

12. Ibid. Augustine writes of the spiritual body: "They will be spiritual, not because they shall cease to be bodies, but because they shall subsist by the quickening spirit" (*The City of God*, XIII:22, in Philip Schaff, ed., *Nicene and Post-Nicene Fathers*, First Series,

vol. II [Grand Rapids: Wm. B. Eerdmans Publishing Co., reprinted 1983], 257). When Paul says, "flesh and blood cannot inherit the kingdom of God," (1 Corinthians 15:50), he is not denying the physical nature of the resurrection. Rather, he is using a common Jewish metaphor to express mortality. "Flesh and blood" is "perishable," while the "kingdom of God" is "imperishable." His point is that it would be impossible for mortal humans to inherit the new heaven and new earth without a metamorphosis. Edmond C. Gruss writes that the expression *flesh and blood* "appears in four other places in the New Testament (Matt. 16:17; Gal. 1:16; Eph. 6:12; Heb. 2:14. The words in the last two verses are inverted). In all the passages just mentioned, it is obvious from the context that 'flesh and blood does not denote the substance of the human body.' What then is the meaning? It is an expression which 'belongs to the Rabbinic vocabulary' which placed 'particular emphasis on man's earthly condition as a frail and perishable creature, in contrast to the eternal and almighty God.' What then is the meaning of 'flesh and blood cannot inherit God's kingdom'? Just what Paul says is the meaning, namely, that a change is necessary (15:51, 52): ['For the perishable must clothe itself with the imperishable, and the mortal with immortality' (v.53)]. The passage does not teach that one must be deprived of a body of flesh, but that the body must be changed to fit it for the new realm where it will spend eternity. . . . Christ's body was changed to fit it for heaven. Christ's body was a glorified body of 'flesh and bones' (Luke 24:39)." (Edmond Charles Gruss, *Apostles of Denial* [Grand Rapids: Baker Book House, 1978 reprint], 136–37.)

13. Kreeft, *Everything You Ever Wanted to Know about Heaven*, 90.

14. Ibid., 91.

15. Anthony A. Hoekema, *The Bible and the Future* (Grand Rapids: Wm. B. Eerdmans Publishing Co., 1979), 250.

16. Geisler, *The Battle for the Resurrection*, 109–10.

Chapter 7. Physical Resurrection of Unbelievers to Eternal Torment

1. Leland Ryken, James C. Wilhoit, Tremper Longman III, gen. ed., *Dictionary of Biblical Imagery* (Downers Grove, Ill.: InterVarsity Press, 1998), 376.
2. R. C. Sproul, *Essential Truths of the Christian Faith* (Wheaton: Tyndale House Publishers, 1992), 286.
3. Dante Alighieri, *Inferno*, Canto III:7.
4. This passage teaches the physical resurrection of both believers and unbelievers. The biblical arguments for the continuity and physicality of the believer's resurrection body apply to the unbeliever as well. Thus, even those in hell will have imperishable physical bodies. (See pp. 68–74 for a discussion of the nature of the resurrection body.) Dr. Norman Geisler notes, "Hell is . . . depicted as a place of eternal fire. This fire is *real* but not necessarily *physical* (as we know it), because people will have imperishable physical bodies (John 5:28–29; Revelation 20:13–15), so normal fire would not affect them. Further, the figures of speech that describe hell are contradictory, if taken in a physical sense. It has *flames*, yet it is outer *darkness*. It is a dump (with a *bottom*), yet a *bottomless* pit. While everything in the Bible is literally true, not everything is true literally." (*Baker Encyclopedia of Christian Apologetics*, 312, emphasis in original.)
5. See Matthew 5:22, 29, 30; 7:13, 19, 23. To these explicit warnings about hell, Christ added many implicit warnings as well in his Sermon on the Mount (see Matthew 5:13, 19, 20, 26; 6:15; 7:27; cf. Matthew 5:18; 6:30).
6. Geisler, *Baker Encyclopedia of Christian Apologetics*, 313.
7. Kreeft, *Everything You Ever Wanted to Know about Heaven*, 218.
8. C. S. Lewis, *The Problem of Pain* (New York: Collier Books, 1962), 118.
9. Geisler, *Baker Encyclopedia of Christian Apologetics*, 314–15.

10. Ibid., 313–14.

11. Ibid., 311.

12. Jonathan Edwards, *The Works of Jonathan Edwards* (Edinburgh, Great Britain: The Banner of Truth Trust, reprinted 1992), 883–84.

13. Kreeft, *Everything You Ever Wanted to Know about Heaven*, 226.

14. Gary R. Habermas and J. P. Moreland, *Beyond Death: Exploring the Evidence for Immortality* (Wheaton: Crossway Books, 1998), 296.

15. Geisler, *Baker Encyclopedia of Christian Apologetics*, 314.

16. Habermas and Moreland, *Beyond Death*, 309. See Luke 12:47–48.

17. Lewis, *The Problem of Pain*, 118–19 (emphasis in original).

18. C. S. Lewis, *The Great Divorce* (New York: Collier Books, 1946), 72. Also quoted in Geisler, *Baker Encyclopedia of Christian Apologetics*, 311.

Chapter 8. Physical "Resurrection" of the Cosmos

1. John Piper, *Future Grace* (Sisters, Ore.: Multnomah Publishers, 1995), 374.

2. Anthony A. Hoekema, *The Bible and the Future* (Grand Rapids: Wm. B. Eerdmans Publishing Co., 1979), 280. Cf. G. K. Beale, who writes: "In the light of the qualitative nature of the contrast between 'new' creation and 'first' creation, it is likely that the meaning of the figurative portrayal is to connote a radically changed cosmos, involving not merely ethical renovation but transformation of the fundamental cosmic structure (including physical elements). Furthermore, 'there will be no more night' ([Revelation] 22:5; cf. 21:25), which indicates another difference, especially in contrast to Gen. 8:22: 'While the earth remains . . . day and night will not cease.'

"Despite the discontinuities, the new cosmos will be an identifiable counterpart to the old cosmos and a renewal of it, just as the body will be raised without losing its former identity (*b. Sanhedrin* 92a-b and *Midr.* Pss. 104.24 see the future resurrection of the body as part of the larger 'renewal' of the earth). That a renewal or renovation is in mind is evident from 21:5: 'I make all things new' (so likewise in Jewish writings . . .). The allusions to Isaiah . . . in 21:1, 4–5 probably understand Isaiah as prophesying the transformation of the old creation rather than an outright new creation *ex nihilo.*" (*The Book of Revelation* [Grand Rapids: Wm. B. Eerdmans Publishing Co., 1999], 1040.)

3. Piper, *Future Grace,* 376 (emphasis in original).
4. Ibid., 378.
5. J. A. Schep, *The Nature of the Resurrection Body* (Grand Rapids: Wm. B. Eerdmans Publishing Co., 1964), 218–19. Schep writes, "The world to come is a *new* world, so thoroughly different from the present that any adequate description or conception of it is utterly impossible. It is a world so entirely different from ours that Scripture can say that God will *create* new heavens and a new earth. The creative power of almighty God is needed to bring about this change.

    "Nevertheless, it is *this* world that will be redeemed. Romans 8:18ff. shows that there is the closest connection between the redemption of creation and that of our bodies. The two will take place simultaneously (vv. 21, 23). The redemption of our bodies . . . does not mean the annihilation of our present bodies and their replacement by newly created ones, but rather their . . . renewal, glorification. In the same way this present creation would not be truly 'delivered from the bondage of corruption' (v. 21) if it were to be destroyed and replaced by something utterly different, without any material connection with this present world. Here also we may expect . . . renewal, glorification.

    "It is on *this* earth, transformed by God's almighty power into a suitable dwelling place for believers in their glorified bodies, that 'God himself shall be with them, and be their God . . . ' (Revelation 21:3ff.).

    "It is *this* earth that the meek will inherit, according to the promise of Jesus (Matthew 5:5)." (Ibid., 218 [emphasis in original].)

6. Hoekema, *The Bible and the Future*, 281. Hoekema adds, "The view that the new earth will be the present earth renewed is clearly affirmed by a well-known Reformed creed, the Belgic Confession, Art. 37, par. 1; [Christ will return] 'burning this old world with fire and flame to cleanse it.'"

7. Piper, *Future Grace*, 377–78.

8. Eareckson Tada, *Heaven . . . Your Real Home*, 68–71.

9. Lewis, *The Great Divorce*, 28, 30; quoted in Eareckson Tada, *Heaven . . . Your Real Home*, 71.

10. Dr. Anthony Hoekema argues that the expression "heaven and earth" in both Isaiah 65:17 and in Revelation 21:1 "should be understood as a biblical way of designating the entire universe: 'Heaven and earth together constitute the cosmos'" (*The Bible and the Future*, 279).

Chapter 9. Physicality: *Was Christ's Physical Body Resurrected from the Dead or Did He Rise an Immaterial Spirit?*

1. Thomas Jefferson, *The Jefferson Bible* (Boston: Beacon Press, 1989), 147. Also quoted in Geisler, *The Battle for the Resurrection*, 69.

2. *The Truth Shall Make You Free* (Brooklyn: Watchtower Bible and Tract Society, 1943), 264.

3. *Let God Be True*, second edition (Brooklyn: Watchtower Bible and Tract Society, 1952), 138.

4. J. F. Rutherford, *The Harp of God* (Brooklyn: Watchtower Bible and Tract Society, 1921), 172. Cf. *The Kingdom Is at Hand* (Brooklyn: Watchtower Bible and Tract Society, 1944), 258–59; *Reasoning from the Scriptures* (Brooklyn: Watchtower Bible and Tract Society, 1985), 334.

5. Christian philosopher and apologist Dr. Norman Geisler has identified three essential characteristics of the bodily resurrection of Christ that are commonly compromised, confused or contradicted.

Historicity. It has become common for neoorthodox theologians to assert that Christ's resurrection was *supra*-historical (that it happened outside of history). In truth, however, Christ's resurrection was a historical event that took place in our space-time continuum. From the embryonic stages of Christianity to the present it has always been affirmed as happening "on the third day" (1 Corinthians 15:4). Says Geisler, "Regardless of the supernatural nature of the event, the resurrection was as much a part of history as was His incarnation before His death" (*The Battle for the Resurrection*, 64).

Identity. Today the orthodox Christian perspective of identity or the one-to-one correspondence between the body of Christ that died and the body that rose is under siege. Orthodox Christians, however, have always affirmed numeric identity. As Geisler notes, "It has always been part of orthodox belief to acknowledge that Jesus was raised immortal in the *same physical body* in which he died. That is, *His resurrection body was numerically the same as His pre-resurrection body*" (Ibid., 63; emphasis in original).

Materiality. Like historicity and identity, the material nature of Christ's resurrection body is axiomatic to Christianity. As Geisler puts it: "The orthodox fathers unanimously confessed belief in 'the *resurrection of the flesh*.' They believed that flesh was essential to human nature and that Jesus, being fully human, was not only incarnated in, but also resurrected in, the same human flesh He had before His death. A resurrected body can be seen with the naked eye. If a picture were taken of it, the image would appear on the film. As Anselm affirmed, it is just as material as Adam's body was and would have remained if Adam had not sinned. It was so physical that were someone to have seen it arise in the tomb, it would have caused dust to fall off the slab from which it arose!" (Ibid.; emphasis in original)

6. Justin Martyr, *Fragments of the Lost Work of Justin on the Resurrection*, ch. II, in Alexander Roberts and James Donaldson, eds., *The Ante-*

Nicene Fathers, vol. I (Grand Rapids: Wm. B. Eerdmans Publishing Co., reprinted 1985), 295. Also quoted in Geisler, *The Battle for the Resurrection*, 53.

7. Cyril of Jerusalem, *The Catechetical Lectures*, XIV:21, in Philip Schaff and Henry Wace, eds., *Nicene and Post-Nicene Fathers*, Second Series, vol. VII (Grand Rapids: Wm. B. Eerdmans Publishing Co., reprinted 1983), 99. Also quoted in Geisler, *The Battle for the Resurrection*, 56.

8. St. Augustine, *City of God*, XXII: 5, in Schaff, *Nicene and Post-Nicene Fathers*, 481. Also quoted in Geisler, *The Battle for the Resurrection*, 57.

9. Thomas Aquinas, *Summa Contra Gentiles*, IV:79; as quoted in Geisler, *The Battle for the Resurrection*, 59. See http://books.mirror.org/ gb.aquinas.html.

10. The Belgic Confession, in Philip Schaff, *The Creeds of Christendom*, vol. III (Grand Rapids: Baker Book House, reprinted 1985), 433–34. Also quoted in Geisler, *The Battle for the Resurrection*, 61.

11. The Westminster Confession of Faith, in Schaff, *The Creeds of Christendom*, vol. III, 621. Also quoted in Geisler, *The Battle for the Resurrection*, 62.

Chapter 10. Soul: *Does the Soul Continue to Exist after the Death of the Body?*

1. Matt is not his real name.

2. Some might try to argue that the mind is identical to the brain because the brain has a causal connection to the mind, or vice versa. However, Dr. J. P. Moreland and Dr. Gary Habermas explain: "It may be that for every mental activity, a neurophysiologist can find a physical activity in the brain with which it is correlated. But just because A causes B (or vice versa), or just because A and B are constantly correlated with each other, that does not mean that A is *identical to* B. . . . Therefore, and this is critical, physicalism [which holds that humans are completely physical without a mental component] cannot be established on the basis that mental

states and brain states are causally related or constantly conjoined with each other in an embodied person. *Physicalism needs identity* [between the mind and brain] *to make its case, and if something is true or possibly true of a mental substance, property, or event that is not true or possibly true of a physical substance, property, or event, then physicalism is false*" (Habermas and Moreland, *Beyond Death*, 48; emphasis added).

3. Ibid., 52.

4. Moreland and Habermas explain: "Mental events are feelings of pain, episodes of thoughts, or sensory experiences. Physical events are happenings in the brain and central nervous system that can be described exhaustively using terms from chemistry and physics. However, physical events and their properties do not have the same features as do mental events and their properties. . . . An experiment will help you see the difference. Picture a pink elephant in your mind. Now close your eyes and look at the image. In your mind, you will see a pink property (a sense datum or a sensory way of experiencing). There will be no pink elephant outside you, but there will be a pink image of one in your mind. However, there will be no pink entity in your brain; no neurophysiologist could open your brain and see a pink entity while you are having the sense image. The sensory event has a property—pink—that no brain event has. Therefore, they cannot be identical. The sense image is a mental entity, not a physical one" (Habermas and Moreland, *Beyond Death*, 49).

5. Ibid., 59.

6. Moreland and Habermas write, "Physicalists and property dualists [property dualists hold that the mind, while distinct from the brain, is a property or attribute of the brain and the mind depends on the brain for its existence] have no alternative but to hold that personal identity through change is not absolute"(Habermas and Moreland, *Beyond Death*, 58). In essence, they are relegated to the unenviable task of trying to rationalize what are called "person-stages"; the "self" is really a contiguous series through time of

closely resembling but not identical "selves". Continuity of self can be accounted for only by positing an immaterial self, i.e., a soul (see Ibid., 57–60).

7. See Ibid., 60–62.

8. Greg Cesario, former PGA tour member and National Product and Sales Manager for Titleist and Foot-Joy Worldwide.

9. Dr. J. P. Moreland (who has greatly enhanced and expanded my thinking on the existence and nature of the soul) and Dr. Gary Habermas define the human soul as "a substantial, unified reality that informs its body. The soul is to the body what God is to space—it is fully 'present' at each point within the body. The soul occupies the body, but it is not spatially located within it, just as God occupies space but is not spatially located within it." Moreland and Habermas further point out that to say the soul occupies the body means "that it has *direct, immediate* conscious awareness of each and every part of the body, and it can *directly* and *immediately* will to move the various parts of the body" (Habermas and Moreland, *Beyond Death*, 68, emphasis in original).

10. While biblically we continue to exist in a conscious state after the death of our physical bodies, we are not complete until we are reunited with our resurrected bodies (see Philippians 1:23; 2 Corinthians 5:8; Revelation 6:9). The sum substance of the self is a *psyche/soma*—a soul and a body.

11. Discussion and endnotes adapted from Hank Hanegraaff, *The FACE That Demonstrates the Farce of Evolution* (Nashville: Word Publishing, 1998), chaps. 4 and 5.

12. Michael J. Behe, *Darwin's Black Box: The Biochemical Challenge to Evolution* (New York: The Free Press, 1996), 22.

13. *The Wonders of God's Creation: Planet Earth*, vol. 1 (Chicago: Moody Institute of Science, 1993), videotape.

14. Fred Heeren, *Show Me God*, rev. ed. (Wheeling, Ill.: Day Star, 1997), 88.

15. Henry M. Morris, *Scientific Creationism*, public school edition (San Diego: C.L.P. Publishers, 1981), 19–20.

16. Kenneth Boa and Larry Moody, *I'm Glad You Asked* (Wheaton: Victor Books, 1982), 38–39.

17. See Carl Sagan, *Cosmos* (New York: Random House, 1980), 4.

18. Source unknown. A solipsist is a person who believes that the self is the only thing that exists.

19. The law of entropy is a bullet to the head of evolution. Not only is the universe dying of heat loss, but according to entropy—also known as the second law of thermodynamics—everything runs inexorably from order to disorder and from complexity to decay. The theory of biological evolution directly contradicts the law of entropy in that it describes a universe in which things run from chaos to complexity and order. In evolution, atoms allegedly self-produce amino acids, amino acids auto-organize amebas, amebas turn into apes, and apes evolve into astronauts.

   Mathematician and physicist Sir Arthur Eddington demonstrated that exactly the opposite is true: The energy of the universe irreversibly flows from hot to cold bodies (Heeren, 129). The sun burns up billions of tons of hydrogen each second, stars burn out and species eventually become extinct (Heeren, 129). Evolution requires constant violations of the second law of thermodynamics in order to be plausible. In the words of Eddington, "If your theory is found to be against the second law of thermodynamics I can give you no hope; there is nothing for it but to collapse in deepest humiliation" (Arthur S. Eddington, *The Nature of the Physical World* [New York: Macmillan, 1930], 74; as quoted in Scott M. Huse, *The Collapse of Evolution*, 3rd ed. [Grand Rapids: Baker Book House, 1997], 113).

   Rather than humbling themselves in light of the second law of thermodynamics, evolutionists dogmatically attempt to discredit or dismiss it. They contend that the law of entropy cannot be invoked because it merely deals with energy relationships of matter, while evolution deals with complex life forms arising from simpler ones. This, of course, is patently false. As a case in point, contemporary information theory deals with information entropy and militates against evolution on a genetic level (see A. E. Wilder-Smith, *The Natural Sciences Know Nothing of Evolution* [Costa Mesa, Calif.: T.W.F.T. Publishers, 1981], 69–73). While in an energy conversion system, entropy dictates that energy will decay; however, in an informational system, entropy dictates that information will become distorted. As noted in *Scientific American*, "It is certain that the conceptual connection between information and the second law of thermodynamics is now firmly established" (Myron Tribus and Edward C. McIrvine, "Energy and Information," *Scientific American* 224 [September 1971]: 188; as quoted in Morris, *Scientific Creationism*, 39 [see 38–40]).

It is boldly asserted that entropy does not prevent evolution on earth, since this planet is an open system that receives energy from the sun. This, of course, is nonsense. The sun's rays never produce an upswing in complexity without teleonomy (the ordering principle of life). In other words, energy from the sun does not produce an orderly structure of growth and development without information and an engine (see Morris, *Scientific Creationism*, 43–46). If the sun beats down on a dead plant, it does not produce growth, but rather speeds up decay. If, on the other hand, the sun beats down on a living plant, it produces a temporary increase in complexity and growth. In the *Origins* film series, Dr. A. E. Wilder-Smith explains that the difference between a dead stick and a live orchid is that the orchid has teleonomy, which is information that makes the live orchid an energy-capturing and order-increasing machine (Willem J. J. Glashouwer and Paul S. Taylor, *The Origin of the Universe*, videotape [Mesa, Ariz.: Eden, 1983]). Adapted from Hanegraaff, *The FACE That Demonstrates the Farce of Evolution*, 85–87.

20. Thousands of years before empirical science formally codified the law of entropy, however, Scripture clearly communicated it. The prophet Isaiah and King David both declared that the heavens and the earth would "wear out like a garment" (Isaiah 51:6; Psalm 102:25–26). Likewise, in the first century, the apostle Paul

looked forward to the day when "the creation itself will be liberated from its *bondage to decay*" (Romans 8:21; emphasis added).

21. Strobel, *The Case for Christ*, 251.

22. Geisler, *Baker Encyclopedia of Christian Apologetics*, 354.

Chapter 11. Timing: *Do Believers Receive Resurrected Bodies When They Die or When Christ Returns?*

1. Geisler, *The Battle for the Resurrection*, 211.

2. Ibid., 212.

3. Ibid., 213.

4. Ibid., 212.

5. Theologian Millard Erickson writes, "Paul . . . makes clear that the view that resurrection has already occurred, that is, in the form of a spiritual resurrection not incompatible with the fact that the bodies are still lying in their graves, is a *heresy*. He makes this point when he condemns the views of Hymenaeus and Philetus, 'who have swerved from the truth by holding that the resurrection is past already. They are upsetting the faith of some' (2 Timothy 2:18)" (*Christian Theology* [Grand Rapids: Baker Book House, 1985], 1197 [emphasis added]).

6. Geisler, *The Battle for the Resurrection*, 211 (emphasis in original).

Chapter 12. Boring: *If Heaven Is Perfect, Won't It Be Perfectly Boring?*

1. Kreeft, *Everything You Ever Wanted to Know about Heaven*, 27.

2. A. A. Hodge, *Evangelical Theology*; as quoted in Peter Toon, *Heaven and Hell* (Nashville: Thomas Nelson Publishers, 1986), 158.

3. Toon, *Heaven and Hell*, 158.

4. Kreeft, *Everything You Ever Wanted to Know about Heaven*, 28.

Chapter 13. Animals: *Will God Raise Pets and Platypuses from the Dead?*

1. Joni Eareckson Tada, *Holiness in Hidden Places* (Nashville: J. Countryman, 1999), 133.

2. Ibid., 135.

3. Ibid., 133.

4. Both the Hebrew noun (*nephesh*) and the Greek noun (*psyche*) specifically refer to the essence of life.

5. Habermas and Moreland, *Beyond Death*,107.

6. See Ernst Mayr, *This Is Biology* (Cambridge, Mass.: The Belknap Press, 1999), 8–9; John W. Cooper, *Body, Soul, and Life Everlasting* (Grand Rapids: Wm. B. Eerdmans Publishing Co., 1989), 17–22.

7. Habermas and Moreland, *Beyond Death*, 106.

8. While I have significant theological differences with both Lewis and Kreeft, I greatly admire their writing prowess, mental acumen, and philosophical sophistication.

9. Lewis, *The Problem of Pain*, 139–40.

10. Ibid., 141.

11. Kreeft, *Everything You Ever Wanted to Know about Heaven*, 45.

12. Ibid., 45–46.

Chapter 14. Reincarnation: *Are Reincarnation and Resurrection Mutually Exclusive?*

1. Adapted from Hank Hanegraaff, "Is Jesus the Only Way?" *Christian Research Journal* (Summer 1995): 50.

2. John Leo, "I Was Beheaded in the 1700s," *Time* (10 September 1984): 68.

3. Ibid.

4. Geisler, *Baker Encyclopedia of Christian Apologetics*, 639. According to a 1994 Barna Research Group survey on reincarnation, 18 percent of Americans in general and 7 percent of "born again Christians" agreed with the following statement: "After death people are reincarnated, that is they return to life in another form" (phone conversation with Barna Research Group representative, 17 November 1999).

5. See, e.g., Sybil Leek, *Reincarnation: The Second Chance* (New York Stein and Day Publishers, 1974), 161–62.

6. See, e.g., Quincy Howe Jr., *Reincarnation for the Christian* (Philadelphia: The Westminster Press, 1974), 93–94.

7. See, e.g., Ibid., 94–96.

8. According to reincarnation, anyone who helps the blind or beggars is working against the law of karma. The downtrodden must work off their own karmic debts. Thus, by healing the blind man, Jesus would have caused him more suffering in a future incarnation.

9. John the Baptist came "in the spirit and power" of Elijah's ministry (Luke 1:17). Other passages typically cited are just as easy to explain. For example, it is suggested that Jesus is referring to reincarnation in John 3:3 when he says, "except a man be born again, he cannot see the kingdom of God." In reality, the context of John 3 refers to spiritual, rather than physical rebirth.

10. Geisler, *Baker Encyclopedia of Christian Apologetics*, 643.

Chapter 15. Cremation: *Is Cremation Commensurate with the Christian Concept of Resurrection?*

1. Norman L. Geisler and Douglas E. Potter, "From Ashes to Ashes: Is Burial the Only Christian Option?" *Christian Research Journal* (July–September 1998): 29.

2. Ibid., 33.

3. Ibid., 33–34.

4. See Ibid., 31–35 for a full-orbed defense of the arguments against cremation and for burial.

5. In 1 Corinthians 15:3–6, Paul is repeating a creedal statement that can be traced back to the formative stages of the early Christian church, see pp. 38–40.

6. For a fuller discussion regarding reincarnation, see pp. 123–28.

7. Geisler and Potter, "From Ashes to Ashes," 34 (emphasis in original).

8. Ibid., 34. See Genesis 1:27; 9:6; cf. 1 Corinthians 6:19–20.

9. A note of reassurance: God will resurrect and glorify all believers, including those who have been cremated.

Chapter 16. Age: *Will We Be Resurrected at the Same Age That We Died?*

1. The natural reading of the Genesis account indicates that Adam was not created as an infant or child, but created physically mature directly from "the dust of the ground": "The LORD God formed the man from the dust of the ground and breathed into his nostrils the breath of life, and the man became a living being" (Genesis 2:7). Similarly, God created Eve physically mature directly from part of Adam's side: "The LORD God caused the man to fall into a deep sleep; and while he was sleeping, he took one of the man's ribs and closed up the place with flesh. Then the LORD God made a woman from the rib he had taken out of the man, and he brought her to the man" (Genesis 2:21–22).

2. Luke tells us Jesus began his earthly ministry at about age thirty (see Luke 3:23), thus Jesus must have died in his thirties. His resurrected body looked enough like his earthly body to be fully recognizable by his disciples (see Luke 24:31, 35; John 20:14–16, 27–28). Concerning the issue that some of the disciples did not initially recognize Jesus in his post-resurrection appearances, Dr. Norman Geisler writes, "The initial inability to recognize Jesus may have been due in part to the fact that the disciples were spiritually dull (Luke 24:25–26) and disbelieving (John 20:24–25). However, the fact that they eventually recognized Him from His appearance, voice, scars, and the like is ample indication that He was resurrected in the same physical body in which He had died" (*The Battle for the Resurrection*, 46).

3. This refers to the original intention God had for our DNA before the Fall. It should also be noted that to say our DNA comprises the blueprints for our glorified bodies is based on sanctified speculation—if this is the case it would justify believing that those who die as infants and those who die in old age will be resurrected physically mature and perfect, as God had originally intended them to be.

4. Justin Martyr, *Fragments of the Lost Work of Justin on the Resurrection*,

ch. IV, in Alexander Roberts and James Donaldson, eds., *The Ante-Nicene Fathers*, vol. I (Grand Rapids: Wm. B. Eerdmans Publishing Co., reprinted 1985), 295.

5. Kreeft, *Everything You Ever Wanted to Know about Heaven*, 99 (emphasis in original).

Chapter 17. Sex: *Will There Be Sex after the Resurrection?*

1. *The Student Bible* (Grand Rapids: Zondervan, 1986), 598.
2. Ed Young, *Pure Sex* (Sisters, Ore.: Multnomah Publishers, 1997), 21–22 (emphasis in original).
3. Kreeft, *Everything You Ever Wanted to Know about Heaven*, 118–19.
4. Ibid., 119.
5. In his post-resurrection appearances, Jesus appeared to the disciples in the very body in which he was crucified (see pp. 95–99).
6. Kreeft, *Everything You Ever Wanted to Know about Heaven*, 131.
7. C. S. Lewis, *Miracles* (New York: Collier Books, 1960), 159–60.
8. Kreeft, *Everything You Ever Wanted to Know about Heaven*, 127.
9. Ibid., 128 (emphasis in original).
10. Ibid., 121 (emphasis in original). Kreeft notes that "Saint Paul's frequently quoted statement that 'in Christ . . . there is neither male nor female' [Galatians 3:28] does not mean there is no sex in Heaven. For it refers not just to Heaven but also to earth: we are 'in Christ' *now* [Galatians 2:20]. (In fact, if we are not 'in Christ' now there is no hope of Heaven for us!) But we *are* male or female now. His point is that our sex does not determine our 'in-Christness'; God is an equal opportunity employer. But He employs the men and women He created, not the neuters of our imagination." (Ibid., 122, emphasis in original.)
11. Thomas Aquinas, *Summa Theologiae*, I, I, 8 ad 2; as quoted in Kreeft, *Everything You Ever Wanted to Know about Heaven*, 121.
12. Kreeft, *Everything You Ever Wanted to Know about Heaven*, 128.
13. In saying that we will be like the angels, Jesus is not suggesting that we will be like angels in every way. For example, angels are non-

physical, while, from a biblical perspective, we will clearly be physical in the resurrection (see pp. 68–69).

14. Lewis, *Miracles*, 160.

Chapter 18. Rewards: *What about Rewards in the Resurrection?*

1. Discussion and quotes adapted from "Yardage Guide" (Pebble Beach, Calif.: Cypress Point Club, 1999).

2. Christian theologian Millard Erickson puts it this way: "A bit of speculation may be in order at this point. . . . Speculation is a legitimate theological activity, as long as we are aware that we are speculating. May it not be that the difference in the rewards [in heaven] lies not in the external or objective circumstances, but in the subjective awareness or appreciation of those circumstances? Thus, all would engage in the same activity, for example, worship, but some would enjoy it much more than others. Perhaps those who have enjoyed worship more in this life will find greater satisfaction in it in the life beyond than will others. An analogy here is the varying degrees of pleasure which different people derive from a concert. The same sound waves fall on everyone's ears, but the reactions may range from boredom . . . to ecstasy. A similar situation may well hold with respect to the joys of heaven, although the range of reactions will presumably be narrower. No one will be aware of the differences in range of enjoyment, and thus there will be no dimming of the perfection of heaven by regret over wasted opportunities" (*Christian Theology*, 1234).

3. Hoekema, *The Bible and the Future*, 261.

4. Hoekema explains, "When one has studied music and has attained some proficiency in playing a musical instrument, his capacity for enjoying music has been greatly increased. In a similar way, our devotion to Christ and to service in his kingdom increases our capacity for enjoying the blessings of that kingdom, both now and

in the life to come. Leon Morris puts it aptly: 'Here and now the man who gives himself wholeheartedly to the service of Christ knows more of the joy of the Lord than the half-hearted. We have no warrant from the New Testament for thinking that it will be otherwise in heaven'" (*The Bible and the Future*, 264).

5. Hoekema explains that "a pound here stands for an amount of money equal to about three months' wages for a laborer" (*The Bible and the Future*, 262). The King James Version translates the Greek word as "pound"; the New International Version transliterates it as "mina."

6. Hoekema, *The Bible and the Future*, 262–63.

7. I am in no way communicating that we work for our salvation— we are saved by grace alone through faith alone because of Christ alone (see Romans 4:3–5; Ephesians 2:8–9). Rather, our works are the evidence that our faith is genuine and that we have been saved. John Piper illustrates the role of our works in the final judgment: "Recall the story of how two harlots brought a baby to King Solomon, each claiming that the baby was hers (1 Kings 3:16–27). They asked King Solomon to act as judge between them. In his extraordinary wisdom, he said that a sword should be brought, and that the baby should be divided, with half given to the one woman and half to the other. The true mother cried out, 'O, my Lord, give her the living child, and by no means kill him.' Solomon said, 'give [this] woman the living child . . . she is the mother.' What was Solomon looking for? He was *not* looking for a deed that would earn the child, or would *create* a relationship that didn't already exist. He was looking for a deed that would *demonstrate* what was already true, namely, that the child was truly this woman's child by birth. That is the way God looks at our deeds on the judgment day. He is not looking for deeds that purchase our pardon in his judgment hall. He is looking for deeds that prove we are already enjoying the fruits of our pardon. . . . The purchase of our salvation was the blood of Jesus, sufficient

once for all to cover all our sins. We do not add to the worth of his righteousness imputed to us by God for our justification" (*Future Grace*, 366–67, emphasis in original).

8. It should be noted that, in context, Paul is writing to slaves who had little incentive to work for earthly masters who rarely allowed them to share in the fruit of their labors. Thus, Paul encourages them to look beyond the temporary to the eternal. It is also noteworthy that slavery in the context of Scripture is not always charged with the same sociological overtones as in our society. In Scripture, slavery was frequently a direct result of economic hardship. Because bankruptcy laws were not in vogue, when people got into financial problems they sold themselves as slaves to discharge their debt. Thus, whether you were a doctor or a doorman you would use your skills to repay your debt. Also, unlike slavery in America, the slavery of the ancients was not typically tied to race. In any case, from the perspective of Scripture, "There is neither Jew nor Greek, slave nor free, male nor female," but we are all one in Christ (Galatians 3:28). However, lest one think Scripture encourages slavery, Paul puts "slavetraders" in the category of murders, adulterers, perverts, liars, and perjurers (1 Timothy 1:10).

9. *The Student Bible*, 1076.

10. Eareckson Tada, *Heaven . . . Your Real Home*, 59–60.

Epilogue

1. Philip Schaff, *The Person of Christ* (n.p.: American Tract Society, 1913), as quoted in McDowell, *The New Evidence That Demands a Verdict*, 15.

Appendix A. Receiving the Resurrected Redeemer

1. Adapted from Hanegraaff, *The FACE That Demonstrates the Farce of Evolution*, 108–20.

2. Romans 3:9–20 shows that all people, Jew or Gentile, atheist or pagan, are separated from God by their sin. Romans 3:23 uses the

same theme but refers specifically to sinners who, by the grace of God, are not condemned, but redeemed.

3. Regarding Christ's claims to be God in human flesh, see Mark 2:1–12; 14:61–63; John 5:16–20; 8:58. For a helpful treatment of the doctrines of the deity of Christ and the Trinity, see White, *The Forgotten Trinity*.

4. Some argue that this verse applies only to believers. However, I'm convinced that anyone who takes the time to examine Revelation 3 in context would agree that the church of Laodicea was spiritually pitiful, poor, blind, and naked. While in context the passage is applied to the Laodicean church corporately, it most certainly has personal application as well.

Appendix B. Resurrection of Christ

1. Selected Scripture passages

Appendix C. Resurrection of Creation

1. Selected Scripture passages

BIBLIOGRAPHY

✢

Books

Aid to Bible Understanding. Brooklyn: Watchtower Bible and Tract Society, 1971.

Albrecht, Mark C. *Reincarnation.* Downers Grove, Ill.: InterVarsity Press, 1982.

Ankerberg, John, and John Weldon. *Encyclopedia of New Age Beliefs.* Eugene, Ore.: Harvest House Publishers, 1996.

Aquinas, Thomas. *Summa Contra Gentiles,* at http://books.mirror.org/gb.aquinas.html.

Augustine. *City of God,* in Philip Schaff, ed., *Nicene and Post-Nicene Fathers,* First Series, vol. II. Grand Rapids: Wm. B. Eerdmans Publishing Co.: reprinted 1983.

Barker, Kenneth, gen. ed. *The NIV Study Bible.* Grand Rapids: Zondervan, 1985.

Barna, George. *The Index of Leading Spiritual Indicators.* Dallas: Word Publishing, 1996.

Barnett, Paul. *Is the New Testament Reliable?* Downers Grove, Ill.: InterVarsity Press, 1992.

Baudouin, Charles. *Suggestion and Autosuggestion.* London: George Allen and Unwin, 1954.

Beale, G. K. *The Book of Revelation.* Grand Rapids: Wm. B. Eerdmans Publishing Co., 1999.

Behe, Michael J. *Darwin's Black Box: The Biochemical Challenge to Evolution.* New York: The Free Press, 1996.

Benner, David G., ed. *Baker Encyclopedia of Psychology.* Grand Rapids: Baker Book House, 1985.

Boa, Kenneth, and Larry Moody. *I'm Glad You Asked.* Wheaton: Victor Books, 1982.

Borg, Marcus J. *Meeting Jesus Again for the First Time.* San Francisco: HarperSanFrancisco, 1995.

Boyd, Gregory A. *Cynic Sage or Son of God?* Wheaton: BridgePoint, 1995.

Brown, Raymond E. *The Virginal Conception and Bodily Resurrection of Jesus.* New York: Paulist Press, 1973.

Buswell, James Oliver, Jr. *A Systematic Theology of the Christian Religion.* Vol. 1. Grand Rapids: Zondervan, 10th edition, 1976.

Clement of Rome. *First Epistle to the Corinthians*, in Alexander Roberts, ed. *The Ante-Nicene Fathers* Vol. 1. Grand Rapids: Wm. B. Eerdmans Publishing Co., reprinted 1985.

Clifford, Ross. *Leading Lawyers Look at the Resurrection.* Claremont, Calif.: Albatross Books, 1991.

Comfort, Philip Wesley, ed. *The Origin of the Bible.* Wheaton: Tyndale House Publishers, 1992.

Cooper, John W. *Body, Soul, and Life Everlasting.* Grand Rapids: Wm. B. Eerdmans Publishing Co., 1989.

Copan, Paul, ed. *Will the Real Jesus Please Stand Up? A Debate between William Lane Craig and John Dominic Crossan.* Grand Rapids: Baker Book House, 1998.

Craig, William Lane. *Reasonable Faith.* Wheaton: Crossway Books, 1994.

———. *Assessing the New Testament Evidence for the Historicity of the Resurrection of Jesus (Studies in the Bible and Early Christianity)*. Lewiston, N.Y.: Edwin Mellen Press, 1989.

Cullmann, Oscar. *Immortality of the Soul or Resurrection of the Dead?* New York: Macmillan Publishing Co., 1964.

Cyril of Jerusalem. *The Catechetical Lectures*, XIV:21, in Philip Schaff and Henry Wace, eds., *Nicene and Post-Nicene Fathers*, Second Series, vol. VII. Grand Rapids: Wm. B. Eerdmans Publishing Co., reprinted 1983.

Dahl, M. E. *The Resurrection of the Body.* London: SCM Press, Ltd., 1962.

Davis, Stephen, Daniel Kendall SJ, and Gerald O'Collins SJ, eds. *The Resurrection.* New York: Oxford University Press, 1997.

Edwards, Jonathan. *The Works of Jonathan Edwards.* Edinburgh, Great Britain: The Banner of Truth Trust, reprinted 1992.

Edwards, Paul. *Reincarnation: A Critical Examination.* Amherst, N.Y.: Prometheus Books, 1996.

Elwell, Walter A., ed. *Evangelical Dictionary of Biblical Theology.* Grand Rapids: Baker Book House, 1996.

———. *Topical Analysis of the Bible.* Grand Rapids: Baker Book House, 1991.

Erickson, Millard J. *Christian Theology.* Grand Rapids: Baker Book House, 1985.

Eusebius. *History of the Church*, in Philip Schaff, ed., *Nicene and Post-Nicene Fathers*, second series, vol. I. Grand Rapids: Wm. B. Eerdmans Publishing Co., reprinted 1982.

From Paradise Lost to Paradise Regained. Brooklyn: Watchtower Bible and Tract Society, 1958.

Fudge, Edward William. *The Fire That Consumes.* Carlisle, U.K.: The Paternoster Press, 1994.

Fuller, Daniel P. *Easter Faith and History.* Grand Rapids: Wm. B. Eerdmans Publishing Co., 1965.

Funk, Robert W. *Honest to Jesus.* San Francisco: HarperSanFrancisco, 1996.

Funk, Robert W., Roy W. Hoover, and THE JESUS SEMINAR. *The Five*

Gospels. New York: Macmillan Publishing Co., 1993.

Gaebelein, Frank E., ed. *The Expositor's Bible Commentary.* Grand Rapids: Zondervan, 1981.

Geisler, Norman L., and Abdul Saleeb. *Answering Islam: The Crescent in Light of the Cross.* Grand Rapids: Baker Book House, 1993.

—— and Thomas Howe. *When Critics Ask.* Wheaton: Victor Books, 1992.

——. *Baker Encyclopedia of Christian Apologetics.* Grand Rapids: Baker Book House, 1999.

——. *The Battle for the Resurrection.* Nashville: Thomas Nelson Publishers, 1992.

Green, Michael. *The Empty Cross of Jesus.* Downers Grove, Ill.: InterVarsity Press, 1984.

Greenleaf, Simon. *The Testimony of the Evangelists: The Gospels Examined by the Rules of Evidence.* Grand Rapids: Kregel Classics, 1995; originally published 1874.

Gruss, Edmond Charles. *Apostles of Denial: An Examination and Exposé of the History, Doctrines and Claims of the Jehovah's Witnesses.* Grand Rapids: Baker Book House, reprinted 1978.

Gundry, Robert H. *Soma in Biblical Theology.* Grand Rapids: Zondervan, 1987.

Habermas, Gary R. *Ancient Evidence for the Life of Jesus.* Nashville: Thomas Nelson Publishers, 1992.

—— and Antony G. N. Flew. *Did Jesus Rise from the Dead?* San Francisco: Harper and Row, 1987.

—— and J. P. Moreland. *Beyond Death: Exploring the Evidence for Immortality.* Wheaton: Crossway Books, 1998.

——. *The Historical Jesus: Ancient Evidence for the Life of Christ.* Joplin, Miss.: College Press Publishing Co., 1996.

——. *The Resurrection of Jesus.* Grand Rapids: Baker Book House, 1980.

Halverson, Dean C., gen. ed. *The Compact Guide to World Religions.* Minneapolis: Bethany House Publishers, 1996.

Hanegraaff, Hank. *Counterfeit Revival: Looking for God in All the Wrong Places.* Dallas: Word Publishing, 1997.

———. *The FACE That Demonstrates the Farce of Evolution.* Nashville: Word Publishing, 1998.

Harris, Murray J. *From Grave to Glory.* Grand Rapids: Zondervan, 1990.

———. *Raised Immortal.* Grand Rapids: Wm. B. Eerdmans Publishing Co., reprinted 1983.

Heeren, Fred. *Show Me God*, rev. ed. Wheeling, Ill.: Day Star, 1997.

Hendriksen, William. *More Than Conquerors.* Grand Rapids: Baker Book House, 1986.

———. *The Bible on the Life Hereafter.* Grand Rapids: Baker Book House, 1975.

Henry, Carl F. H., ed. *Basic Christian Doctrines.* Grand Rapids: Baker Book House, 1971.

Hillstrom, Elizabeth L. *Testing the Spirits.* Downers Grove, Ill.: InterVarsity Press, 1995.

Hodge, Charles. *Systematic Theology.* Vol. 3. Grand Rapids: Wm. B. Eerdmans Publishing Co., reprinted 1977.

Hoekema, Anthony A. *The Bible and the Future.* Grand Rapids: Wm. B. Eerdmans Publishing Co., 1979.

Hoerth, Alfred J. *Archaeology and the Old Testament.* Grand Rapids: Baker Book House, 1998.

Howe, Quincy, Jr. *Reincarnation for the Christian.* Philadelphia: The Westminster Press, 1974.

Huse, Scott M. *The Collapse of Evolution*, 3rd edition. Grand Rapids: Baker Book House, 1997.

Jefferson, Thomas. *The Jefferson Bible.* Boston: Beacon Press, 1989.

Josephus. *The Works of Josephus.* Peabody, Mass.: Hendrickson Publishers, 1987.

Keener, Craig S. *The IVP Bible Background Commentary: New Testament.* Downers Grove, Ill.: InterVarsity Press, 1993.

Kingdom Is at Hand, The. Brooklyn: Watchtower Bible and Tract Society, 1944.

Kreeft, Peter. *Between Heaven and Hell*. Downers Grove, Ill.: InterVarsity Press, 1982.

——. *Everything You Ever Wanted to Know about Heaven . . . But Never Dreamed of Asking*. San Francisco: Ignatius Press, 1990.

——and Ronald K. Tacelli. *Handbook of Christian Apologetics*. Downers Grove, Ill.: InterVarsity Press, 1994.

Ladd, George Eldon. *I Believe in the Resurrection of Jesus*. Grand Rapids: Wm. B. Eerdmans Publishing Co., 1975.

Leek, Sybil. *Reincarnation: The Second Chance*. New York: Stein and Day Publishers, 1974.

Lenski, R. C. H. *The Interpretation of St. John's Revelation*. Minneapolis: Augsburg Publishing House, 1963.

Let God Be True, 2nd edition. Brooklyn: Watchtower Bible and Tract Society, 1952.

Lewis, C. S. *The Great Divorce*. New York: Collier Books, 1946.

——. *Mere Christianity*. New York: Collier Books, 1962.

——. *Miracles*. New York: Collier Books, 1960.

——. *The Problem of Pain*. New York: Collier Books, 1962.

——. *The Screwtape Letters*. New York: Collier Books, 1961.

Lutzer, Erwin W., and John F. DeVries. *Satan's Evangelistic Strategy for This New Age*. Wheaton: Victor Books, 1989.

MacArthur, John F. *The Glory of Heaven*. Wheaton: Crossway Books, 1996.

——. *The MacArthur Topical Bible*. Nashville: Word Publishing, 1999.

Marks, Robert W., *The Story of Hypnotism*. Grand Rapids: Prentice-Hall, 1947.

Martin, Michael. *The Case against Christianity*. Philadelphia: Temple University Press, 1991.

Martin, Walter. *The Kingdom of the Cults*, Revised, Updated, Expanded Anniversary Edition. Minneapolis: Bethany House Publishers, 1997.

——. *The New Age Cult*. Minneapolis: Bethany House Publishers, 1989.

Martyr, Justin. *Fragments of the Lost Work of Justin on the Resurrection*, ch. IV, in Alexander Roberts and James Donaldson, eds., *The Ante-*

Nicene Fathers. Vol. 1. Grand Rapids: Wm. B. Eerdmans Publishing Co., reprinted 1985.

Mayr, Ernst. *This Is Biology*. Cambridge, Mass.: The Belknap Press, 1999.

McDowell, Josh, and Bill Wilson. *He Walked Among Us*. San Bernardino, Calif.: Here's Life Publishers, Inc., 1988.

McDowell, Josh. *The New Evidence That Demands a Verdict*. Nashville: Thomas Nelson Publishers, 1999.

McGrath, Alister E. *Intellectuals Don't Need God*. Grand Rapids: Zondervan, 1993.

———. *Christian Theology: An Introduction*. Malden, Mass.: Blackwell Publishers, 1997.

Meier, John P. *A Marginal Jew: Rethinking the Historical Jesus*. Vol. 1. New York: Doubleday, 1991.

Metzger, Bruce M. *Breaking the Code*. Nashville: Abingdon Press, 1993.

Montgomery, John Warwick. *Faith Founded on Fact: Essays in Evidential Apologetics*. Nashville: Thomas Nelson Publishers, 1978.

———. *History and Christianity*. San Bernardino, Calif.: Here's Life Publishers, Inc., 1965.

Moreland, J. P. *Scaling the Secular City: A Defense of Christianity*. Grand Rapids: Baker Book House, 1987.

Morris, Henry M. *Scientific Creationism*, public school edition. San Diego: C.L.P. Publishers, 1981.

O'Collins, Gerald, SJ. *The Resurrection of Jesus Christ*. Valley Forge, Penn.: Judson Press, 1973.

Orr, James. *The Resurrection of Jesus*. Grand Rapids: Zondervan, 1965.

Pannenberg, Wolfhart. *Jesus God and Man*. London: SCM Press Ltd., 1968.

Passantino, Robert and Gretchen. *Answers to the Cultist at Your Door*. Eugene, Ore.: Harvest House Publishers, 1981.

Piper, John. *Future Grace*. Sisters, Ore.: Multnomah Books, 1995.

Ramsay, William M. *The Bearing of Recent Discovery on the Trustworthiness of the New Testament*, reprint ed. Grand Rapids: Baker, 1953.

Reasoning from the Scriptures. Brooklyn: Watchtower Bible and Tract Society, 1985.

Rhodes, Ron. *The Complete Book of Bible Answers*. Eugene, Ore.: Harvest House Publishers, 1997.

———. *The Counterfeit Christ of the New Age Movement*. Grand Rapids: Baker Book House, 1990.

———. *Reasoning from the Scriptures with the Jehovah's Witnesses*. Eugene, Ore.: Harvest House Publishers, 1993.

Richards, Larry. *735 Baffling Bible Questions Answered*. Grand Rapids: Baker Book House, 1997.

Rutherford, J. F. *The Harp of God*. Brooklyn: Watchtower Bible and Tract Society, 1921.

Ryken, Leland, James C. Wilhoit, Tremper Longman III, gen. ed. *Dictionary of Biblical Imagery*. Downers Grove, Ill.: InterVarsity Press, 1998.

Sagan, Carl. *Cosmos*. New York: Random House, 1980.

Schaff, Philip. *The Creeds of Christendom*. Vol. 3. Grand Rapids: Baker Book House, reprinted 1985.

Schep, J. A. *The Nature of the Resurrection Body*. Grand Rapids: Wm. B. Eerdmans Publishing Co., 1964.

Schonfield, Hugh J. *The Passover Plot: A New Interpretation of the Life and Death of Jesus*. New York: Bernard Geis Associates, 1965.

Smith, Morton. *Jesus the Magician*. San Francisco: Harper and Row, 1978.

Smith, Wilbur M. *The Biblical Doctrine of Heaven*. Chicago: Moody Press, 1976.

Spong, John Shelby. *The Easter Moment*. San Francisco: Harper and Row, 1987.

Sproul, R. C. *Essential Truths of the Christian Faith*. Wheaton: Tyndale House Publishers, 1992.

———. *Knowing Scripture*. Downers Grove, Ill.: InterVarsity Press, 1977.

———. *Now, That's a Good Question!* Wheaton: Tyndale House Publishers, 1996.

———, John Gerstner, and Arthur Lindsley. *Classical Apologetics: A Rational Defense of the Christian Faith and a Critique of Presuppositional Apologetics*. Grand Rapids: Zondervan, 1984.

Strobel, Lee. *The Case for Christ.* Grand Rapids: Zondervan, 1998.

Student Bible, The. Grand Rapids: Zondervan, 1986.

Studies in the Scriptures, Series II. Allegheny, Penn.: Watchtower Bible and Tract Society, 1908.

Swindoll, Charles R. *Improving Your Serve.* Waco: Word Publishing, 1981.

Tada, Joni Eareckson. *Heaven…Your Real Home.* Grand Rapids: Zondervan, 1995.

———. *Holiness in Hidden Places.* Nashville: J. Countryman, 1999.

———. *When God Weeps.* Grand Rapids: Zondervan, 1997.

Tenney, Merrill C. *The Reality of the Resurrection.* San Francisco: Harper and Row, 1963.

Tertullian, *The Prescription Against Heretics*, in Alexander Roberts, *The Ante-Nicene Fathers.* Grand Rapids: Wm. B. Eerdmans Publishing Co., reprinted 1986.

Thiede, Carsten Peter, and Mathew d'Ancona. *Eyewitness to Jesus.* New York: Doubleday, 1996.

Thiering, Barbara. *Jesus and the Riddle of the Dead Sea Scrolls: Unlocking the Secrets of His Life Story.* San Francisco: HarperSanFrancisco, 1992.

Things in Which It Is Impossible for God to Lie. Brooklyn: Watchtower Bible and Tract Society, 1965.

Toon, Peter. *Heaven and Hell.* Nashville: Thomas Nelson Publishers, 1986.

Truth Shall Make You Free, The. Brooklyn: Watchtower Bible and Tract Society, 1943.

Vermes, Geza. *Jesus the Jew.* Philadelphia: Fortress Press, 1973.

Wenham, John. *Easter Enigma.* Grand Rapids: Baker Book House, 1993.

———. *Redating Matthew, Mark & Luke.* Downers Grove, Ill.: InterVarsity Press, 1992.

White, James R. *The Forgotten Trinity.* Minneapolis: Bethany House Publishers, 1998.

Wilckens, Ulrich, Gerhard Delling, Willi Marxsen, and Hans-Georg Geyer. *The Significance of the Message of the Resurrection for Faith in Jesus Christ.* London: SCM Press, 1968.

Wilckens, Ulrich. *Resurrection.* Atlanta: John Knox Press, 1978.

Wilder-Smith, A. E. *The Natural Sciences Know Nothing of Evolution.* Costa Mesa, Calif.: T.W.F.T. Publishers, 1981.

Wilkins, Michael J., and J. P. Moreland, eds. *Jesus Under Fire: Modern Scholarship Reinvents the Historical Jesus.* Grand Rapids: Zondervan, 1995.

Wilson, A. N. *Jesus.* New York: W. W. Norton and Company, 1992.

Yardage Guide. Pebble Beach, Calif.: Cypress Point Club, 1999.

Young, Ed. *Pure Sex.* Sisters, Ore.: Multnomah Publishers, 1997.

Youngblood, Ronald F., gen. ed. *Nelson's New Illustrated Bible Dictionary.* Nashville: Thomas Nelson Publishers, 1995.

Articles

Craig, William Lane. "Contemporary Scholarship and the Historical Evidence for the Resurrection of Jesus Christ." *Truth* 1 (1985): 89–95. From the Leadership University Web site at http://www.leaderu.com/truth/1truth22.html

Davis, C. Truman. "The Crucifixion of Jesus: The Passion of Christ from a Medical Point of View." *Arizona Medicine.* Arizona Medical Association (March 1965).

Edwards, William D., Wesley J. Gabel, and Floyd E. Hosmer. "On the Physical Death of Jesus Christ." *The Journal of the American Medical Association* (21 March 1986).

"Facts About the Jesus Seminar and Founder Robert W. Funk." Answers in Action Web site, www.answers.org/Apologetics/jesuseminar.html

Ganaway, Dr. George. "Historical versus Narrative Truth." *Journal of Dissociation* II, no. 4 (December 1989): 205–20.

Geisler, Norman L. and Douglas E. Potter. "From Ashes to Ashes: Is Burial the Only Christian Option?" *Christian Research Journal* (July–September 1998): 29.

Gomes, Alan W. "Evangelicals and the Annihilation of Hell." *Christian Research Journal* (Spring 1991): 15–19.

Hanegraaff, Hank. "The Indwelling of the Holy Spirit." *Christian*

Bibliography

Research Institute Web site, www.equip.org/news/spirit.html

Leo, John. "I Was Beheaded in the 1700s." *Time,* 10 September 1984, 68.

Lynn, Steven Jay, and Judith W. Rhue. "Fantasy Proneness." *American Psychologist* (January 1988): 35–44.

Ostling, Richard N. "Jesus Christ, Plain and Simple." *Time,* 10 January 1994. From the *Time* Web site at http://cgi.pathfinder.com/time/magazine/archive/1994/940110/940110.religion.html

Price, Reynolds. "Jesus of Nazareth: Then and Now." *Time,* 6 December 1999, 84–94.

Rhue, Judith W., and Steven Jay Lynn. "Fantasy Proneness, Hypnotizability, and Multiple Personality" in John F. Schumaker, ed., *Human Suggestibility.* New York: Routledge (1991).

Sheler, Jeffrey L. "Is the Bible True?" *U.S. News and World Report,* 25 October 1999, 58.

Tart, Charles T. "Transpersonal Potentialities of Deep Hypnosis." *Journal of Transpersonal Psychology*, no. 1 (1970): 37.

Trott, Jon. "The Grade Five Syndrome." *Cornerstone*, vol. 20, no. 96.

White, James R. "The Jesus Seminar and the Gospel of Thomas: Courting the Media at the Cost of Truth." *Christian Research Journal* (Winter 1998): 51.

Yamauchi, Edwin M. "Easter—Myth, Hallucination, or History?" *Christianity Today.* 15 March 1974, 4–16.

Audiotapes

Craig, William Lane, and Robert Greg Cavin. "Dead or Alive? A Debate on the Resurrection of Jesus." Anaheim, Calif.: Simon Greenleaf University, 1995.

Joyner, Rick. "The Heart of David: Worship and Warfare." Conference Report (April 1996).

Videotapes

Glashouwer, Willem J. J., and Paul S. Taylor. *The Origin of the Universe.* Mesa, Ariz.: Eden, 1983.

Rajneesh, Baghwan Shree. *Fear is the Master.* Jeremiah Films, 1986.

The Wonders of God's Creation: Planet Earth, vol. 1. Chicago: Moody Institute of Science, 1993.

SCRIPTURE INDEX

6:9; 111
8:9; 121
19:12; 145
20:10; 76
20:12–15; 150
20:14; 130
21:1; xxii, 68, 87, 116,
243
21:1–5; xvi, 86
21:3–5; 92
21:4; 74, 134
21:5; 86
21:8; xxii
21:27; 74
22:12; 150
22:12–14; 143

SUBJECT INDEX

✜

ABOUT THE AUTHOR

Hank Hanegraaff answers questions live as host of the *Bible Answer Man* radio broadcast, heard daily throughout the United States and Canada. He is president of the famed Christian Research Institute headquartered in southern California. He is author of the best-selling Gold Medallion winner *Christianity in Crisis* as well as the award-winning bestsellers *Counterfeit Revival* and *The FACE That Demonstrates the Farce of Evolution*.

As author of *Memory Dynamics*, Hank has developed memorable tools to prepare believers to effectively communicate what they believe and why. He has also developed fun and easy techniques for memorizing Scripture quickly and retaining it forever.

Hank is a popular conference speaker for churches and conferences worldwide. He resides in southern California with his wife, Kathy, and their eight children: Michelle, Katie, David, John Mark, Hank Jr., Christina, Paul, and Faith.

For a list of stations airing the *Bible Answer Man* broadcast, log onto CRI's Web site at www.equip.org, contact CRI at P.O. Box 7000, Rancho Santa Margarita, CA 92688-7000, (949) 858-6100, or fax CRI at (949) 858-6111. To contact the *Bible Answer Man* broadcast with your questions, call toll-free (888) ASK-HANK, Monday through Friday, 2:50–4:00 P.M., Pacific Time. To listen to the broadcast live via the Internet, tune in at 3:05 P.M., Pacific Time at www.equip.org.

Contact CRI's Resource Center twenty-four hours a day at (949) 858-6100 or visit CRI's online bookstore at www.equip.org.

RESURRECTION ON TAPE

✠

Hank Hanegraaff is passionate about *Resurrection!* In the audio pages of *Resurrection* you can experience that passion for yourself. Your ability to absorb this memorable material will be greatly enhanced as it enters your mind through both the *ear* gate and *eye* gate. For an audio sample, log onto www.equip.org. Or you can order *Resurrection*, the audio pages, by calling or writing the Christian Research Institute. Available in bookstores everywhere.

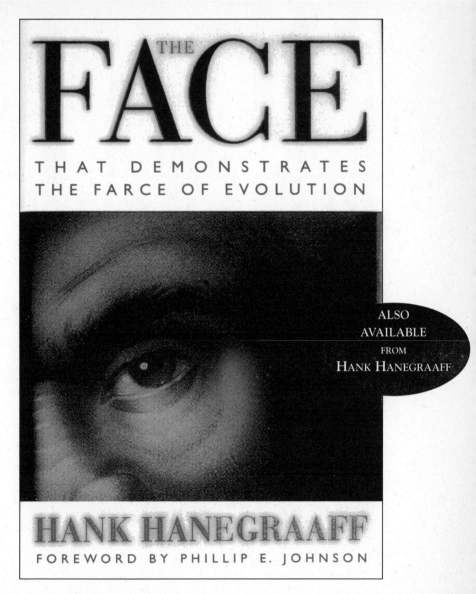

LOOKING FOR GOD IN ALL THE WRONG PLACES

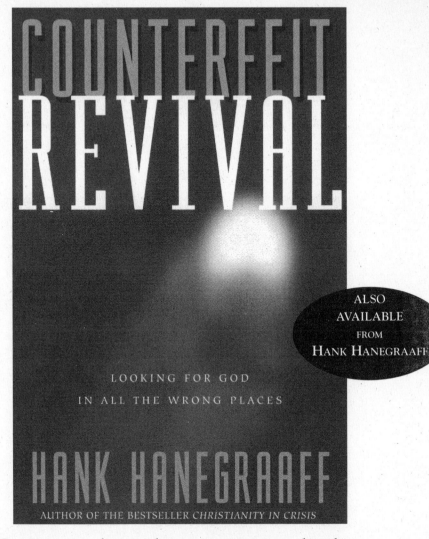

How can you discern between true revival and mere emotional experience?

In *Counterfeit Revival*, "Bible Answer Man" Hank Hanegraaff goes behind the scenes and uncovers the contradictions, spiritual deception and seductive allure of the wildly popular and bizarre world of contemporary revivalism. By comparing modern "revivals" with scriptural and historical examples of God's movement among his people, Hanegraaff teaches you to be on your guard against esoteric experiences masquerading under the banner of truth.

 WORD PUBLISHING
Available at Bookstores Everywhere.

www.wordpublishing.com